Women, Leadership, and the Bible

Women, Leadership, and the Bible

How Do I Know What to Believe?

A Practical Guide to Biblical Interpretation

NATALIE RUTH WILSON EASTMAN

Foreword by
Alice P. Mathews

CASCADE *Books* • Eugene, Oregon

WOMEN, LEADERSHIP, AND THE BIBLE
How Do I Know What to Believe? A Practical Guide to Biblical Interpretation

Cascade Books
An Imprint of Wipf and Stock Publishers
199 W. 8th Ave., Suite 3
Eugene, OR 97401

www.wipfandstock.com

ISBN 13: 978-1-60899-913-2

Cataloguing-in-Publication Data

Eastman, Natalie Ruth Wilson

Women, leadership, and the Bible : how do I know what to believe? a practical guide to biblical interpretation / Natalie Ruth Wilson Eastman

xxiv + 298 p. ; 23 cm. Includes bibliographical references and indexes.

ISBN 13: 978-1-60899-913-2

1. Bible—Hermeneutics. 2. Women in the Bible. 3. Leadership in the Bible. I. Title.

BS575 E188 2014

Manufactured in the U.S.A.

For the Lord.
For the church.
For women who want to know for themselves.

. . . so that the body of Christ may be built up until we all reach unity in the faith and in the knowledge of the Son of God and become mature, attaining to the whole measure of the fullness of Christ. Then we will no longer be infants, tossed back and forth by the waves, and blown here and there by every wind of teaching . . .
Ephesians 4:12b–14a

Contents

Figures

Tables

IN THE APPENDICES

Foreword

Years ago the search committee of a very large evangelical church contacted me for the names of some qualified women they could consider hiring as director of their women's ministry program. Hoping to match what they were looking for, I asked for a copy of the job description (which I was sure a church of that size had developed). As I read through their very long list of qualifications for the job, I was struck by the fact that nowhere was there any requirement for biblical or theological training. When I mentioned this to a member of that committee, she looked at me as if I had two heads. Why would they require any kind of formal biblical training for that position?

Why indeed. We wring our hands about the shallow quality of many church ministries to women without connecting the dots between a leader's solid biblical knowledge and ministry programs with depth. This becomes particularly problematic for women attending churches and ministries if their women's ministry leaders, indeed if they have a women's ministry, are not trained, either. We often end up with the well-intentioned blind leading the blind.

This is not to say that God cannot or does not use untrained people in kingdom service. Most of us have benefited from the ministry of such faithful men and women. At the same time, we are all instructed in Scripture to learn God's Word in order to understand it correctly and minister it appropriately. In his second letter to Timothy, Paul is clear in his instruction: "work hard so you can present yourself to God and receive his approval. Be a good worker, one who does not need to be ashamed and *who correctly explains the word of truth*" (2 Tim 2:15, NLT).

The problem for many *women* is that the opportunity for formal biblical training is often not available in their communities. How are women to learn how to understand and communicate biblical truth accurately?

Natalie Eastman has given us an excellent tool for that purpose. *Women, Leadership, and the Bible: How Do I Know What to Believe? A Practical Guide to Biblical Interpretation* is an amazingly detailed manual for developing the skills in biblical study that would otherwise be available only in a Bible school or a seminary. Step by step, Natalie walks us through a process any person can follow in order to interpret and apply God's Word with integrity.

Theologically trained herself, Natalie combines in this book both the theory and the practice of Bible study for leading others in understanding and applying God's Word. To this she adds down-to-earth insights from a host of Christian women leaders candidly talking about their ups and downs as they walked through a process for doing solid biblical exposition. The combination moves the reader through each step with real-life examples for sometimes very complicated ideas. This is one "how-to" book that works!

There are two other important things that I want to say about this book. First, even if you don't think of yourself as a "leader," this book *is* for you. Every Christian is a teacher at many points and in many contexts, whether in a Bible study or around the breakfast table with our family. Any person who loves God's Word, wants to understand it better, and desires to apply it more effectively to the questions that life throws at us will find a goldmine in this book.

Second, this is not another book telling the reader what to think about women in church leadership. There are no normative conclusions here. This book is about the *process* of interpreting Scripture around any issue. Natalie's goal is to empower us to engage this question in a way that is theologically informed and exegetically sound. (The bonus is we can apply this method to any other theological or scriptural question that we want to explore.)

Thank you, Natalie, for giving us such a useable tool for ministry and for life.

I know I will recommend this book to women everywhere because women are thirsty to understand the word, because the need for skilled women Bible teachers and theologically informed women in the church is great, and because the process laid out in the book is clear and do-able. For the academically inclined, the information in the footnotes is excellent. For the rest of us, her five-step approach to solid interpretation will enable us to handle God's Word correctly and with confidence.

Alice P. Mathews, PhD
South Hamilton, MA

Acknowledgments

FIRST THANKS GO TO . . .

The Lord for caring so much about women that he gave himself for them and for entrusting me with the task of writing this book to encourage them to live their best for him and give him their sharpest thinking.

The women who consented to an interview and to share their lives with other women.

Cascade Books for giving this idea a foot in the publishing-world door and my editor, Robin Parry, who helped it become all it could be.

Many additional thanks go to . . .

Mom, who cheers me on, no matter what.

Dad, who, much to my childish dismay, never merely "gave me the answer."

Dr. Alice Mathews, who taught and modeled for me how to think biblically and theologically for myself.

The Wonderful Writers group in Shelton, CT, especially Ed and Janet Waggoner. The WWs read many portions of the book and gave excellent feedback, as well as much encouragement along the way to keep writing.

Many other friends, family members, and colleagues who read portions of this book, or even the proposal for it, and offered helpful comments, encouragement, and necessary editing: Valerie Andruss, Lynn Bell, Elisabeth Belton, "Auntie" Stacia Birdsall, Kelly Boyce, Sharon and Jeff Brantley, Laura Cooper, Kay Daigle, Janet Eastman, Kristi Eastman, Cynthia Fantasia, Jeanie Ganssle, Sandi Glahn, Jen Hartley, Amy Heck, Jane Hendrickson, Anita Hinkson, Jewel Hyun, Andrea Keeler, Cricket Lomicka, Anne McMurry, Jackie Roese, Jen Rosner, Brian Stiltner, Linda Triemstra, Nicole Unice, Peggy Wiley, Christi Wilson, Hannah Wong, Marsha Wood, Kim Yates, and Charmain Yun.

My doctor of ministry cohort colleagues, who encouraged this idea in its infancy and provided support and feedback along the way.

Canfield Christian Church and my father-in-law, Jay Eastman, for use of the pastor's study, where I could hole up and write.

The *many* friends and family members who babysat or otherwise cared for our family over the past twelve years while this project inched forward. Special thanks to Maureen Sharp, who supported me in tons of practical ways, including volunteering numerous times to take my kids or run errands for me so I could write.

Now for a bit more of the story.

Some years ago, my Ohioan mother-in-law put up wallpaper in their "Ohio State Buckeyes" room (a requisite room in nearly every Ohioan's house, I've come to see) that displays quips and quotes on success and persistence in sports. One that caught my eye—attributed to an anonymous track coach—says, "The race does not always go to the swift, but to the one who keeps running."

I am a person who is fantastic at imagining and starting projects, but not so strong on finishing. In God's grace, he has allowed (perhaps sometimes forced) me to keep running the race of writing this volume. When I finally see it in print, I will give every praise and thanks to the Lord for carrying me through these years of laborious writing. Indeed, writing has not come easily but has often felt painful, even torturous. In the midst of this, God has surprised and sustained me in this journey with an ongoing, surprising enthusiasm for the project itself and for the women who will, Lord willing, read and benefit from it. This vision has kept me going.

I am not the only one God has sustained in this journey, either. The process has also felt torturous to my husband at times. My life's love, David, is a linear, follow-through, get-it-done kind of guy. Five masters' degrees and a Yale PhD, while typically working two to three jobs simultaneously and starting a family—does this give you the picture of his task-oriented nature? Watching his hard-working yet global-thinking, imaginative wife write in her—ahem—less-linear way has been, well, hard. Yet, no one has been more supportive than he has been. To say that he has supported this project sacrificially would dramatically understate his contribution.

So it is that I thank David from the bottom of my heart for (1) supporting, encouraging, and pushing me to faithfully follow God's call to write this book; (2) sacrificing speed in his own PhD work and career in order to partner faithfully and significantly with me in raising and caring for our kids; and (3) contributing editorially to this work at several critical points, each time making it a much better work than it was before.

The other person who has sacrificially supported this book—and me—is my mother-in-law, Beulah Eastman. Indeed, she has stepped in and done the physical acts my own mother would love to have done, but could not due to physical limitations and distance. Over the course of these years of writing, Beulah has logged more babysitting hours, days, and weeks-amounting-to-months of our children than any other person alive. As a writer and lifelong pastor's wife, herself committed to ministry, she has done all this and more with the goal of helping me write this book and encourage other women—women much like herself.

Beulah also transcribed over a third of the thirty-five mentor interviews used for this book, many of which were two to three hours long. On top of that, due to a delay in our home renovations, my kids and I lived with Beulah and my father-in-law, Jay (a.k.a. "Nannaw and Tattaw") for what unexpectedly turned out to be nearly ten months during part of the last phase of writing and editing. Every Tuesday and Thursday, and many other times in between, she kept all three kids so I could write.

So, this book you hold in your hands has been a labor of love, a compelling call from the Lord, sustained to the end by his provision of just the right helpful people.

Perhaps he had you in mind when he laid the idea on my heart and in my lap and said, "Write."

For we are his workmanship, created in Christ Jesus for good works, which God prepared beforehand, that we should walk in them.

—Ephesians 2:10

Introduction

THE YOUTH DIRECTOR SHUFFLED, fingered, and stacked the three-by-five note cards with an air of anticipation. During every moment of preparation for this retreat, she had specifically envisioned this panel discussion. Women in the college ministry had anonymously written their most pressing questions for the eight women on the panel. Finally, the college women (and she, only a few years out of college herself) were going to get some solid answers to some touchy questions.

She'd handpicked the women on the panel. All of them were spiritual exemplars at their large, Bible-believing, evangelical church. A few were wives of elders, a couple held leadership positions in the women's ministry, and several led women's Bible studies that had been meeting for years. One of them, a feisty Latina, read theological books voraciously, rarely being seen without the latest read tucked under her arm. To the youth minister, each woman embodied the epitome of a thinking, spiritual Christian woman and leader. A perfect set-up for this forum.

Secretly, the youth minister hoped to get answers to some of her own questions. Primarily, she wanted answers to the probing questions the young women had been asking her for the several years of her ministry. She'd lost count of the girls in junior high, senior high, and college, along with many of their mothers, other church women, boys, and men, who'd asked her what the Bible said about various issues—but one particularly nagged at her. She finally admitted to herself that she really didn't know how to answer their questions.

Oh, she tried. She looked up all the pertinent texts she could find, but didn't understand their apparent contradictions. She asked her boss, who was one of the pastors, and received some helpful information, but perceived disagreement between his personal interpretation and what he described the church's position as being. He cautioned that she ought to be careful discussing this issue around the church just now, because people were divided about it due to some recent staffing changes. He advised that she remain slightly under the radar by not raising too much of a ruckus about it.

She listened for clues in the buzz around the church and, indeed, perceived strong disagreement. She read a couple of chapters in a few relevant books; but all the theological and Bible interpretation information confused her, because she didn't have any formal training in those methods. The differing views of those books perplexed her, too, because she couldn't tell who was right. The authors argued their positions from the Bible and everybody's position seemed at least somewhat plausible. Evaluating these opinions in a meaningful way evaded her.

In the end, she found herself unable to give a comprehensive, biblical understanding for the young women's questions, not to mention her own. So, loading the panel with these quality women—role models all—promised some straight talk for answers.

At least, that's what she expected.

Card by card, they made their way through the stack of questions while the room buzzed with lively, informal discussion.

Then came the card exposing the elephant-in-the-room question. It loomed large in the minds of everyone present.

She read slowly and clearly: "What does the Bible say about the roles of women in the church and the home?"

The young women waited.

The panelists froze in their seats.

Silence intruded on the gathering like an unwelcome visitor. Growing more and more taken aback as the seconds ticked away and the silence roared, the youth minister repeated the question and waited. The panelists looked at the floor, at the walls, at the ceiling—anywhere but at her or at the other women.

At last, the theology-reading Latina moved to speak.

The youth minister thought, "Finally!"

But, the panelist jarred the room as she exclaimed, "I'm not touching that one with a ten-foot pole!"

MY OWN AWAKENING

Ever been there? Have you seen or experienced anything like that? Christians—even mature ones, even leaders—clam up when it comes to talking about women's roles in the church. For a long time, I avoided the topic myself, because I didn't have a good understanding of it. Digging into it in public situations intimidated me, partly because I saw what a touchy subject it was and partly because I didn't have a theological understanding of it, so I really couldn't biblically engage in any kind of meaningful way.

You were right if you guessed that the young youth minister was me. That weekend retreat occurred nearly twenty years ago. Much has happened since then in terms of my own learning and development. Yet, I still see the intimidation factor, and the silence it causes among Christians, especially women, everywhere. They tend to clam up, like the panel of women at the retreat.

Why is the topic so difficult? Originally, my experience showed me, but then my research confirmed, three reasons for the discomfort:

- Lack of agreement. This one is fairly obvious. The old saying goes, "Never discuss religion or politics at family gatherings"—Miss Manners might add, ". . . or with anyone." Why? Disagreement brings discomfort for most—bristling discomfort. Hardly anyone enjoys conflict. The women's issue involves people, rather than ideas, although the result is no different. However, the next two reasons exacerbate the discomfort.
- Lack of widespread *ability* among Christians to do their own work of responsible Bible interpretation.
- Lack of a full understanding of the issue itself. People say "ignorance is bliss"; but I don't believe that holds true when people approach this issue in a group, or even in personal reflection, and find they have nothing but misinformation to contribute. People who genuinely want to sort through an issue feel embarrassed and intimidated when they don't know any facts and can't engage meaningfully.

What happened at our retreat? Did we ever get any answers? Well, one of the elder's wives courageously stepped in and offered our denomination's position. That certainly shed some light on the issue. But our denomination's position was generous enough on the issue that, at least in theory, there shouldn't have been such a high level of tension. Obviously, this was caused by other dynamics the in-the-know panelists couldn't discuss.

We engaged in some dialogue but, due to some staffing changes my boss had previously told me about, the sensitivity of the issue at that time limited our discussion.

In my own journey, there was a time—a very long time—during which I was paralyzed by ambiguity and uncertainty when it came to questions concerning women's roles in the church. I exemplified a sincere, biblically oriented, ministry-active, conservative Christian woman. Yet, like many Christian women in churches everywhere, I had little understanding of theology, much less Bible interpretation.

As a woman heavily engaged in ministry activity from my junior year of high school onward, I energetically attended and taught numerous youth and women's Bible studies and Sunday school classes, initiated ongoing discipleship relationships with women, evangelized many women, and walked alongside many others in their faith. Retreat organization and leadership; workshop instruction; worship team leading, guidance, and training; campus ministry; missions trips; seminars—hardly a ministry activity existed in which I was not involved or leading at some point in my life. Yet, throughout all of this Christian initiative, I never had the personal wherewithal to explore the theological bases for my own beliefs, aside from basic apologetics skills and arguments.

This leads me to another disheartening aspect of discussing this issue with others at church: often people believe things without a solid biblical basis and then *act upon* that faulty foundation. They rely instead, knowingly or unknowingly, upon emotion, culture, or tradition when determining their beliefs about women's roles in leadership, rather than on responsible, evenhanded interpretation of God's Word. I know this, because I have done all of this myself.

One major problem with this is that people often enact policies based on these assumptions. Entire congregations then adopt those policies without any critical analysis of where and how Scripture addresses those issues, often relying instead on the writing and oratory skills of those who drafted the policy. For most, a few supportive, obvious verses will do. In fact, that'll *have* to do, because most churchgoers, men or women, aren't trained in serious Bible interpretation—much less systematic, analytical approaches to discerning answers to questions about theological issues. In most cases, experience will tell you this is certainly true for the issue of women's roles in church leadership.

In my own case, I had few skills for understanding or sorting through conflicting interpretations of biblical passages. Even though I was a ministry director at a large evangelical church, I had no formal theological training and very little informally. After a few years on staff, my boss encouraged me to take some courses of interest at a seminary supported by our church, particularly counseling, which I happily and thankfully did. It was a good start. Yet, sometimes, I felt actively discouraged from serious theological development. The folks who discouraged me were certainly the exception; but this did happen with some degree of regularity. Also, the below-the-surface tensions simmering among the leaders in our congregation over this issue confused me.

I *struggled* to help women and men in my ministry areas who came to me with their questions about women's roles and the particular conflicts in our church. My primary responses involved parroting the denomination's position or whatever interpretation I had most recently heard.

After just over a decade in ministry—four years as a lay volunteer and six years as a full-time staff member—the Lord provided the way for me to begin full-time seminary study, with my church's complete support.

It was during my years of study toward the Master of Divinity degree that I felt an awakening to theology through understanding formal approaches to Bible interpretation ("hermeneutics" and "exegesis"— we'll discuss both terms and practices later in this book) and learning how to do it. While there, I was blessed to be mentored both formally and informally by a female professor and Radio Bible Class expositor, Dr. Alice Mathews, who trained and encouraged me toward developing theological critical thinking skills.

What do I mean by "critical thinking skills"? For our purposes in this book, I define critical thinking as the process of thoughtfully weighing ideas by passing them through the sifter of what one knows about the Lord, his Word, people, church history (and history in general), and one's world. It extends to evaluating conflicting opinions and teachings from various authorities or sources about those ideas. Thinking critically also includes forming a thoughtful opinion about an issue, having considered it in the context of all of these other inputs.

Eventually, I gained confidence and knowledge in this arena. I was finally able to make sense of the many conflicting opinions and interpretations I had heard and continued to hear about women's roles.

Ultimately, I was able not only to make my own biblically informed decision about women's roles but to begin learning more about other theological issues and applying the same sifting strategy to them. I have since had the opportunity to serve other women in their theological development through informal mentoring relationships, helping them learn to think theologically through issues and questions. Many other Christian women want the same understanding and discernment that I craved, that the girls and women—and many men—who came to me during my church ministry years craved.

I represent a classic case of "If only I knew [how to do] *then* what I know [how to do] *now*." I hope to pass along the opportunities of learning and training with which I've been blessed—to "pay it forward" to sisters to whom I can give a leg up in this area.

I *don't* want to tell women what to think. Plenty of Christian resources and people are quite ready to tell women exactly what to think about theological issues.

I want to help women learn to *think for themselves*. This book exists to help equip women to move beyond surface Bible study into a deeper understanding of how to "do" interpretation and how to "do" theology. In this book, I help women learn those skills in the process of exploring and discerning biblical and theological answers to their questions about the issue of women's roles in church leadership.

As you read this book, I sincerely hope you will feel encouraged to go forward in your biblical development. I hope you will feel stimulated to believe that you can—and should—learn to discern answers biblically and theologically for yourself. And I want to give you as many important and necessary skills as I can, so that you will be *able* to develop and discern as you seek God's heart on this and many other of your most pressing life questions.

Abbreviations

SCRIPTURE ABBREVIATIONS

Hebrew Bible / Old Testament:

Gen	Judg	Neh	Song	Hos	Nah
Exod	Ruth	Esth	Isa	Joel	Hab
Lev	1–2 Sam	Job	Jer	Amos	Zeph
Num	1–2 Kgs	Ps (pl. Pss)	Lam	Obad	Hag
Deut	1–2 Chr	Prov	Ezek	Jonah	Zech
Josh	Ezra	Eccl (or Qoh)	Dan	Mic	Mal

New Testament:

Matt	Acts	Eph	1–2 Tim	Heb	1–2–3 John
Mark	Rom	Phil	Titus	Jas	Jude
Luke	1–2 Cor	Col	Phlm	1–2 Pet	Rev
John	Gal	1–2 Thess			

BIBLE VERSIONS

ESV	English Standard Version
NASB	New American Standard Bible
NASV	New American Standard Bible
NIV	New International Version
RSV	Revised Standard Version

Chapter 1

Where Many Women Begin with "The Women's Issue"

Margi slid into the comfortable, green-velvet-covered auditorium chair. The conservative evangelical church she'd been attending for a few months gathered for worship in the auditorium of the local middle school. After the opening set of worship songs, a call to worship, and Scripture readings, a lovely silver-haired woman stepped to the podium. Making neither apologies nor any claims to be "sharing," the woman opened a Bible and began to speak. She rightly divided the Word of God, so far as Margi could tell. But, what was this?

None of the other churches she'd attended over the course of her life ever had a female preacher. Some had women who sang solos, led in prayer, gave personal testimony, or read Scripture, but none who preached. Margi wasn't sure how she felt about it, what she believed about it, or even what she *thought* about it. A woman preaching outright in the main worship service? Should she be offended? Should she walk out?

WHAT WOULD YOU TELL Margi? More importantly, *why* would you tell her that?

What do *you* think about that woman preaching? Are *you* offended? Would *you* leave? Why? What do *you* think the Bible says about it? *Why?*

Let's take this one step further. What if you later learned that this woman who spoke was ordained as a pastor or teaching elder or minister? Again, what do you think? What do you believe the Bible says about ordination, generally, and then about women in particular being ordained? Why do you think the Bible says that?

Stepping back a bit, what do you think, in general, about women ministering in the church? What roles are okay for them to assume? Is it biblically acceptable for a woman to lead? In which ministries or areas? Do you think women can be elders in the church?

Again, I ask, *why* do you think that?

Do you know what you believe the Scriptures say about women and women's ministry roles? Do you know what ministry roles are open to you, biblically, as a woman? If so, *how* do you know?

Do you know what 1 Timothy 2:12 means? How about 1 Corinthians 11:5 or 14:34–35? If you do, *how do you know*?

In short, have you taken an opportunity to think through this issue biblically and theologically, in depth, *for yourself?*

Do you find the many conflicting opinions about women's ministry roles confusing or frustrating?

In light of Scripture and theology, how do you sort through it all to come to your own conclusion?

Speaking as a woman interconnected with other women, I can say with some experience that we women tend to race along in our full everyday lives. We're filled to the absolute maximum with obligations, relationships, and ongoing issues of all kinds. Personal goals are often driven downward on our already-long daily to-do lists.

Who's got time for personal goals when there's ministry to be done, careers to manage, families to raise, aging parents to care for, husbands to love, friends to hold on to, jobs to report to? Some days my only goal is to make it *through* that day!

Further, if we barely have time for thinking about personal goals and issues, who has time or energy for thinking about theological questions like those surrounding the "women's issue"? Why reinvent the wheel? Our denominations, or maybe our pastors, already did the study about the theological issues we're facing. Can't we just go with that?

Have you ever heard (or said) anything like these statements:

- "Our church already ordains women, so I don't have to worry about that."

- "Our denomination follows the Westminster Confession, so I know I'm Reformed (whatever *that* means). I think that's why we don't ordain women . . ."

Margi's story represents only one of many kinds of situations that the Christian women you and I know face. From each situation we encounter arise a number of questions and issues about God—our relationship to him, to the church, to our ministries, to our very selves. These questions are theology. They are theology because they relate to God, his Word, and our relationship to God. The questions surrounding women's roles in the church are theological questions. And they demand answers from you and me.

Yet, I find that many women face strong intimidation factors when it comes to finding answers to their big life questions. I had a hunch about this, because I experienced it personally and saw it in women around me. However, I also conducted a formal, extensive survey of nearly four hundred women from many denominations and traditions. That research confirmed my hunch.

Some women feel paralyzed by their own questions concerning whether or not women ought to be in ministry leadership, whether women ought to lead men, or whether women should be in leadership of any kind.

Some women feel paralyzed by fears that hold them back from asking even initial questions. "What if people think I'm getting too big for my britches? What if people think I'm becoming liberal? What if people think I'm becoming too literal and narrow?"

Some women feel paralyzed by what they might learn, as in, "What if I study the Scriptures and they tell me something different from what I believe now? Then what?"

Some women are paralyzed by the conflict over the issue.

Yet, no matter why they initially feel paralyzed by the issue, numerous women *remain* paralyzed because the topic—and people who discuss it—intimidate them. Many women experience hindrances, doubts, and fears about doing serious theological thinking for themselves. "Theology is for smart people; I'm not that smart. Theology is for men. I don't have time. I can't go to seminary. I don't know how. I just can't 'go there'; it hurts too much. What if . . . ?"

Yet, as Carolyn Custis James gently informs in her book *When Life and Beliefs Collide*, "The moment the word 'why' crosses our lips, we are doing theology."[1]

How, then, if we are busy or intimidated by the prospects, do we consider those theological questions in order to figure out what God intends for women—for us—in our lives and ministries?

Unfortunately, until something happens that affects us directly—in personal, possibly painful ways—dealing with theological issues is typically far off our radar screen. Most of the time, it takes a conflict to get us to step up to the start line. Yet, whether the conflict strikes in our own lives or the lives of those we love or care about, we can't write off thinking through these issues as someone else's responsibility. It is precisely when we are personally confronted with the issue, problem, question, or pain that we want and need answers. Others' words often don't cut it. We need to know what God says to us, about us, about himself, about his will.

Waiting until we're in the middle of a sticky or painful situation to know what theology we're leaning on is dangerous. At best, we find ourselves ill prepared for facing the situation. We reach for the Bible to find verses that will make us feel better, but it only "band aids" the hurt. At worst, we find ourselves not prepared at all. Our hearts and minds go completely empty and ready for the taking by despair, pain, numbness, or rage at God. We are unable to tap into truth from God's Word in a meaningful, dependable way to bring any kind of balm to the situation. We open ourselves to being "tossed to and fro by the waves and carried about by every wind of doctrine" (Eph 4:14).

We're obliged to begin the thoughtful process of biblical and theological discovery about what God's Word says about women's roles in the church now—before things happen. And I'll state it even more strongly: we are *responsible* for thinking through these questions biblically and theologically. We're responsible not only to ourselves, but to God.

It would benefit us, then, to develop our theological thinking and our Bible-studying skills. And this takes some effort and study. Some knowledgeable modeling, as well as out-and-out encouragement, couldn't hurt, either. These factors—effort, study, modeling, and encouragement—reflect the guts of this book. It is designed to help you through these in two primary ways: by giving you a discernment process to use and by giving

1. James, *Life and Beliefs*, 64.

you models to see. In addition, you will find plain language throughout and unabashed cheering, along with spurring, at strategic points.

A DISCERNMENT PROCESS TO USE

The primary "how" aspect of this book concerns the process of discernment. This is the heart and soul of this volume. It comes in the form of a repeatable five-step process for researching, understanding, evaluating, and making a decision about what Scripture has to say about women's roles in church leadership. This discernment process gives you a framework for sorting through the issue of women's roles in church leadership. You will be able to find answers to your questions about women's roles and make critical biblical decisions about the issue for yourself. You will learn to discern it fully and arrive at a biblically grounded, theologically thoughtful decision.

Having a step-by-step process by which you can think clearly about a difficult issue will help toward freeing you from any ambiguity you may feel. It will help you prayerfully process the many conflicting voices that address this issue in light of Scripture. It will help clear up the confusion that surrounds this issue.

Yet, what you'll find in these pages is a *plan*, not a *position*.

There are no easy *responsible* answers. However, you will learn how, by the enabling of and in the power of the Holy Spirit, to sift and sort through conflicting opinions and interpretations—and find for yourself what you believe the Bible says about women's roles in the church.

The great news is that this process of discernment applies to all kinds of theological questions, not just those about women's roles. Perhaps you're pondering the degree to which good works or social justice play a role in our spiritual lives as you form a plan for a women's ministry. Maybe you are discipling a younger Christian who is asking lots of challenging questions about what role, if any, the Bible tells us we play in our salvation. Whatever questions you might be asking, this process of discernment can help you begin to formulate your own biblically grounded, theologically sound thinking on that issue.

MODELS TO SEE

In preparing for this book, my interest was in the *process*, because that's where women seem to get hung up. Although the thought of formal theological study intimidates many women, those same women tend to flourish in mentoring relationships, particularly when they see another woman walking all the way through some particular process before they try it out themselves. We tend to learn well by watching, talking with, and walking with other women in action.

There are times when I need to watch someone else do an action to get me going in that area. When I'm able to walk closely with and observe a person who already knows how to do something, I more easily and quickly learn how to do it myself. I wanted to learn how women develop themselves biblically and theologically. So, I looked for women who've "gone before" in this arena.

Once I found some, I interviewed them—extensively. I asked them a host of questions about their own processes, to find out how they worked through their questions with regard to women's involvement in church leadership. The women you will meet in this book have "been there and back" in their search for theologically sound answers to their questions about women's involvement in church ministry. I called them the mentors. They share with us, in their own words, the stories of their theological development.

In, "Appendix A: Meet the Mentors," you will find a brief introductory biography for each mentor found in the book.[2] In the pages of this book, you'll find portions of the mentors' stories, captured in first-person style, no-holds-barred. They share what happened after they awakened to the issue, telling us *how* they

- Developed their knowledge of the biblical and theological concerns,
- Investigated biblical possibilities,

2. Although I interviewed more than thirty-five women, I have only included biographies for those twenty who are quoted or their stories referenced in this book—and those only in part. Yet, the contribution of every woman interviewed influenced the direction, tone, and messages contained in these pages. Some readers may be interested to read more of their interviews. Therefore, several appendices containing additional portions of mentor stories are located at www.womenleadershipbible.com. You will find much more there, as well, including several downloadable e-books and articles related to *Women, Leadership, and the Bible*. See the "Keep in Touch" page (at the end of this book, just before the Bibliography) for further instructions and to see all that you will find on the website.

- Explored theological concepts,
- Evaluated others' opinions about Bible interpretation,
- Worked through fears and concerns,
- Formed their own opinions, and
- Made a personal decision about the issue.

Additionally, they share some of the resources they found most helpful during their discernment and disclose many lessons learned as they tested their theories and beliefs, especially as they lived out their decisions within the body of Christ.

Sometimes we'll be able to identify with them and sometimes we won't; but we will learn a great deal through reading about their experiences and the ways they tried to make an intelligent, faithful, informed decision about this issue. Through the diversity of the women's backgrounds and traditions, their study approaches, and their decisions, we can learn more about how to make our own theological decisions. Their examples help us consider the complexity of the issue with greater competence.

COMMUNITY RECOMMENDED

This discernment process is not a passive exercise. Thinking through this or any other theological issue demands activity—mental, spiritual, and, typically, physical, in terms of study and written reflections, as well as talking with other people. It is difficult to read a few books and truly know what you think about this issue biblically.

Even though you will meet many mentors in the pages of this book, it helps to think through complex ideas with others as or after you've mulled them over a while. For this reason, unless you are an extremely self-directed person, you might consider surrounding yourself with others who also want to walk through this issue for themselves. In fact, I strongly encourage you to pursue this within a group or community to keep you going and to find encouragement along the way. The mentors' stories and my own voice are meant to provide you with a sense of "virtual sisterly relationship"; but we all know there is no substitute for real-time relationships—someone you can call, and say, "What did you think about that *ridiculous* idea Natalie presented on page 97? What *was* she thinking?"

If you do choose to pursue this with a group, you all will benefit from journeying together, keeping each other going and encouraging each other along the way. That said, the book is written so that you can read it alone if you choose that approach. Also, it is written in such a way that you might pick it up and put it down, pursuing sections as your time and energy allow.

UNITY

You will find an undercurrent throughout this book that stems from a disheartening aspect of the discussion among Christians on women's roles in the church. *Problem*: this issue is *divisive*—it has been historically, and is currently. It has divided denominations, churches, friendships, and marriages. Other big-question issues have, too. However, no matter how much research you do and no matter what position you end up believing is scriptural, none of us—not one, *according to Jesus* in John 17[3]—is allowed to be out of fellowship with another faithful believer over this issue. That displeases our Lord, who desires our unity.

One important goal of this book is for you not only to learn how to know what you believe, but know why you believe as you do. If the subject arises, you can participate thoughtfully and knowledgably. In this way, you can more effectively contribute to the unity and maturity of the body of Christ.

THE BOOK'S LAYOUT

Throughout *Women, Leadership, and the Bible*, we address the million-dollar question:

> ***"How would I know?"***
>
> **In other words:** How do I face my intimidation factors and also develop myself biblically and theologically such that I can explore my deep biblical and personal questions about women's roles and make my own thoughtful decision about it?

3. The emphasis on unity may also be found throughout Ephesians, not to mention most of the New Testament.

The anchor points of *Women, Leadership, and the Bible* are comprised of the five steps in this discernment process:

Step 1: Prepare

Step 2: List

Step 3: Study

Step 4: Filter

Step 5: Choose

"Step 3: Study" and "Step 4: Filter," easily make up the bulk of the book, for good reason: they're the most labor-intensive. In step 3, we focus on our top-priority filter for discerning theological answers: God's Word. The Bible is our *primary* determining factor when discerning answers to these questions—not our feelings or our experiences, although we inevitably factor in other influences as we move through the entire discernment process.

Discernment is a spiritual process; yet, it cannot be accomplished without intellectual effort and focus. Therefore, this process includes teaching you how to do your own biblical work—how to "chew your own food," as one mentor described the process of thinking for yourself. "Step 3: Study" helps you learn how to find answers in God's Word using the thorough, systematic analyses used by theology students, seminarians, academics, and others who "do this for a living." This will give you solid traction toward doing your own deep, exegetical Bible study. Because all prayerful discernment must begin with truth, your study is critical to your entire process.

Step 4 then highlights filters, both internal and external, through which you can process everything you learned and the facts you gathered in steps 1 through 3. In Step 5, you make your own decision and consider its implications.

The "Your Turn" Exercises

An old proverb, attributed to the Chinese, says, "Tell me and I'll forget; show me and I may remember; involve me and I'll understand."

Reading a book about biblical and theological development is good; but digging in and doing it yourself is better. (Turning around and teaching it to someone else is the best!)

Throughout *Women, Leadership, and the Bible*, you will encounter this little icon: ✍📖. This writing hand and book icon indicate that there is an exercise, question, or action point that correlates to what you just read. These "Your Turn" exercises will help you engage directly with the ideas presented.

Those who wish may read straight through, of course, and then revisit the application points afterward. Some people prefer this method of learning. You can, of course, go through the book without doing the "Your Turn" exercises; however, they are here to help you along exactly in this way. Remember, the most growth comes from active practice, not passivity.

In addition to the "Your Turn" exercises, you will also find other text boxes that provide more detailed examples, and in-depth explanations.

SHALL WE?

Discover for yourself, not simply receiving what someone tells you she thinks you should believe the Bible says about women's roles in church leadership. Know how to know for yourself what the Bible says. Indeed, you will also discover more about yourself: how you know what you know; what assumptions you have consciously or unconsciously made; *why* you believe what you believe; and, best of all in my opinion, that you can do it.

Will you move forward with me now? Let's start discerning answers. We'll begin by cutting to the chase: what is this discernment plan?

Chapter 2

The Plan, Introduced

> *Five easy steps to going green!*
> *Five easy steps to effective study habits!*
> *Five easy steps to creating a small business marketing plan!*
> *Five easy steps to growing beautiful roses!*
> *Five easy steps to get that red-carpet hair style!*

In less than one second on Google, a search entry for "five easy steps" results in 81 million listings. *81 million!* What does this say? We want answers and we want them in five steps. And we want those steps to come easy.

Ahem. *Well* . . .

The Plan

1. Prepare
2. List
3. Study
4. Filter
5. Choose

If you look at the box on this page ("The Plan"), you'll notice that five steps also comprise this simple plan. It's simple, yes, but I wouldn't try to sham-wow you by saying it's easy. It's not easy. But, listen: you have chosen to read this book for your own good reasons and you are to be congratulated! You can do it! *You can.* And won't it feel *good* when you find some answers for yourself that you can truly stand by biblically.

Perhaps you have felt stymied by the conflict surrounding women's roles for a long time and believe it's time to get to the bottom of it. Perhaps you are in ministry and women and men alike ask you what you think about it, yet you feel unprepared to answer their questions. Perhaps you have wanted to sort this out for yourself for a long time, but didn't know where to begin. Or, perhaps you are in or are leading a Bible study group that decided to study this issue and you want some fodder for a thoughtful approach.

I don't know your reasons for reading this book, but I congratulate you and cheer you on! Jump in and get going. Let God deepen your walk with him, ground you further in his Word, broaden your theological insight, and, as an added bonus, strengthen your confidence in your own ability to sort through this big, often very personal issue.

BAD NEWS AND GOOD NEWS

One of the primary goals for this book is to give you a plan for forming your own theologically and biblically grounded understanding concerning women's roles in church leadership. As you read in chapter 1, what you'll find here is a *plan*, not a position. There are no easy responsible answers. That's the bad news, if you consider that bad.

The good news is that through this process you will learn how to evaluate and integrate what you already know about Scripture with what you will study in the future. You'll learn how to give numerous factors, interpretations, and opinions their fair chance and make your own solid, biblically informed decision.

When you do the work yourself, this benefits you because your decision will be defensible, educated, and flexible.

- **Defensible**. If the situation arises (and, chances are, it will), you will be able to explain your thoughts clearly to someone inquiring about your beliefs or practices, because you will have thought clearly about it. The goal is not to be able to argue about it; rather, if a discussion arises, you can speak your biblical mind with theological thoughtfulness.
- **Educated**. You'll have done the research and thinking yourself, so you'll be standing on your own two theological feet. You can know not only *what* you believe, but *why*.
- **Flexible**. Although you'll make a solid, biblically based working decision about women's roles, you'll still be able to leave room for grace. You'll need this grace for both yourself and others, and also to welcome the further work of the Holy Spirit in your mind, heart, and life when it comes to this issue. This gives you the mental and spiritual space to learn, study, pray, and think about women's roles

in church leadership, realizing you'll grow more in your understanding of God's heart, and this issue, over time.

As a bonus, you'll be acting *responsibly* before God by inquiring of the Lord above all other inputs and influences. It's appropriate for a Christian to take a systematic approach to making a decision, especially concerning issues theological in nature. In our grappling with and taking responsibility for our own decisions, we honor the Lord with our minds and our faithfulness, as well as our discipline.

Also, when we do the work ourselves, we are better prepared to live with those women and men around us who are dealing with and asking big questions. Adela Carter spoke about this necessity:

> When we train Christian women and prepare them to go out and reach lost women, part of the process of training is a lot about gender, about feminism, and about what the Bible says about gender. I do teach on this, because if they are going to go out and minister to the women we are ministering to, these questions are out there. They are going to come up and you need to know what they are and grapple with them in your own life first. You don't have to have all the answers, but you have got to be willing to understand that things are not always as they seem. And you have to take responsibility for your own position . . . and you need to explore it.

Although you won't find any "right answers" in this plan, you will find assistance toward

- *Sifting* through Scripture and other people's opinions about Scripture.
- *Analyzing* and *filtering* those opinions.
- *Forming* your own opinion on women's roles in the church.

In short, this involves *discerning* solid answers to your questions about women's roles.

EVERY LIFE FACTOR COUNTS WHEN DISCERNING

When discerning, every life factor counts, although some take priority. Culture and our sub-cultures are helpful and can give us interpretations and beliefs to consider, but shouldn't be our foremost guides in belief and action. Likewise, your gut instincts are good and God-given, but must not be your only criteria for deciding what your beliefs and practices should be. Prayer is crucial, absolutely, but is not the only means God gave us to know how he wants us to act and what we should believe.

As people who believe that God's Word should be our foremost guide for life, it would make sense that Scripture study should form the central basis for a decision. Indeed, it should. But discernment doesn't stop with a mental assessment of facts. It involves much more:

> Discernment seeks to get at the heart of our relationship with ourselves, others, and God, and to help us determine the moral response most consistent with who we are as people made in God's image. . . . The goal is always to select from the possible options the action that best promotes right relationships with others and leads us more deeply into communion with God. . . . For this we need to engage the whole network of human capacities.[4]

This "whole network" includes both internal and external input such as Scripture, prayer, faith, reason, facts, emotions, intuition, study, research, church, and community, as well as a personal, settled peace.

We are not creatures who operate solely on facts. We're spiritual. We're moral. We're social and emotional. So, we need to take the facts, opinions, and interpretations of Scripture we gather, along with our own conclusions, and assess them all using the other inputs available to us, both internal and external. We must sift through them in light of the impact different conclusions can have. Then we decide.

WE SEEK TO ASSIMILATE WHAT WE FIND

When you make a discerning theological decision, you're not going through the process simply for the fun of it (at least most of us aren't). The decision we make typically impacts our lives to its core. We are talking about informed beliefs here. These beliefs affect our actions at a fundamental level. We assimilate, we absorb, and we incorporate these beliefs into our existing life structures and live with them.

Frankly put, this is a big deal. Because it is a big deal, it might take a few rounds of a discernment process to find a decision that brings you a settled peace you can live with before God, within the body of Christ,

4. Panicola, "Good Decisions," 66, 67.

and in the world at large. That is okay. The process is as important as the decision itself.

Before we are ready to move forward into the plan, however, we need to examine where our real hope lies for sorting through this issue: the Holy Spirit.

THEOLOGY OF THIS PLAN: YOU HAVE A GUIDE!

Your foundational theology for this plan, and your hope for coming to any kind of biblical understanding of this issue, or any other, is the guidance of the Holy Spirit.

When you need to figure out something that's theological in nature, begin with prayer and ask the Holy Spirit for guidance. His help is assured when we bring our questions to him, because he is the one who gives us wisdom and illuminates our minds, hearts, and spirits (e.g., John 16:13; Eph 1:17). So, bring the questions you have about women's roles in the church to God in prayer. Weave prayer into the very fabric of your discernment. Resist launching into something and getting caught up in it without praying.

Remember who this is all about. Consider the story of LaVerne Tolbert (see the box, this page). Although God didn't answer every question for her and she did go on to study the issue in great depth, she began with prayer, and God gave her a starting point.

> **Along the Path: Prayer**
>
> When LaVerne Tolbert sensed issues arising in her church about women's roles, she was unsure about it. Her first instinct was to pray and seek God's heart. In Laverne's words . . .
>
> "I prayed about it. I did not have any ambition—*ever*—to be a Senior Pastor or anything like that. That was *never* my ambition, but this situation just didn't sit right with me. I asked the Lord in my time with him whether women were supposed to be pastors.
>
> The answer I received was Jeremiah 3:15: 'I will give you shepherds [in the New King James, this Word is "pastors" with a small "p"] according to my heart who will feed you with knowledge and understanding.'
>
> God was telling me he had called me to be a 'pastor' with a small 'p' and I could not grasp it at first."

Jesus has provided a miraculous and wonderful gift to all who believe in him as the Christ, the Son of God: that of his very own presence, assurance and guidance in real-time. This is what the Spirit does; this is who the Spirit is: Jesus' gift of himself after his bodily presence on earth ended.

When we recognize and acknowledge personally that Jesus is the Son of God, repent, and are baptized, the Spirit marks us like a seal, stating "This one belongs to God in Christ" (Eph 1:13–14). That's a one-time deal.

But it's not like Neo in the movie *The Matrix*.[5] In *The Matrix*, when freed humans like Neo and his compatriots needed to learn a new skill or knowledge set, those who knew how could upload a program into their electrical systems and they could instantly fully function with that skill set inside the computer-generated reality called the Matrix. Unfortunately, it doesn't happen that way in our non-computer-generated reality. In fact, not much happens in our Christian life that's instantaneous (outside of miracles, but that's another book)! The reality involves slow, faithful seeking alongside growing in understanding and faith. And along the way, the Spirit educates us about who God is and how we live for his glory. He also empowers, sustains, and grows our faith in Christ.

So, our theology for discerning answers to our questions is that the Holy Spirit helps us discern those answers. The entire plan rests on this belief. We don't solely ask teachers, experts, and mentors in our life for the "right answer"; we ask the Spirit. Yet God, like an excellent teacher, doesn't just outright tell us the answers to our questions. We must use our minds, along with our hearts. And, while we live and learn within a community, the community of believers in Christ, we do seek counsel there, but we don't rely 100 percent on the community for our beliefs and practices. We take our community's beliefs, teaching, and practices to the Word of God for checking and to the Spirit for leading as we discern.

Now, the Holy Spirit does many things, and for every action of the Spirit, there are active responses we can make. To learn how the Spirit leads and helps us toward biblical, workable answers to our questions concerning women's roles in church leadership, along with how we can respond, let's look at four of the Spirit's functions.

The Holy Spirit **unites**. We can respond to others with humility and grace and we promote unity among believers.

5. *The Matrix*, directed by A. Wachowski and L. Wachowski.

The Holy Spirit **loves**. We can respond by loving and promoting loving relationships.

The Holy Spirit **illuminates** our minds. We can respond by being diligent to know the Lord.

The Holy Spirit **grows** and **matures** us. We can respond similarly by encouraging and supporting human growth and maturity.

Let's look briefly at each of these in turn.

Unity

The Holy Spirit is the Lord's gift to us and for us, accomplishing the work in us that Jesus began. The Spirit unites believers because Jesus desires the unity of all who believe in him and are one with the Father and him. How do we know this? Primarily from John 17, the prayer Jesus prayed on the eve of his crucifixion. (See especially John 17:20–23.) But Paul also prominently and frequently emphasizes unity among believers in Christ. He teaches that the Spirit's presence and direction are crucial to that unity. His letter to the Ephesians is a shining example, especially chapter 4.

So, because Jesus desires our unity, and the Spirit is working for unity within the body of Christ as well, we can respond by seeking to promote unity among believers.

What does this mean? In general, it means we assess the impact that the possible choices and decisions we make will have on relationships, including relationships with God, self, our local church, the world, and the at-large Christian community. We choose an attitude of grace toward others, considering their understanding of Scripture as well as our own, remaining respectful as far as it is within our ability and as long as it doesn't clearly contradict Scripture. And even if it does appear to us to contradict Scripture, we can still treat others with respect. This can take on different forms and definitions for different people.

Susan McCormick discerns whether her decisions reflect Jesus' desire for our unity by considering the overall impact of her presence for good to the body of Christ. In ministering, she wants to do good to the body and not cause a rift: "If a point came that created harm or dissension in the body because of my presence, I would leave."

This kind of leaving, by the way, is not for the sake of running away from tension or because of fear of engaging the issue with brothers and sisters who disagree. Sue has certainly engaged, steadily and faithfully, with the other leaders in her church on the issue of women's leadership roles in the church. Instead, Sue was referring to the value of unity in that church over her personal call to ministry in that church.

Love

The Holy Spirit loves because Jesus loves and because, well, he's God. More than a mere affection, Paul describes love (*agape*) as the supreme, most enduring aspect of life, belief, and relationship (1 Cor 13:13). Much more than a warm, fuzzy feeling, it encompasses self-sacrifice and the promotion of another or others' best interest. Alice Mathews once described this to me: "We can't always drum up the warm emotion, but we can always do what is in the other person's best interest." Jesus desires us to love and, yes, commands us to love in this manner (e.g., John 13:34–35). So we love and promote loving relationships. And the Spirit enables us to do this (Rom 5:5).

When we read about early Christian communities, we see how they diligently tried to understand God's Word and to live out its message in their own context. Many times (e.g., 1 Cor 5–6; Phil 4:2–3), the biblical writers had to say to the believers, in effect, "Hey, the way you're living and acting is not bringing honor to the name and message of Jesus as Christ and you're not being ruled and guided by love. So, stop it (or try doing it another way)!"

I like what my friend Dr. Kathryn Greene-McCreight said about interpretation during a conversation we had one day over coffee: "The early church had to discern how their actions and their interpretation of God's Word reflected on Christ to their world. We have to work out the same thing and consider it when we interpret Scripture. In our living out of what we believe the Bible to say, how are we being witness to the world around us to the charity and forgiveness we have in Christ?"

I eventually learned that Kathryn did her doctoral dissertation on issues that arise when people interpret the Bible using a plain-text reading.[6] In her studies, she learned that St. Augustine, early church father and one of the most influential theologians in the history of the church, taught that interpretation of the Bible must propel us toward two facets of faith:

6. More on plain-text reading interpretation in chapter 10, page 102

1. Faith in God, as supported by the historic teaching of the church, which strove to identify and preserve apostolic teaching, and
2. Love of God and love of neighbor. This is two-pronged and reflects Jesus' summary of the Law in the Gospels (Matt 22:37–40; Mark 12:28–31). Augustine called this the "Rule of Charity."

Kathryn summarized Augustine's outlook this way: according to Augustine, "biblical interpretation that does not build us up in the faith of the church and the love of God and neighbor is faulty. Augustine says this in *De Doctrina Christiana*."

We can probably accept that fairly readily: our Bible interpretation should form people in both faith and love and its results in us should project that same faith and love to the world. Here's a little twist, though: he went as far as saying that if what you come up with does *not* form you in faith and love, what you came up with was *wrong*. Period. Um, that's not politically correct! But political correctness was not his concern; spiritual formation and good interpretation were.

His suggestion was either to go back and try it again or leave interpretation to someone else who knows better! However, please don't take that as a suggestion to give up trying to understand Scripture for yourself. I do not believe that was Augustine's intention!

Illumination

When it comes to understanding and discernment, the word "illumination" gorgeously captures what we're trying to achieve—or rather, to receive. In one dictionary, "illumination" means "the act of making understood; clarification."[7] This describes the Holy Spirit's work.

Another part of the definition describes illumination as "spiritual or intellectual enlightenment; insight or understanding." That is what we receive from the Spirit as he makes God's truth understood to us and glorifies Jesus, helping us know him more. Paul was fairly clear on this aspect of the Holy Spirit's work in his first letter to the Corinthians:

> But, as it is written,
> "What no eye has seen, nor ear heard,
> nor the heart of man imagined,
> what God has prepared for those who love him."

7. "Illumination," *Collins English Dictionary*.

> These things God has revealed to us through the Spirit. For the Spirit searches everything, even the depths of God. For who knows a person's thoughts except the spirit of that person, which is in him? So also no one comprehends the thoughts of God except the Spirit of God. Now we have received not the spirit of the world, but the Spirit who is from God, that we might understand the things freely given us by God. And we impart this in words not taught by human wisdom but taught by the Spirit, interpreting spiritual truths to those who are spiritual. (1 Cor 2:9–12, ESV)

The Holy Spirit illuminates our minds because we need it. Jesus desires that we continue to grow in our understanding of who he is (John 14:25–27; 17:2–3) and wants his followers to remain in his love (John 15; 17:6–24). To remain in Jesus and grow in our understanding, we need the Spirit's power, guidance, and insight. The Holy Spirit gives us our understanding of him. That is his gift and his job—his continuation of the job Jesus began.

I love the entire concept of "illumination" and the word itself. To me, it conveys light, life, wonder, mystery, knowledge, intensity, revelation, passion, and enlightenment all at once. But what does illumination produce in us? How do we respond?

In response to these gifts from the Spirit, we strive diligently to know the Lord more fully through his Word and through the relationship of prayer. The really wonderful thing is that the Holy Spirit not only gives us understanding of God's Word, but also provides us with the ability and strength to respond. He aids our diligence. How's that for a deal? You *can* have your cake and eat it, too.

I see two sides to this coin. One side is, for lack of a better word, wonderfully passive. We receive what the Holy Spirit teaches us, such as revealing Jesus to us and literally helping us understand what God is saying in his Word and how it applies to us. (See Isa 11:2; Acts 15:28; 2 Cor 3:3; Eph 1:17; 1 John 5:6.) What a joy, encouragement, and, frankly, relief.

The other side of the coin is our active, diligent response to the awakening of our hearts and minds to know the Lord further, as well as help others know him more fully (Col 1:28–29). In our response, we diligently pray and study the word—"diligently" being the key word here. We do our best to present ourselves as "work-women approved," rightly dividing the Word of God (this is a play off of 2 Tim 2:15).

As my personal trainer (okay, she's on a DVD I got from Sam's Club) says to me Tuesday, Thursday, and Saturday mornings, "Don't phone it in!" This is your spiritual life and your own accountability to God. No one gets to stand behind anyone else when we account for our lives and our works to God (1 Cor 3:10–14).

Throughout her life, Karen Moy often heard that women's mental capacity was insufficient for understanding theological matters. So, she made it her goal in life to be diligent in handling Scripture, so a woman's mental capacity could not be blamed for her beliefs.

> Over time, it became apparent (although it wasn't *always* true) that I was chiefly arguing against men, part of whose criticism was that women were insufficiently intellectually rigorous to handle Scripture. So I realized that part of the best way for me to refute that argument was for me to be intellectually rigorous in my own handling of Scriptures so there was no weakness, so there was no opportunity for that argument to come to the fore.
>
> I don't use "I feel" words any more. I don't even use "I think" words. I use "I've concluded," "I believe," "I've studied," "It seems to me that . . ."
>
> This way my argument is intellectually rigorous, so that no one can say, "She's just another weak woman with strong emotions who works from her intuition."
>
> I get that from women, as well. In fact, what I get from women is, "You don't seem emotional *enough*."
>
> I say, "Well, I sat down and studied."

So, be diligent and attend to the quality of your work, and seek and enjoy the Spirit's illumination. By the power of the Spirit, "build with care" (1 Cor 3:10).

Growth and Maturity

By the power of the Spirit, God brings us along in our maturity as believing people (Eph 4:1–16). God uses everything to take us toward that maturity. This is one of the main ideas conveyed in Romans 5:1–5 and 8:18–39. In cooperation with him, we promote human growth and maturity, too.

What does this look like for us? Michael Panicola speaks of human flourishing as being one of the primary goals of Christian ethical and moral discernment.[8] I'm inclined to agree. What does this mean? Let's unpack the idea.

Jesus says that loving God with all our heart, soul, and mind and loving our neighbor as we love ourselves are the two greatest commandments found in the Old Testament Law. These "laws of love," according to Jesus, are foundational to the rest of the entire Law. These laws of love root and establish us in relationship. It is not so much whether we're doing something "right" according to the Law; rather, it's whether we are "doing right" toward God and toward other people.

We can see this from the way Jesus answers the Pharisees' question about the greatest commandment in Matthew 22:23–40. First, the Sadducees pose a puzzle to him about which person a certain widow would be married to at the resurrection. This was a ridiculous question in their minds, because they didn't even believe in a resurrection. The Sadducees only honored the books of Moses, called the Pentateuch, which are the first five books of the Hebrew Bible (Genesis, Exodus, Leviticus, Numbers, and Deuteronomy). In these, Moses never speaks directly of a resurrection.

I imagine Jesus restraining himself from saying, "You schmucks. You really don't get it, do you?" He does essentially tell them this, but declares it in a much more tactful way than I would: "You are in error because you do not know the Scriptures or the power of God." Okay, maybe that wasn't so tactful, but he educates them in the process. He establishes to them that marriage as we know it won't exist in heaven—it will be something different and better. ("*Bam!*" Imagine the 70s Batman TV show special effects flashing on the screen to the sudden screech of trumpets!) Then he points out that elsewhere in the Pentateuch (Exod 3:6) God speaks of being the God of Abraham, Isaac, and Jacob in a very present tense: "I am."

Jesus declared, "He is not the God of the dead but of the living." If the resurrection did not exist, how could this living, present-tense relationship continue? ("*Pow!*" Batman-trumpets scream again!) Ouch. Everyone's astonished, and the Sadducees skulk away licking their wounded prides.

8. Panicola, "Good Decisions," 65–66.

Directly following the Sadducees' trickery, the Pharisees, who honored the Old Testament Law in all of its infinitesimal commands, come through with their own specially concocted question designed to trip Jesus: "Teacher, which is the greatest commandment in the Law?"

Jesus summarizes all of the Law by summarizing the Law's capstone set of laws, the Ten Commandments, and by setting those commandments in the context of love, that is, the Law's command to love God and neighbor. They are about love, he declares.

Basically, both groups, the Pharisees and the Sadducees, tried hard to trap Jesus theologically. They were nit-picking the Law and Jesus responded by taking it to a higher level: where is the love that gives glory to God and his power and causes people to flourish in that love?

When we love our neighbors as ourselves in every situation, we promote right relationships among people. When we promote right relationships among people, we reflect the love of God. This right-ness causes us, and others around us, to grow, mature, and flourish.

Therefore, as you examine various interpretations and positions on the question of women's roles, you might ask, "Does this position promote right relationships and human growth and maturity, and encourage the deepening of our relationship to God?"

THE FIVE-(NOT-SO-EASY)-STEP PLAN, REVISITED

The *(Simple, but Not Easy)* Plan

1. Prepare
2. Identify
3. Study
4. Filter
5. Choose

Returning to the idea of this plan being "five *not*-so-easy steps," although this plan isn't easy and it is challenging, you *can* do it by the power of the Spirit! Pause a minute, if you haven't already, and let this theology of the Holy Spirit sink into your soul. You can be at peace knowing and trusting that the Spirit guides you and gives you illumination and strength for this journey. The Lord himself, by the power of his Spirit, guides us in our inquiry.

Your Turn:

As you discern, ask, "Does this option unite? Am I willing to extend grace to others as they seek the Lord? Does this idea (or practice) reflect and promote love? Am I diligently seeking God's heart through fervent prayer and responsible study? Does this alternative promote human growth and maturity?"

It's time to begin—and we must begin by getting our head in the game. To *be* ready, we must *get* ready. That's our job in step 1: "Prepare."

STEP 1

Prepare

METHODS TO CONSIDER ADOPTING

When it comes to football, if you ever stumbled across me watching it, you're just as likely to find that there's a crowd of people there I'm enjoying, along with a crock full of little smokies and a pile of barbecued meatballs. Admittedly, I'm not there to watch the game on the television. However, occasionally, I try to bond with my husband a bit by sitting with him and watching football.

One evening, I watched Sunday Night NFL with him—Ravens v. New England. For one moment (there *are* actually moments when I watch), the camera zoomed in on the Ravens' captain, Ray Lewis, who was practically preaching a sermon to the squad preparing to take the field. His goals? To inspire, to refocus the squad after their moments on the sideline, to direct their thinking toward their on-field goals—basically, to get their heads in the game.

The Plan

1. **Prepare**
2. Identify
3. Study
4. Filter
5. Choose

It struck me: that is precisely what we must do as we begin this process. However, instead of huddling and then slapping each others' tighties, let's look at some methods to adopt for this process. You may want to consider adopting them for the rest of your life, too; they'll come in handy for just about everything. You might think of these methods as perspectives—ways of looking at the world and at the subjects you study. Adopt them and you will gain solid footing for proceeding in your discernment process. In the next three chapters, we'll discuss three methods:

Chapter 3—Prep Method 1. Ask Questions. Assume Nothing.

Chapter 4—Prep Method 2. Get out of (Your) Town!

Chapter 5—Prep Method 3. Plan for Ambiguities.

Chapter 3

Prep Method 1

Ask Questions, Assume Nothing

A GOOD INVESTIGATOR ASKS, "What's the full scoop?" She doesn't quit until she asks every question she can think of. Then, she asks other people for questions she may not have thought of and asks those as well.

I readily admit that I'm a big Nancy Drew fan. I read and reread the series when I was a girl, along with the Hardy Boys, the Bobbsey Twins, Encyclopedia Brown, and whatever other kid-detective books I could find. A few Christmases ago, while in Austin at my brother's family home, I found myself sneakily rereading my three nieces' Nancy Drew books whenever I could, usually when I was nursing my baby in a quiet room. Nancy couldn't help herself from asking questions when something was afoot. Her father, Carson Drew, "the prominent lawyer," as the books always describe him, praised her for her inquisitive nature. And, as we all know, Nancy always solved her mystery.

When it comes to finding biblical answers, as far as you're concerned you're the Nancy Drew of Bible study. Adopt her strategy and you'll solve some of your own personal biblical mysteries. Ask all the good "Who? What? When? Where? Why? How?" questions you can conjure up and dig, dig, dig until you find solid answers.

Candie Blankman asked questions and then asked more questions:

> I asked questions about everything.
>
> I went through the whole Pentecostal analysis thing when I was in high school, studying to find out, "What is this 'tongue' thing, and does everybody have to do it, and is it this or is it that?"

Even as a teenager I was involved in serious Bible study, challenging "What does it really say?"

I was always challenging what the leader was telling me. One time we had a Pentecostal, Foursquare Gospel woman who was leading the coffee house in the town where I graduated from high school. She was telling everyone they had to speak in tongues as the initial evidence of the Holy Spirit—everyone needed to do it.

And I thought, "Hey, wait a minute. I've known Christ for many years and that's not been a part of my experience and I don't feel like I'm 'less than.'" But, I had to go to the Scriptures to find out.

Something in me—maybe it was something my parents taught me or something I was born with—was really bent on knowing for myself and not just accepting what someone else said. That started pretty early.

So regarding these issues about women, I just didn't see anywhere in Scripture this over-arching thing everyone talked about in my evangelical community. I certainly saw Timothy and the different passages that said a woman ought not to do this or that, but I had also been taught enough Bible exegesis to know you don't just take a verse on first reading—at face-value—and assume that is what it means.

Go ahead. Challenge everyone's presuppositions. Challenge your own while you're at it. That's what Adela Carter did:

You talk about ordination, and I say, "What is ordination, anyway? Why should *anybody* be ordained? What is it? Why can't you ordain the doorman?"

I question the whole thing. To me it's not a matter of a *woman* getting ordained, but why is *anyone* getting ordained? Why are certain people ordained and not others? And why for certain things and not other things? Why do nursery workers not get ordained if they are called to work with little children?

I'm not necessarily saying I'm against it, but I don't give it as much importance as other people do. They think it's a very important issue; but I don't know if it is or not. Is it really? Biblically, is it really an important issue? I can see why it has social importance and cultural significance for how church systems get set up. I understand the politics of it. There are systems to keep certain kinds of people in and other people out and all that.

So, I question it *all.*

Karen Moy shared how she developed in this area of asking good questions:

I believe an awful lot of churches, and an awful lot of Christians, would like their pastors and their preachers to chew the food for them. And the pastors and preachers are happy to do that. In particular, I fault *most* of the women I have met in my life for either (A) it doesn't occur to them to ask questions, or (B) they are afraid to.

In retrospect, I think perhaps my experience was unusual, in that I had a father who simultaneously *always* asked questions and yet still had respect for authority. He "chewed his own food" is my expression for it.

He had ten years in the military so we had a very authoritarian household, but there *weren't* questions you *couldn't* ask. In fact, you were *expected* to figure something out for yourself.

That was probably important in my spiritual development. I wasn't ever expected to swallow something just because my parents believed it.

So, my whole premise is that I am going to ask questions. I want to make sure. Also, along the way I learned that people lie to you and people can be mistaken. So they *could* be wrong about Jesus; they *could* be wrong about the Bible. They also *could* be wrong about, "This is how you do marriage"; "This is how you do parenting"; "This is how you do work." Or even, "When you graduate from college, if you really want to serve Jesus, you need to be a missionary."

So, I have a questioning approach. I am thoughtful and purposeful. I want to know *why* I am doing something. I don't want to do something just because we have been doing it this way for 400 years. I might well continue doing it that way, but I want to "chew my own food." I want to see original source material, read it, and figure it out for myself, because—and I go back and remember the other things I've learned—people *lie* to you and people can be *mistaken.*

✍📖Your Turn:

List any questions that arise in your mind. Write them all down and try to answer them as you study.

Remember the old adage, "There's no such thing as a dumb question!"[9]

9. During my years of intensive study, I wrote a list of all of the questions I could think of that we can legitimately ask of the scriptural texts. If you would like to see that list to spur your thinking, you can find it in the article "Questions We Can Ask of the Text" at www.womenleadershipbible.com or through www.natalieeastman.com.

Chapter 4

Prep Method 2

Get Out of (Your) Town!

Our perspective on Scripture can easily be influenced, even skewed sometimes, by the perspective of the group(s) we live in and associate with day-to-day. These groups are our subcultures. It's normal to be affected by them. As investigators, though, we need to attempt to have as much objectivity as possible. To do this, we can apply some correctives to our investigation. We'll discuss two here that are very helpful: variety and fairness.

VARIETY

To make sure your subculture influences you in healthy ways, but doesn't hold complete sway over your thinking, occasionally get out of your subculture. Become familiar with different viewpoints and interpretations.

This, like the discernment plan overall, is fairly simple, but not always easy. Some groups honestly don't appreciate thinking outside their own box. You might find yourself swimming upstream in your own subculture simply by exposing yourself to other viewpoints, even if you don't adopt them. But, don't give up. It's the right thing to do. Consider Kay Daigle and Karen Moy's comments and encouragement.

> [Kay] To women who want to figure out what they believe about something theological, but who don't have the time, money, inclination, or whatever to go to seminary, at the very least it's helpful to

read a resource that gives more than one side, so that you have an understanding of the other perspectives.

Most of us are given a perspective by our church or our friends or those in a Bible study with us or somewhere—or just by the tradition we are in. We're taught a perspective by the person who gets up on every Sunday and who leads the church.

I think it's important to understand the perspectives of other people, so that we're not making this a cause of division. There are a lot of people who are very adamant about this issue who do not understand—don't even take the time to try to understand—what the other group believes about it. It's important at least to understand where the other side is coming from, simply to understand each other better.

[Karen:] [When I'm facing an issue,] I go look into Scriptures. I read them all.

I read exhaustively from every particular direction until I see, "Yep, this is what I thought it said. It does seem to be confirmed in Scripture and now I can define it and defend it and explain the other person's point of view any time this comes up."

FAIRNESS

Plainly put, be fair. You're not doing yourself any favors by studying the other perspective, whatever that other perspective may be, only to shoot it down. Misrepresenting what someone is saying simply because you don't want to believe it doesn't help, either. Kay Daigle found that people liked to argue against things people weren't saying or nit-pick little points of the argument, but not the whole argument.

I have found many of the arguments on both sides frustrating, because they *all* would often set up these "strawman" arguments that the other side wasn't arguing in the first place, and then argue against it. In doing that, *both* sides tried to make the other side look more extreme than they really were, instead of just dealing with what they're really saying.

I found myself really frustrated and angry as I read books on *both* sides. I would find myself saying (a *lot*), "That's *not* what the other person *said*! *Why* are you suggesting that that's their position?"

I have also observed the kinds of things that Kay pointed out. Honestly, I've probably done them myself at different times. Learn and grow, I always say. I'm learning and growing—in grace—right alongside everyone else. I've learned, often the hard way, that this kind of unfairness and misrepresentation, even if it exists solely in my mind and I never speak the words aloud, does not help me truly understand an issue. I'm sure it doesn't glorify the Lord, either.

I must be willing to look a view squarely in its face, metaphorically speaking. I imagine myself looking my friends who hold a contrary view squarely in the face and loving them because I am actively attempting to understand them as fully as I possibly can.

Chapter 5

Prep Method 3

Plan for Ambiguities

WHEN IT COMES TO Bible interpretation, there is much room for ambiguity. I see ambiguity occurring nearly equally in three different, but related scenarios. These don't necessarily occur in a particular order and may even occur mutually exclusively; but they all occur.

In this chapter, we'll look at examples of these ambiguity-inducing scenarios; then, some plans for facing them.

AMBIGUITY-INDUCING SCENARIOS

Scenario 1. Your Own Interpretation

This first scenario is the solo attempt: attempting on your own to understand what the Bible seems to be saying. Obviously, a lot of ambiguity can occur here, especially if one has no training in interpretation.

Example of Scenario 1

Sandra Glahn nailed one of the major difficulties with going solo when trying to understand what the Bible is saying: what do you do when the Bible seems to say two different things, depending on which verses you look at?

> There are so many good issues where you can line up your verses on both sides and pretend the other ones aren't there. For example, take

> the issue of "eternal security," meaning "once saved, always saved, no matter what."
>
> In our Christian culture, if you doubt your salvation, people question you: "Well, do you have a story in the first place, meaning, 'Well, were you really ever saved?'! Didn't you 'receive Jesus into your heart?'"
>
> But, looking at it from another perspective, still biblical, it seems like James said, "Well, let's see here. . . . Are you loving your brother? Are you lying? Are you . . . ?" It's not merely a question of whether you "accepted Jesus." It's more than that.
>
> The issue's not as clear-cut as we'd like it to be. God is much more into mystery.

Does the Bible say, "Only receive Jesus and that's all you need to do to be saved?" Or, does it say that there's something eternally important about what happens after you "go forward" to receive Christ? This ambiguity leads to not knowing what to believe, quite frankly, and to a classic reaction: paralysis! Augh!

Ambiguity Scenario 2. Your Interpretation of Other People's Interpretations

You might think of this scenario as hearsay. In other words, attempting to understand what the Bible seems to be saying through what another person—perhaps your pastor, a friend, or an author—believes the Bible says. There's a lot of room for ambiguity to occur here, depending on how much more expert one perceives the other person to be.

Example of Scenario 2

In addition to understanding what God is saying, we have the added bonus of potential confusion caused by conflicting interpretations by various scholars, pastors, and other interpreters. Kay Daigle described facing this kind of discrepancy over the word *kephale* (the Greek word found in Ephesians 5:23 and other places):

> I've read a lot of things on both sides of the whole "headship" argument regarding the Greek word *kephale*. You can find Greek scholars saying both "head" and "source." The ones that have been

the most convincing to me are the ones that admit you can find support for *either* "head" or "source" and that context decides. That makes the most sense to me and it seems that's the way it is with most languages, especially when you're dealing with ancient texts.

Ambiguity Scenario 3. Your Interpretation of What a Whole Group of People Says the Bible Seems to Be Saying

When a whole group of people decides firmly on an interpretation, they may agree that their set of interpretive beliefs will serve as the group's platform. This puts you in the position of attempting to understand all the nuances of that platform. Think of how a politician running for office identifies with a political party. When they identify with that party, they identify themselves with the particular issues, projects, and beliefs—the platform—that party espouses. That platform (or perhaps platforms) serves as their primary identifier as a group.

In terms of conservative Christian groups that have established beliefs on women's roles in the church so firmly that it has become their stated platform, primary examples would be Christians for Biblical Equality (CBE) and the Council on Biblical Manhood and Womanhood (CBMW). Each of these organizations represents a platform: CBE, egalitarianism; CBMW, complementarianism. Just as voters must examine a candidate's voting record, policies, official and unofficial practices, speeches, and debates, students of God's Word must attempt to understand the ins and outs of a Christian group's set of beliefs.

Example of Scenario 3

Then there's the issue of "positions" or stances people take on various interpretations. These are labels that tend to minimize individual thought under a ready-made interpretive position. Think, for example, of the terms "egalitarian" or "traditionalist." Somewhere along the line, different people coined these terms in attempts to name an identity that describes their interpretation of the Bible. For example,

- "I'm an 'egalitarian,' *because* I believe the Bible says that women and men are gifted equally and should be allowed to serve in any role for which they are gifted."

- "I'm a 'traditionalist,' *because* I see a correlation between the order among Father, Son, and Holy Spirit and among Christ, husband, and wife and, therefore, male-female relationships in the church and in the home.

Admittedly, *you're* actually aiming for finding a position of your own using this book. Just know in advance that even ready-made positions have lots of room for ambiguity. Karen Mains experiences this when it comes to defining her own position on women's roles:

> To call me an "egalitarian" would be fair, except that it's far too simple. I have a high regard for paradox, so I think some of this is not definable.
>
> We have to live within what I call "the complementary contradictions," which most theology is. For example, Jesus as both God and man is a complementary contradiction and we can't really define where that thing ends. We just have to learn to live with it.
>
> *All* of our theology is based on complementary contradictions. Think of predestination or free will. What usually happens is that the church generally argues one side or the other, because they can't stand the tension.
>
> There's much tension in what people call "egalitarianism" that is probably too simple. And how it works its way out is in reality—the reality of experience and of life.

The church generally handles ambiguities and other difficulties that cause any level of tension with kid gloves, at best. We church folk often feel we need to draw lines very distinctly because the mental tension causes emotional tension between people in Christ's body. Drawing lines and creating very clear definitions help everyone know what's expected. But, as we've seen, understanding God's truth is not that simple. Yet, we can still move forward, as long as we have a plan.

DEALING WITH THE AMBIGUITIES

Because there's so much room for ambiguity in Bible interpretation, I can pretty much guarantee you'll eventually encounter something that initially confuses you or creates tension in your mind and/or heart. It's good to have ways to deal with your own ambiguity. So, let's talk about some ways to face those inevitable situations:

1. Find a way to face the tension
2. Recognize the sliding scale
3. Suspend your judgment
4. Draw your own lines (to an extent)

All four plans focus on managing and working through your internal tensions. Let's look at each in turn.

Dealing with Ambiguities 1: Find a Way to Face the Tension

Occasionally I annoy my husband, David, when we're watching a dramatic thriller. It feels like the suspense almost literally kills me. I have a psychosomatic stress reaction. My body trembles uncontrollably. I have to urinate frequently. I leap in fright when the main characters leap, scream when they scream, and yell out to them, "Don't go in there!" David's a good sport about it, being my husband and all, but I know sometimes it gets on his nerves. It gets on *my* nerves! So, I've developed a plan for these types of scenarios. When I know I'm going to watch a thriller with David or with friends, I do two things:

First, I recognize that "tension is coming." It's a suspense movie. Duh. It's going to scare me. Get ready. I need to empty my bladder beforehand. I need a warm blanket. I need David or some other sucker—er, friend—to grab onto and hide behind (I cannot watch a scary movie alone). I also practice slow, steady, deep breathing.

Second, if I feel it's necessary, I go read the plot summary on Wikipedia.com. I read at least the ending, if not the whole thing. Once I know what's ultimately going to happen, I can relax and experience a more normal person's level of tension. I can settle in to the movie.

This all may sound silly, but if I really want to watch it, I physically and mentally need to prepare for it. There's a principle in this for you and your tensions when it comes to Bible interpretation: tension is coming; just count on it, settle in for the duration and find ways to face it.

Obviously, every analogy breaks down at some point. You can't read the plot summary ahead of time on this one. I wish I could send you to a wiki site on which you could read the end of this particular story and get "the 'right' answer." Sadly, that site doesn't exist. (That's why books like this do exist!)

However, when the puzzle pieces you find in the Bible and in the way people are interpreting and living out the Bible's words don't seem to fit initially, it's okay to feel tension. It's natural. For most people it's inevitable, as we've discussed already. You are going to come across something in the Bible itself or in people's discussion of the Bible that confuses you or doesn't seem to fit together easily and it will create tension in your mind and heart.

As Karen Mains said, most of theology consists of what she called "complementary contradictions." Two ideas may seem contradictory at first blush, or even at second or third or thirtieth blush, but they definitely go together scripturally. Our job is to try to understand how that can be biblically possible and figure out how to live within its reality.

So, you know it's coming. Now you can settle into experiencing it and dealing with the tension itself instead of fearing the possibility that something in or about the Bible might seem confusing or contradictory.

Dealing with Ambiguities 2: Recognize the Sliding Scales

Very rarely are issues definitively black or white, right or wrong, this way or that. Most typically, things occur along a spectrum, or sliding scale, of possibilities. When it comes to women's roles in the church, very few people exclusively hold the "extreme-extreme" possibilities of beliefs and practices.

For example, even in the most conservative settings, women are not entirely silent and it would be rare to find a worship setting in which women never ever lead in any way, shape, or form. More often, there are slight variations and nuances of understanding or practice one way or another.

These variations create a spectrum of possibilities for one basic idea. What we can do is

- Identify and study the variations on the main positions,
- Line up the variations according to the degree of the presence of certain factors,
- Understand the variations and where they come from, and
- Assess them in light of a number of different factors and filters.

Later in the Plan (in "Step 2: Identify"), you'll create your own spectrum of possible positions that you find in your research about women's roles. It'll help you sort through the various possibilities and see that this isn't just a "complementarian-egalitarian" debate. You'll find those aren't the only two positions. A large number of folks embrace a Christian feminist or biblical feminist view that differs in subtle but significant ways from the Christian egalitarian view. Others hold to a patriarchal vision that is not the same as the complementarian view.

Not only are there a few other perspectives to consider, but you'll see that within each of the major positions numerous sub-positions are created by what I call "tweaking." It's like when you go to the hairdresser for a cut and style. Think of how the operator dries and styles your hair, but stands there for ten extra minutes doing tiny little adjustments, or "tweaks," until she achieves the exact look she wanted. Or think of when your committee at work creates a nearly-right marketing statement for the firm's new product within the first five minutes, yet you all spend three more hours brainstorming minor adjustments in word order that make a major difference.

Tweaking takes you from "nearly-right" to "exactly-right," at least in your own mind. And with just a little change of an idea here and a slight adjustment to an application there, sub-positions of the major positions become "tweaked" right into existence.

Once you can visualize on a spectrum the many "tweaks" people put on others' interpretations, you'll understand more fully the different shades of thought and practice concerning women's roles in the church, along with where each comes from scripturally. Our job is to assess each variation and weigh its merits. You'll do this in a future step in the plan ("Step 4: Filter").

Dealing with Ambiguities 3: Suspend Your Judgment

Some foods taste better after sitting in the refrigerator a day or two, because the various ingredients have time to blend and work their flavor-producing chemical reactions. Sometimes *ideas* are more palatable, too, or just more understandable, after a few days (or months or years) of sitting with the overall mix of ideas.

Instead of dismissing out-of-hand an idea that seems illogical or that you don't understand or that even seems wrong at first glance, you can set it aside for further consideration and exploration. You suspend your judgment on that idea until you've had more opportunity to understand it, compare it to other ideas, or study further the concepts involved in the idea. At times, you'll decide to discard that idea; other times, you'll adopt it and integrate it into your belief system. Or maybe you just let it continue to simmer on the back burner of your mind.

Edward De Bono, a contemporary thinker about creative thinking, suggests that even if an idea seems wrong and you think you will eventually dismiss it, you can still examine it for what usefulness it may have.[10]

When Grace May wondered about becoming an ordained pastor, she compared Scripture to what her church was practicing and teaching and couldn't make the pieces fit initially. She had to put some concepts in suspended judgment for quite some time: "I had to put that idea on hold or put it in the back of my mind and let it just sit there for years."

It can be as simple as putting the idea on a mental shelf and letting it rest there a while. You can then occasionally pick it up, dust it off, and study its facets again.

Your Turn:

As you reconsider an idea you previously shelved, consider these questions:

- Have you gained any new information in the meantime that sheds light on the idea and allows you to understand it?
- Does this idea illuminate, support, or disprove one of the other ideas you have been considering?
- Can you dismiss or accept this idea at this point or do you need more stewing time on it?

At this point, you either accept and assimilate the idea, reject and discard it, or put it back on the shelf of suspended judgment. You can repeat this process as many times as you feel is necessary.

10. De Bono, *Lateral Thinking*, 110.

Dealing with Ambiguities 4: Draw Your Own Lines (to an Extent)

I learned something fairly shocking recently. According to the *Handbook of Denominations in the United States*,[11] well over two hundred denominations exist in our fair country. That number doesn't even count other denominations worldwide! And I suspect there are actually more in the United States than are identified in the handbook. We Christians are good at drawing lines, aren't we?

I'm not necessarily saying it's an inherently bad practice; we've been doing it since the earliest churches gathered. The creeds (Nicene and Apostles') attempted to clearly define who the authentic Christians were. They drew definitive lines. Who are the true believers? The ones who believe this and that; say this, that, and the other; and do these certain things. This protects the church from heresies that can easily invade people's thinking, especially when those heresies seem close to the truth.

The danger to drawing distinct lines is that those lines may sometimes cause not only the intended distinctions, but also division and disunity. This is a big rabbit-trail issue I'm not going to address further in this book. Suffice to say that I've often thought that creating lines and distinctions is many times the easy way out. Admittedly, drawing a new line with a biblical "tweak" and creating a new church or denomination is much easier than the slow process of working through an issue biblically with folks who see an issue differently. That process takes lots of time, energy, and emotion and it requires navigating a lot of conflict. It's a huge investment.

Unfortunately, I can't say to you, "Watch how I do it, because I'm good at this," because I'm not. I dislike conflict, to put it mildly. But when I can't make the investment (or won't, for whatever reason), this is my concession and commitment: I support unity and charity over my personal distinctions and position as much as I possibly can. At the very least, I know where I stand and what I believe, but am committed to continuing to build the church to maturity right along with those who understand the Bible differently from me.

✍📖Your Turn:

Know where you stand at this moment. What are your lines? How flexible are they? Under what conditions can they flex? Think this through for a bit and move forward.

11. Atwood et al., *Handbook of Denominations*, 13th ed.

At this point, you have considered and perhaps adopted some methods that can be helpful to you as you discern the issue of women's roles in the church. Now you are ready to get some traction in your investigation. Let's move to the next step: "Identify."

STEP 2

Identify

The Plan

1. Prepare
2. **Identify**
3. Study
4. Filter
5. Choose

At this point, you have prepared well for interpreting. You have shifted your mindset and freed yourself to begin asking as many questions as arise in your mind and assume absolutely nothing. You have put yourself into the position—physically, emotionally, and mentally—of considering a variety of interpretive thinking on the issue. And, as much as you are able, you have prepared a self-aware plan to deal with your ambiguities. You are ready to go.

So, let's go! In Step 2, you will begin to identify various views and Bible interpretations on the issue of women's roles in church leadership.

Chapter 6

She's Got a Little List

THE FIRST BIG MUSICAL I performed in, during the summer after my seventh grade year, was the comic opera *The Mikado* by Gilbert and Sullivan. In it, Ko-Ko, the Lord High Executioner of the town of Titipu, sings, "I've got a little list" of everyone whose head he thought should roll.

> If someday it may happen that a victim must be found,
> I've got a little list; I've got a little list.
> Of society offenders who might well be underground
> And who never would be missed, they never would be missed![12]

He was ready and "they'd none of them be missed."

Let's make some lists of our own, although hopefully not as gruesome as Ko-Ko's. In this step, you will identify as many *positions* as you can find, along with their variations, and create a graphic that readily shows how they all relate to each other.

A *position* is simply a person or group's *interpretation* of what the Bible says about women's roles in the church (or another issue). It also includes how they *apply* it, or believe it should be applied, in church life today.

Position = Interpretation + Application

Begin *your* identification process by making some lists. In this chapter, we will walk through the initial list-making process. You'll begin to flesh out existing interpretive ideas about women's roles in

12. Gilbert and Sullivan, "I've Got A Little List," from *The Mikado*.

church leadership and graph them in such a way as to understand their relationships to each other.

LIST IT

You probably know of a position or two already, so you can simply add to that number. Here are two particular lists to make in this step:

List 1: Identify Existing "Camps"

Who are the major players (groups, organizations, or individuals) that are verbalizing, promoting, and publishing their interpretation(s) of the Bible on this issue? These will be your main anchor points on your spectrum. You can identify them by asking your pastor(s), good friends, professors, or anyone else you think may have already thought or read about this topic. Ask them to identify the major people and groups voicing their interpretations today. Also, ask for the names of one or two of their favorite books on it. (Then ask if you can borrow those books!)

List 2: Identify Each Camp's Position

What major ideas are these camps espousing? What are unique identifiers that separate their beliefs on women's roles in the church from those of others? Below each of the major positions, list the major interpretive points to which they hold and the Scriptures they understand to say that. For example, you might start a position labeled 100 percent silent. Under that heading, you might begin a list with "Women to be silent during worship gatherings—1 Timothy 2:12; 1 Corinthians 14:34–35."

As you research each position, list their major concerns and emphases on this issue and the verses/passages from which they derive their understanding and practices. You may even know of a specific group, organization, or famous individual that holds this position. If so, place the name under the positions. If it makes more sense to you, list the name, then the position. Format it however it works best for your thinking.

SPECTRUMIZE IT!

You now have an initial list. At this point, you will lay it out graphically so you can visualize where each position stands in relation to the others. I call this "spectrumizing," which is a word I made up to refer to the process of creating a spectrum. A spectrum is a range or continuum of related items, sorted and ordered according to "least to most" or "most to least" or some other form of "from this to that." You are going to spectrumize your list of positions and their various tweaks.

For example, you might place on the right-hand side of a page "Women's 'Full Inclusion.'" This label would mean that, according to this understanding of Scripture, women can hold any position, office, or role including, for example, an ordained, "solo" senior/head pastor of a church. They can officially and non-officially lead women or men in any way and in any context. On the left hand side of the page, you might put "Women Completely Silent/No Lead," meaning that, according to this understanding of Scripture, women may not speak, share, pray, or lead in any way, at all, in any church-body context.

Example:

Table 1. Example of Spectrum Anchor Points

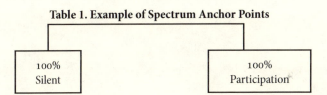

100% Silent	100% Participation
• Women silent in worship setting (1 Tim 2:12; 1 Cor 14:22, 23) • Etc.	• All roles in church filled according to the Spirit's gifting and qualifications, but not gender (1 Cor 12) • Etc.

These would be your two extremes, or "anchor points." You might have a few other major positions between these two that become other anchor points. As you discover other interpretations and practices that are shades, tweaks, and variations of these anchors, place them on the spectrum. Position them according to how close or far they are to each of the two end anchor points.

Don't evaluate anything yet as you add positions to your spectrum. That will come in a later step after you've done some serious research, the process of which I'll walk you through. For now, just create your spectrum. In the next step (Step 3: "Study"), you'll begin your research in earnest.

STEP 3

Study

TIME TO GET INTO THE TEXT!

Many people look for ways to get rich without putting in time, effort, or money. It's tempting sometimes, isn't it? A shortcut to the top of the money pile. But even Internet gurus who are making money hand over fist will agree that, while their money is now coming rather easily, it all started with time, effort, or an initial infusion of money. Short of a complete windfall, it takes something to get something.

In this book, we've joked about wishing someone would just give us the answers to our questions about women's roles. That's the tempting siren call when it comes to understanding theological concepts and making biblical decisions. Yet, without firsthand study, you can't make a responsible decision that's backed by personal understanding of and wisdom concerning the nuances of the issue.

The Plan

1. Prepare
2. Identify
3. **Study**
4. Filter
5. Choose

The *foundation* of your decision regarding any theological issue should be your study, rather than how you feel about something, your comfort level, your culture's practices and/or beliefs, or any other influence. Study includes the research you've performed already and whatever study you still need to do. You will certainly take those other items into consideration, but later on in the process. They should not form the basis for your opinions, beliefs, and practices.

YOU, YES YOU, DOING BIBLE INTERPRETATION

As you have been reading, you may have thought, "Wow. Even if I've actually decided to do something, I'm overwhelmed with all of the warnings, challenges, and considerations concerning Bible interpretation. And don't even get me started on this thing I've heard about called exegesis! Just how *do* I interpret the Bible? Specifically, how do those of us without a bunch of academic letters after our names interpret the Bible? Here I am sitting on my bed with my Bible and my journal. What do *I* do?"

Great questions, motivated sister. This portion is specifically for you. To help you move past any lurking intimidation you might have concerning interpreting the Bible and bravely get going, in these next several chapters you will receive

- How-to's for beginning with the nitty-gritty elements of beginning-level exegesis.
- Checklists to keep you on your path.
- Examples of how the mentors worked and thought through many issues.
- Recommendations of resources you will need for your research.

> ✍📖**Your Turn:**
>
> You may want to get out a pen, pencil, or highlighter and be ready to make marks in your margins and take notes in a notebook. You might also keep your computer handy for jotting longer notes. Whatever your system is, start it now.

Basically, we want to answer these two million-dollar questions:

- *The theological question:* "How do we determine what the biblical authors were trying to say to their audiences?"
- *The practical question:* "How do we determine, of all that the biblical authors said, which commands and situations apply to us today?" In other words, how do we live out God's Word?

Paul did this in most of his letters. Many times, he would discuss an Old Testament concept or two for the New Testament church in light of the redemption of the cross of Christ. Then, he would work out for them how the truths concerning their new life in Christ might be fleshed out in day-to-day life and how that Old Testament concept either did or didn't apply anymore. Just read pointedly through Galatians and you'll see him interpreting and working it out, interpreting and working it out.

Want to learn to do something like that?

Step 3, "Study," is here to help you find that solid ground of study by giving you tools to dig into the text. Our goal is for you to move forward with a greater degree of biblical and theological confidence as you discern answers to your questions about women's roles. To make this process more manageable, we will break it down, addressing the Bible study portion of the interpretation process in seven separate chapters within step 3, "Get into the Text!":

Chapter 7–Study Guidelines

Chapter 8–Fundamentals of Interpretation, Part 1: What is Bible Interpretation and Who Does It?

Chapter 9–Fundamentals of Interpretation, Part 2: Challenges to Interpretation

Chapter 10–Fundamentals of Interpretation, Part 3: How Do We *Prepare* to Interpret Well?

Chapter 11–Fundamentals of Interpretation, Part 4: How Do We Interpret Well? Use Basic Exegetical Skills

Chapter 12–Fundamentals of Interpretation, Part 5: How Do We Interpret Well? Understand Categories of Meaning

Chapter 13–Why We Can Yet Hope to Interpret with Confidence (Despite Daunting Challenges)

Let's jump in with some study guidelines. These guidelines will help direct your thinking and your overall approach to your study.

Chapter 7

Get into the Text! Study Guidelines

CONSIDER ADOPTING THESE FOUR guidelines as you become a researcher:

1. Do your personal best.
2. Read, read, read.
3. Read on all sides of the issue.
4. Know when to say *when*.

Let's look at each guideline.

STUDY GUIDELINE 1: DO YOUR PERSONAL BEST

The fitness instructor on my favorite workout DVD repeatedly tells us exercisers as we puff away, "Go! Do it! My job is to push you beyond where you thought you could be, so you realize your personal best. In order to get your body to change, you have to put stress on it. You have to push it beyond where you thought it could be. Then it will change." Come to think of it, a whole lot of fitness instructors say things like that. There's a sermon in there for us, my friends.

Not to sound too much like a self-help fitness guru, but your best is waiting to happen. It really is. Find it. Let the Lord show you what a top-notch critical thinker he's made you to be by really getting in there and exploring your questions about this issue.

Not many of us can devote full-time hours to this research. God simply asks that we do *our* best to present ourselves as work-women approved, correctly handling (dividing, cutting) the Word of truth (2 Tim 2:15).

Sandra Glahn told how she faced teaching a class on women's roles, an issue she hadn't settled for herself yet, with a very short lead-time. Look at how she did it:

> At the seminary where I teach as adjunct professor, the woman who taught the class on women's roles in the church passed away very suddenly and the school asked me to take her class.
>
> And I told them, "You want me to teach—three months from now—the most controversial subject in Christendom? No, I won't. But if you give me a year, I'll gear up. I will spend the year reading everything I can get my hands on, talking to every theologian I can, really exploring this issue. In the meantime, I will handle as an independent study all the students who need this class to graduate. I will gear them toward books and we will have a once-a-month discussion. But I am not ready to approach this issue as a formal class yet."
>
> They agreed.

Don't worry about doing someone else's best. Just do *your* personal best. Roll up your sleeves. Don't run from the challenge; do it. Get in the game. You know your limitations and you know what you can do; you might find you were able to do more study than you believed you could. On top of that, you may surprise yourself and really enjoy this part of the process!

STUDY GUIDELINE 2: READ, READ, READ

No way around this one. You have to read. Every mentor who described her process to me began her study with prayer and then whipped out her library card (metaphorically speaking)! It's as Sue Edwards said:

> My biblical and theological development came about first when I started studying to be a Bible teacher. I began giving Bible lessons as part of the larger Bible study; but when I actually began writing

> my own studies, which I was doing in the mid- to late-1970s, they just threw me right in!
>
> I began on my own to get books and read them and study for myself. I began to develop myself biblically and theologically in my late twenties. We were taught—it was our tradition in that Bible study—that each teacher should write her own studies. The first book I studied was the book of Proverbs. I had to read extensively about wisdom literature in order to prepare to write that study.
>
> As I wrote other studies through the years, I educated myself. I had enough resources and I had good people that I could go to and ask, "What books do I read?" Those people mentored me in that process. But I was biblically and theologically self-taught until I went to seminary in 1985.

Adela Carter is also primarily self-taught and uses reading to further her understanding and development:

> I've never had formal seminary training. I've sat in seminary classes, although not on this topic. I've sat in on college classes. But what I do is I *read*. I read systematic theology. I don't read light stuff.
>
> I also have a lot of friends who are theologians that I talk to and work through things with, that I converse with and have relationships with; but I have had no formal seminary training whatsoever. Probably the only reason I would want to go back to school would be to learn biblical Hebrew and Greek. That's the only part I think is deficient, that I am hurt by. That would be the only reason.

Reading supports your exegesis. Hopefully it doesn't replace it though, especially once you begin to know a bit about how exegesis is done and what it accomplishes.

Find a Reading Starting Point

"Natalie, there is sooooo much reading material on this topic! Where do I begin?" you ask.

To get the ball rolling, find a reading starting point. We'll consider three:

1. Denominational position papers.

2. Footnotes, endnotes, and suggested/further reading.

3. Read on all sides of the issue.

Reading Starting Point 1:
Denominational Position Papers

Mary Ann Hawkins began with her denomination's position:

> I began doing a study by reading everything I could get my hands on, so I could understand this theologically. As I began, the first things I was able to put my hands on were Church of God publications.

I began my initial study this way, too, back when I first became aware that there was controversy about women's roles. I started searching for my denomination's (at that time) position paper on women. It shed a lot of light on the subject. It didn't answer all of my questions by any stretch and it created many more questions, but it got me started.[13]

Reading Starting Point 2:
Footnotes, Endnotes, and Suggested/Further Reading

In a book, booklet, or paper, the author may provide a list of suggested reading for those who wish to pursue the topic further. Check these resources and make a list of the books you want to find and read for yourself.

In a paper or book, the writer may provide a bibliography, which lists the books the author consulted. Bibliographies don't, however, link exact ideas to the book, unless the writer provides that information in a short description of the source, which is called an annotation. Most books utilize either footnotes or endnotes to cite the sources the author has consulted. These notes are wonderful resources, because you can see exactly which book was espousing a certain idea.

13. Several online examples of denominational and seminary position papers are included in the bibliography. See page 286.

Reading Starting Point 3:
Go to "School."

Going to school can be literal or figurative. Literally, you can go to seminary or Bible school if you have the means and ability. Figuratively, you can imitate school by doing many of the same things on your own. Try some of these strategies:

- Go hear a lecture.
- Attend a class at a local church.
- Attend a conference or a short seminar. Many colleges, seminaries, and divinity schools have week-long winter or summer courses.
- Audit a class at a local college or seminary. This is usually cheap and sometimes free (and we love free).
- Organize a small group of interested women and share your research with each other. This approach can be energizing as well as helpful. You might occasionally invite area leaders whom you know have varying understandings of the issue to come speak to your group and share how they came to that understanding scripturally.
- Write an article for a church newsletter.
- Write a paper.
- Teach a class! Remember the old adage: "The best way to learn something is to teach it."

Let's briefly look at some benefits to several of these possibilities.

"Go to School" Possibility: Classes, Seminars, and Conferences

By taking classes and seminars and going to conferences, you can kick-start your studying and direct your reading. Susan McCormick and Jeanette Yep both took this approach.

> [Susan] I attended an Ed Silvoso seminar to get more in-depth scriptural study on these passages and other considerations. I learned more fully about the various viewpoints and interpretations.

> [Jeanette] I guess I'm something of a conference junkie. I've spent maybe five to ten years' worth of time in conferences, many of

> which were on the topic of women, exegeting one or another of the "troublesome" passages. They helped my understanding. I also spent several weeks a year in conferences for InterVarsity staff alone. And I've been on staff twenty-seven years.

Recognize that most conferences, seminars, and classes ultimately present one viewpoint and their goal is to educate the participants in that interpretive viewpoint. So, you might want to take a couple of classes, one each for the two or three main positions. You'd do really well (and save money . . .) by finding a class, conference, or seminar that doesn't promote one position over another, but attempts to present the major issues and, like this book, help you think through them. Kay Daigle described her first experience formally studying this issue:

> When I went to Dallas Theological Seminary, I had to take a class on the role of women in ministry. At that time (and probably still), Dallas Seminary was complementarian, so the class was really taught from that perspective. We did read some egalitarian papers and books, though.

"Go to School" Possibility: Papers

"Papers? Whaaaat? You've got to be kidding!" You shriek in the expectant pain of reliving your middle school, high school, or college misery of paper-writing. However, consider some of the benefits of writing even a one-page reflection paper on something you just read:

- You can process your thoughts.
- You can test an argument a book or article lays out by thinking it through and following the logic to its end.
- You can think about how a book's propositions would work out in real life and ministry.
- You can write a mini article to benefit others with what you just learned in your reading. You might even consider submitting it to your church's newsletter or local paper.

Papers are not only for school kids or grad students. In a paper, you are merely writing down your thoughts on paper, thinking through an idea—either your own or someone else's—and working it out. The goal is active learning and response, rather than passively reading. You can achieve this either by typing up something formally with a couple of drafts or by simply reflecting in your notebook or journal after you've recently read a piece.

You might reflect on some aspect of an idea you just read in a resource. You might argue against a point, attempting to refute it. You might write a persuasive paper on why you think an idea is correct. You name it, you set the terms, because you're your own instructor!

I would draw a simple distinction between "journaling" and "writing a paper" by one primary criterion: rather than a free-flow of thought, in writing a paper you write with the purpose of exploring or analyzing a specific thought or point, or perhaps arguing a single point or idea. You might dissect a single point. You might *begin* a paper with free flowing thought to get the juices flowing, but you might consider that a first draft. In writing with the goal of learning from your reading, you eventually define some type of goal for that writing (exploration, dissection, analysis, proving, etc.), then you work toward accomplishing that goal.

If you're not in school, you can write whatever papers you want, for however many pages you want to write them, on whatever subjects interest you. Whether on your own or in an academic setting, you can write your papers tailored toward answering your own questions. LaVerne Tolbert refined her own vision and calling after being dramatically impacted while writing a paper:

> I did a paper on women in missions in the American Baptist church. In American Baptist churches, when women were not permitted to pastor or lead in the United States, they were sent to Africa to build schools and mission stations and cut down trees and clear the bush and construct living facilities and fight malaria and everything. Obviously, women were leading and doing *great* work in missions! And black women were also doing a tremendous work! I have another paper on women in missions in the African American culture.
>
> I loved the fact that women who loved the Lord and wanted to serve, if they were not allowed to serve here, didn't say, "Oh, I can't teach, so I'm gonna sit and do nothing." These women said, "Where can I serve?"
>
> If they were told, "Africa," then they packed up and went to Africa. They went places that most men probably wouldn't go.

> I always considered myself a missionary called to the inner city of Los Angeles.

Notice that as LaVerne processed her research for her paper, she learned more about her own cultural heritage, observed important historical occurrences, and even found application and comparison to her own life.

If the title "Papers" still fills you with dread, will you just promise me that you will at least keep an open mind to this idea? Remember, your papers don't have to be long. A brief reflection paper even a few paragraphs long (but with some type of goal, as discussed above) can invaluably aid your thinking about an idea you've been considering. Try it! You may like it!

"Go to School" Possibility: Teach a Class!

Another way to "go to school" on this is to teach your own class. When her seminary asked Sandra Glahn to teach their class on women's roles, she thought,

> Okay, I'll teach a study on the role of women in ministry, but I had plenty of questions, too.
>
> I figured, "We'll go ahead and do this study. We might not necessarily have any answers or conclusions, but we will sure raise a lot of questions and challenge some presuppositions."
>
> That beginning research helped me find out what the main organizations debating this issue were, the two main sides, what they were publishing, and what they were saying.
>
> I came out of that period of research thinking, "We 'conservatives' need to be more 'liberal,' if you will; but I am not totally satisfied with how the text is being handled in some of these egalitarian explanations, so I am not ready to go there, either."

You may not be teaching at the seminary level like Sandra, but could you begin a study group or class at your church, in your community, or through a local parachurch ministry?

Teaching a class or leading a small group can help you in a number of ways. It can provide the impetus and accountability for your own study. If you have to teach it, you'll want to know it! And although you don't have to know it perfectly when you teach, or even "know all about it," you'll want to know enough about it to raise good questions in the class and facilitate good guided discussion.

Good group discussion can motivate your own study. The group discussions and students' papers can raise questions and answers you might not have initially found on your own. All educators know they learn a ton from their students. It's a two-way street.

Seriously consider trying this. Who knows? You might even find out you have the gift of teaching!

STUDY GUIDELINE 3: READ ON ALL SIDES OF THE ISSUE

We discussed reading widely in step one's "Prep Method 2: Get Out of (Your) Town!" Still, the idea bears repeating, because it's your best approach for making a truly informed decision about the issue. Jeanette Yep and Adela Carter both emphasized this:

> [Jeanette] Read widely and come to your own conclusions. Don't be afraid of facing the pain that might come from that reading. It's just as painful for a complementarian to read extreme egalitarian positions as it is for the opposite. Yet, it's important to read because it's another perspective. It's important for a woman to use her God-given mind to come to peace on it.

> [Adela] I studied a lot of stuff I got through Christians for Biblical Equality, like *Beyond Sex Roles* by Gilbert Bilizekian. I just read a lot. I read a lot of egalitarian stuff; but I read a lot of traditional stuff, too, like *Recovering Biblical Manhood and Womanhood* by the Council on Biblical Manhood and Womanhood.

Karen Moy's process involved reading, then checking her thinking against Scripture:

> It was only because I had started reading (I have a shelf full of books about all the different positions on women in leadership) that I started realizing that there were all these people who had somehow concluded there was stuff women couldn't do. So, I wanted to understand their position and I wanted to confirm my own, which had started from it never occurring to me there was stuff I couldn't do.

> I thought, "I'd better go check to make sure that my thinking is consonant with Scripture."

For each piece of literature you read, be it a book, article, pamphlet, paper, or whatever, ask some questions about what you're reading and take good notes. Write down your own reactions to the text. If you make reactive comments inside your head as you read, write them down. If you own the item, just make notes right there on the page: underline, draw arrows to connect ideas, highlight, write in the margins, put question marks where you can't figure out what the author's saying. Avoid highlighting or underlining *everything*, though. That becomes as unhelpful as not having any highlighting at all. It becomes distracting to your eyes and your mind.

✍📖Your Turn:

As you read any resource, ask yourself these questions:

- What "camp" is this author in?
- What interpretations/positions do the major camps hold?
- Do this author's ideas create any subtle variations from that camp's main position?
- Can you identify those variations?
- Do you understand why those variations exist?
- How do the applications of the interpretations of both the camp and this individual author impact Christian men and women in "real life"?

These last questions may identify a new "tweak" on your spectrum.

Make notes on all of your observations. I take notes in my book *and* in a loose-leaf notebook (or on my laptop). I can't tell you how many times I've gone back to a book to find an idea I remembered and to see how I interacted with it at the time by reading my notes in the margin. Another little tip is that once you've written or printed out notes on loose-leaf paper, copy and staple them, then fold the copy and store it between the pages of the book. Then, you have all those notes readily accessible when you read that book again or want to review a particular idea in it. However you do it, find a system that works for you.

STUDY GUIDELINE 4: KNOW WHEN TO SAY WHEN

"Have I done enough study?" you ask. "How do I know if I have?"

Great questions. How do you know when to stop? How much is enough? Here are a few considerations for determining when enough is enough.

First, what's your temperament? Are you the type to gather data for thirty years and still feel ill-prepared to make a choice? Conversely, are you one who'll read two denominational position papers and think you know everything you need to know? Consider your temperament and try to compensate for that tendency.

For example, you might employ the help of a friend or colleague who knows you well, understands your particular tendencies, and, importantly, is objective and honest with you. With that friend, you can set goals that will help you gauge over time when you have studied enough.

Next, what are your questions? Begin with an end in mind. Once you've defined the questions you want to answer, then you can gather information toward that question, rather than wander endlessly (although not aimlessly) in the overall subject. What was your original motivation for reading *Women, Leadership, and the Bible*? What's your motivation for finding answers to your questions? You need to give yourself permission to have an end to your information gathering. So, define your questions, list them, and seek to answer them.

If you're looking at the entire picture of women's roles in order to determine your own position, here's a guideline to consider: once you have a good sense of what's on the spectrum of ideas about women's roles in the church and you're able to say what those positions are in your own words, fairly and accurately, then you are ready to make a decision.

No matter your temperament, motivation, or questions, prayer needs to factor in to knowing when you know enough. Ask the Lord to guide you in this. Ask for the ability to give yourself grace, without giving yourself so *much* grace that your diligence lags. Trust the Lord to lead and simply do your best.

Now, let's look at what Bible interpretation is and who does it—you might be surprised by what you learn.

Chapter 8

Get into the Text! Fundamentals of Interpretation, Part 1

What Is Bible Interpretation and Who Does It?

BIBLE INTERPRETATION. IS IT faith, art, science, or guesswork—or some combination of these?

> "God said it, I believe it, and that settles it."
>
> *versus*
>
> "Now these were more noble-minded than those in Thessalonica, for they received the Word with great eagerness, examining the Scriptures daily, to see whether these things were so."
>
> (Acts 17:11, NASB)

Why do we need to interpret the Bible? Doesn't it just mean what it says?

We know that "All Scripture is God-breathed and useful for teaching, for reproof, for correction, and for training in righteousness . . ." (2 Tim 3:16 ESV). However, as Deborah Gill and Barbara Cavaness advise in *God's Women Then and Now*, it doesn't say that all Scripture is equally applicable to every situation.[14] So, figuring out to which situations Scripture does apply and discerning how it applies—along with whether

14. Gill and Cavaness, *God's Women Then and Now*, 26.

it still applies *today* and whether it applies in the same *way* today—are challenges we need to face. These challenges call for interpretation.

Look at the Acts 17 verse at the beginning of this chapter. Who were these noble-minded, eager Scripture-examiners? These were the Bereans. The writer of Acts comments favorably on their character, and then implies that their thoughtful and careful approach to what they were hearing directly resulted from their good character. And what were they lauded for? Examining the Scriptures, which for them would have been what we call the Old Testament, to see if what Paul said was true, particularly about Jesus as the Messiah. They were interpreting the Scriptures.

Look at other people in the Bible who are interpreting the Bible:

- "And they read from the book, from the law of God, translating to give the sense so that they understood the reading" (Neh 8:8 NASV). That's interpretation!
- "And He said to them, 'O foolish men and slow of heart to believe in all that the prophets have spoken! Was it not necessary for the Christ to suffer these things and to enter his glory?' And beginning with Moses and with all the prophets, He explained to them the things concerning Himself in all the Scriptures" (Luke 24:25–27 NASV). That's interpretation!
- "He [Paul] writes the same way in all his letters, speaking in them of these matters. His letters contain some things that are hard to understand, which ignorant and unstable people distort, as they do the other Scriptures, to their own destruction." (2 Pet 3:16 NIV). That's interpretation (Paul, interpreting well; the unstable, interpreting badly)!
- And how about when Philip *explained* Isaiah 53 to the Ethiopian eunuch in Acts 8:27–35? That's interpretation!

Okay, we've determined that interpretation is a biblical practice. However, not only is it biblical, the Bible speaks *positively* of those who interpret thoughtfully and don't indiscriminately believe what someone says the Bible teaches. It also lauds those who do not interpret Scripture in such a way as to twist it. It praises those who carefully weigh what they hear against Scripture, which means that they must attempt to determine for themselves what Scripture says, in addition to listening to what others say about it. So, if we want to be biblical followers of Jesus, we need to learn to do Bible interpretation.

Right. What is it, then?

WHAT IS BIBLICAL INTERPRETATION?

Kathy Keller talked about her initial encounter with a big, fancy word, "hermeneutics":

> I ran into 1 Corinthians 14 about women being silent. Of course, in 1 Corinthians 11, they were all prophesying and praying. Then, in 1 Timothy 2, they weren't allowed to teach with authority. So, I was trying to figure out, *How does one understand that?*
>
> This, of course, takes you straight to hermeneutics. I didn't even know what hermeneutics *was* until I got to seminary. But, it's the whole study of Scripture and how the clear interprets the cloudy and you don't pit one scripture against another.
>
> God's authority is such that even when it touches a part of your life you'd just as soon keep, you don't have that option. It doesn't matter if that's your sexuality or your job plans or your romantic life or whatever; God's Word has the final say.

Perhaps the term "hermeneutics" is already familiar to you. If so, good; that puts you a half-step ahead, because it won't seem as intimidating as it often strikes people hearing it for the first time.

I remember the first time I heard the word, I was with some friends at church who were seminary students. I had no idea what they were talking about; but they used the word freely, as though I should, since I was in full-time ministry and led lots of Bible studies. I felt dumb, although that was not their intention. Still, to spare *you* that feeling, let's discuss the term.

Basically, "hermeneutics" is an impressive word scholars use to refer to the science of interpreting texts. In their book *How to Read the Bible for All Its Worth*, Drs. Gordon Fee and Doug Stuart introduce the practice of hermeneutics as "moving from the 'then and there' of the original text to the 'here and now' of our own life settings."[15] Hermeneutics includes both established Bible study principles for interpretation, as established by scholarly instruction and practice, and one's personal basic interpretive principles. It also involves our viewpoint as we approach Scripture.

To flesh that out: when we read the Bible we approach it from a certain *perspective* that guides our understanding and, ultimately, our personal view of Scripture. That view, then, affects our interpretation of

15. Fee and Stuart, *How to Read*, 10.

Scripture. Scholars have another fancy word for this *view*, or perspective, that influences one's interpretation: they call it a "hermeneutic" (note: no "s" on the end of that word).

Now, notice the subtleties here. Two words are in play so far: "hermeneutics" and "hermeneutic" (one with and one without an "s" on the end). The word that has the "s" on the end—"hermeneutics"—refers to the total process of, or the science of, interpretation. The word *without* the "s"—"hermeneutic"—refers specifically to the interpretive perspective.

What Is Exegesis?

You may also have heard the word "exegesis." Exegesis is the process of exploring the text through various means to attempt to know its clearest meaning, as intended by the original writer. Effective exegesis shows us the significance of the text and leads us toward applying the text correctly to our lives today.

Exegesis offers us our best opportunity for objectivity. For example, ideally, pastors and preachers exegete a passage to discover the meaning of a text before they write a sermon. Hopefully, they try to discern the meaning of the text as the writer intended and as God intended, rather than simply pulling verses together to fit whatever message they want to give in their sermon. (At least, we're basically trusting them to do that.)

Exegesis can fail to help us understand a text's meaning if we do it poorly. We need to follow certain guidelines and principles of interpretation that "level the playing field" and help us exegete passages as objectively and thoroughly as possible.

"Exegesis" is related to hermeneutics, because it is the process of analyzing the text and context using a number of different approaches. They really go hand in hand if you want to do serious Bible interpretation.

Let's be clear: *anyone* reading the Bible approaches it with an interpretive viewpoint that guides their thinking about and affects their understanding of Scripture. Sometimes they identify this; sometimes they don't. It's always a good practice to identify it, though. Identifying it helps you understand why you look at Scripture the way you do, and helps others understand why you look at Scripture the way you do.

This awareness helps you in a conversation with someone about a particular passage or biblical idea. Especially if you're disagreeing, knowing the interpretive viewpoint from which you've each started helps you understand each other's perspective.

WHO DOES BIBLE INTERPRETATION?

Early Christians Did It

Beginning with the apostles and disciples, the church through the ages has endeavored to answer many theological questions. Paul and other New Testament writers interpreted the Old Testament Scriptures for the early church. In fact, most of Paul's letters involve him interpreting Old Testament laws and principles for the church as it was growing in its Christian identity.

Acts 15 gives us an excellent example of the church discerning whether Gentile believers were subject to keeping the Law of Moses. Were they required to be circumcised and follow all of the other laws in order to follow Christ and be saved? They were interpreting Old Testament laws as applied to the Gentiles. Note as you read how they process the situation:

- The apostles and elders met and considered the whole situation. And there was much discussion. I imagine this to be an understatement, because for them to consider that the Gentiles were not required to follow the Law in order to follow the one they believed to be the Messiah—the *Jewish* Messiah—would have been quite radical for them as Jews.
- The preponderance of understanding rested with the believing Pharisees (yes, a number of Pharisees believed). The believing Pharisees, quite logically, proposed that Gentiles must follow all of the Law, including circumcision. Essentially, they were proposing that Gentiles should, no *must*, convert to Judaism in order to follow Jesus as Messiah. It's a logical step, particularly when you look at it from their perspective—the Jewish perspective.
- After "much discussion," Peter reminded the assembly that God gave the Holy Spirit to Gentiles as well as Jews at Pentecost (Acts 2), adding that God "purified their hearts by faith" (v. 9).
- Peter then challenged the group to consider the weight they were considering placing on the Gentiles when they themselves were unable to bear it, particularly when God had already accepted the

Gentiles. He summarized with the irrefutable fact that if they, as Jews, believed and were saved by the grace of God, so were the Gentiles.

- Paul and Silas then brought the up-to-the-minute eyewitness reports of God's work among the Gentiles, testifying to the signs and wonders among Gentiles they had personally witnessed throughout the region. This reinforced, through personal experience, God's acceptance of the Gentiles just as they were.
- James added fodder for further consideration from the ancient Jewish prophets, quoting verses in Amos 9 from the Septuagint (a Greek translation of the Hebrew Bible, which most early Christians used as their Bible).

James' particular words certainly seemed to contribute the final say in a growing preponderance of evidence to the participants in that assembly, because they ultimately came to a consensus. They agreed with James' proposal that they not make it difficult for the Gentiles to follow Christ, but still write them a strong cautionary letter to abstain from certain important things, including food sacrificed to idols and sexual immorality.

Church historians refer to this gathering of church leaders as the council of Jerusalem. It was the first church council of the early church.

During early church councils (held between the fourth and eighth centuries in the cities of Nicaea, Ephesus, Chalcedon, Constantinople), church leaders interpreted many other important biblical and theological issues for the church.

Today, we hardly give a thought to where these ideas came from, outside of thinking, "Well, it must have come from the Bible, I guess." Back then, though, because of harsh persecution of those claiming the Christian faith, there were centuries during which these decisions were matters of life and death. Church fathers and church councils discerned not only basic tenets of theology such as the doctrine of the Trinity and how Jesus could possibly be both God and man, but things like what teachings were they going to call heresy and why.

Also, something near-and-dear to our hearts, they discerned and decided which letters and documents to include as the "God-breathed" books that became our New Testament! (And don't you know there was a *lot* of discussion at those councils!)

Don't be fooled: these issues and questions took centuries to discern.

God didn't just say, "Okay, here are the letters, accounts, and other documents I want included in my Bible."

Wouldn't that have been nice? But, no. Nothing was decided overnight.

So, when you interpret Scripture for yourself, you're following a long tradition of faithful believers who have sought the heart of God through the Holy Spirit's guidance. We and they trust the Lord's leading as to what would make the Gospel of Jesus Christ clearest and the kingdom of God most plain to people.

Professional Scholars Do It

It may already be obvious to you that "professionals," including scholars, translators and other "experts," interpret the Bible, perhaps for a living. But what do they do, exactly? They examine the texts and the manuscripts the texts come from. They think about the texts and formulate theories about the texts. They also formulate theories about reading the texts, as well as theories about interpreting the texts.

Other biblical studies scholars engage in what is called "exegesis." This means they examine the original texts from many angles, including translation. They're often interested in what the Bible can tell us about the theology and practices of the early Christians. For professionals who are purely academic, they may not be very concerned about the application of the text, as in, what the text means for us today. Of course, we are very concerned about that.

You may wonder, "Do professional interpreters approach the text with an interpretive view, too? Do they have biases?"

In short, yes. Scholars are definitely not exempt from having an interpretive viewpoint. They're not magically completely objective just because they have a PhD. In fact, all good scholars *begin with* such a framework.

As a scholar has her preferred interpretive views and principles in mind, either consciously or unconsciously, she begins to study the Bible. It then guides her thinking about Scripture. Good scholars openly acknowledge their approach, declaring it right from the start. That helps a person reading that scholar's work understand that scholar's perspective and take it into consideration.

The Pastors, Preachers, and Teachers at Your Church Do It

What do pastors do all day long in between Sundays? Well, aside from presiding at funerals, marriages, and other life events, think about what the pastor at your church does to prepare for a sermon. At a fundamental level, every Bible teacher, preacher, and expositor interprets the Bible. They try to answer their own questions, as well as predict their listeners' questions, as they study. Then they attempt to communicate their findings to their congregations or audiences.

You Do It

Surprise! Did you realize that you *already* interpret the Bible? When you think about God and try to understand what God is doing in the world and you try to do so by reading your Bible, you are interpreting. Or, when you bring Scripture into conversations to justify your opinions on things, you are interpreting.

Because you chose this particular book, that indicates you are trying to sort through why your particular church, or Christians you have known in other circumstances, have certain beliefs about women's roles and practices.

You want to know, "How *did* we come up with this system, or these practices?" And you want to assure yourself that those practices are scriptural—or to correct a practice if it's not.

The bottom line: you chose to read this book right now, and not that delightful novel sitting on your end table, because you want to find answers to some big questions. You've made your decision; you have decided to do something. And that "something" involves interpreting the Bible.

In order to learn some basics of Bible interpretation, including both hermeneutics and exegesis, let's define some terms we'll use.

DEFINING OUR TERMS

For our purposes, the term "Bible interpretation" includes all of hermeneutics, with all of its principles, guidelines, and practices. This includes the various skills you will learn, including some exegetical tools, to further your interpretive knowledge and ability. As far as a "hermeneutic" goes, we'll call it an "interpretive view" or your "interpretive principles."

I recognize that just reading those descriptions and definitions may give some readers an arrhythmia. I'm sure you're already imagining the complexity of the process. Individuals either knowingly or unknowingly utilize a complex variety of assumptions to arrive at an interpretation of a biblical passage.

Yet, don't despair! Many tools and processes exist that will help us. For now, let's look further at what interpretation is, what it involves, and how we can do it well. We'll find that there are plenty of challenges, but *lots* of help and hope.

Chapter 9

Get into the Text! Fundamentals of Interpretation, Part 2

Challenges to Interpretation

SOME OBVIOUS CHALLENGES TO INTERPRETATION

THE TASK OF INTERPRETATION is not a simple one; nor would I say it is easy. Many factors affect how we decide the answers to our questions. This creates quite a complex scenario. Here are a few of the more *obvious* challenges:

1. Facing down ancient, foreign languages.
2. Our personal skill and comfort level with said ancient, foreign languages.
3. Translating those ancient foreign languages.

Obvious Challenge 1: Ancient, Foreign Languages

Understanding a foreign language presents challenges; understanding an ancient foreign language presents even more. Even to modern Greeks, Koine Greek, the Greek used to write the New Testament documents, is a foreign language! The same is true about the Hebrew found in the Bible for modern Israelis and Jews who speak Hebrew.

They are considered "dead" languages. The term "dead language" refers to a language no longer spoken by any living people as its native language, although the language may still be studied and translated with a degree of certainty.

Obvious Challenge 2: Our Personal Skills with those Ancient, Foreign Languages

Even if we do have some Greek or Hebrew skills, those skills may not be extremely well-developed. That can make us hesitant to use them at all. Barbara Fletcher felt this way:

> I learned Greek, although I have to admit that I have not done any serious Greek analysis since I walked out of seminary. [*Barbara chuckles.*]
>
> My conviction has been, "Who am I to think that in one or two years of Greek I would know enough to go up against some Greek scholar and say, 'My translation's better'?"
>
> That's the bottom line for me! I think I'm just going to accept what they say! *They've* studied a lifetime.

Completely understandable, right? Still, I always encourage women who have even an inkling of motivation in the direction of learning the biblical languages to do it. It will give you a start. At this point in my own development, I would not call myself a Greek or Hebrew "scholar." Yet, learning Greek and Hebrew gave me the ability to look at a Bible passage and know where to begin. It helped me know how to translate and understand key words. It gave me the facility to understand the form and tense of a word. This started me on a solid road to understanding the grammar, too, which is key for sentence diagramming; this, in turn, is key for interpreting and for constructing an exegetical talk or sermon. All of this helps me read the Bible with a more informed understanding.

Obvious Challenge 3: Translating that Ancient Foreign Language

"That word. I do not think it means what you think it means." (*The Princess Bride*, 1987)[16]

16. W. Goldman, *The Princess Bride*.

We can never be 100 percent certain that a translation is absolutely accurate. Why? Because translators face four major challenges.

Translators' First Challenge: Sources

The authors of the sources never intended what they spoke or wrote to be in a book like the Bible as we know it. Much of the Bible first came from stories passed down over centuries, which were eventually written down, and was subsequently copied repeatedly from manuscripts.

Most of us realize, when we really think about it, that the Bible on our nightstands comes entirely from ancient manuscripts. Yet, not a lot of us realize that the stories recorded in those manuscripts, especially from the Old Testament, were first passed down through the tradition of storytelling before being committed to writing.

As for the New Testament documents, they originated from both passed-down stories and written documents. Luke 1:1–4, in particular, gives us a bit of the picture as Luke describes how these two methods of remembering events and lessons often worked together. Scribes (writers) recorded the oral traditions, as well as collected and edited the written documents. And all of this occurred over the course of many centuries.

I find two historic facts about these origins particularly beautiful:

Beautiful Thing 1. Those meticulous scribes attempted to preserve every "tittle and jot" (Matt 5:18; Luke 16:17)[17] as they copied (and they did a *miraculously* good job at it).

Beautiful Thing 2. A surprisingly large number of ancient manuscripts exists to support

For Those Interested . . .

Not only do more manuscripts exist for the New Testament than most other classics, but, interestingly, most of the manuscripts for those classics didn't even appear until many hundreds of years after they were originally told or written. In contrast, the New Testament has manuscripts that were found a "mere" three hundred years after John the Apostle's death.

17. Reference to Matthew 5:18–"Tittle: A point, (Matt 5:18; Luke 16:17), the minute point or stroke added to some letters of the Hebrew alphabet to distinguish them from others which they resemble; hence, the very least point"; Jot: "or *Iota*, the smallest letter of the Greek alphabet, used metaphorically or proverbially for the smallest thing (Matt 5:18); or it may be *yod*, which is the smallest of the Hebrew letters." (Easton, "Tittle" and "Jot" in *Bible Dictionary*, no pages.)

the texts found in the Bible. By the sovereignty of God, there are many manuscripts for individual books of the Bible, particularly for the New Testament documents. In fact, more manuscripts exist for the New Testament than for just about any other text from all time, including classics such as Homer, Cicero, and Virgil! That means translators and scholars can compare these manuscripts with each other so they can know with a greater amount of certainty what the original text most likely said (in the original language). Making such comparisons helps translators have the best possible text from which to translate.

Translators' Second Challenge: Meanings

Over the centuries, the meanings of words vary and change. Think about the word "love" in English. We know that "love" can mean a lot of different things, such as

- "I *love* chocolate!" really means "I really like to eat chocolate a lot."
- "I *love* my new boyfriend. We've been together for two whole weeks!" This really means infatuation.
- The act of sex, as in "making *love*."
- Commitment, as in "to *love* and to cherish."
- I'd really *love* to go on . . .

From this example using the word "love," you can see that a range of definitions and usage exists for a word. Although the word a translator used to translate the text may fit with one of the word's definitions, it is not guaranteed to be the *best* translation to reflect the author's meaning.

Translators' Third Challenge: Nuance

Words in the original languages often contain subtle nuances. Going back to our "love" example, in ancient Greek are several words for "to love" (*agapao, phileo,* and *erao,* whose noun forms are *agape, eros,* and *philia*). Yet, not only are there more than one word for "love," but each has subtle nuances specific to that word that are hard to translate precisely into English.

- *Agapao*–"to love." This love, in both its verb and noun forms, includes the concepts of brotherly love, affection, good will, love, benevolence, and Christian love feasts.[18] It is "distinct from erotic love or simple affection."[19] This kind of love shows commitment through action, and possibly sacrifice. In the New Testament, it can refer to love that is "wholly selfless and spiritual"[20] (e.g., John 13:34; 1 Cor 13; Heb 12:6).

- ***Erao***—"to love." This kind of love indicates "physical love; sexual desire."[21]
- ***Phileo***–"to love." This love suggests traces of other connotations: to approve of, like, sanction, treat affectionately or kindly; to welcome, befriend, show signs of love, kiss, be fond of doing.[22] When we think of "brotherly love" (or sisterly love), this word expresses that kind of committed friendship with a true friend. (Examples: Luke 20:46; John 20:2; Rev 3:19.)

You can see how they differ subtly. Of course, *erao* is the most clearly distinct, as it pertains primarily to sexual desire and physical love. Both *agapao* and *phileo*, each of which are found throughout the New Testament, are most typically translated simply as "love." While they contain a good amount of overlap in their range of meanings and are fairly synonymous, each still has subtle nuances specific to that word that don't always translate easily into English.

One of the hardest words in the Bible to translate is *logos*. Most typically, it is translated as "word," or "Word." One of the "biggie" reference books, *A Greek-English Lexicon of the New Testament and Other Early Christian Literature*, often called by its shorter, easier nickname "the BAG-D," lists ranges of meanings for thousands of ancient words according to how they were actually used both in Scriptures and in the broader culture of that period according to known documents. When you flip to the page for *"logos,"* you see a long list of its documented meanings.

Was it originally speech/"the spoken word"? God's rational thought? Is it a specific spoken word? It is full of meaning and nuance!

Another word is *kosmos*, commonly translated as "world." Think about, "For God so loved the *kosmos*, that whoever believes in him . . ." (John 3:16). You can see an inclusivity in that usage that may be inherent

18. *Oxford Dictionaries*, "*Agape*."

19. Thayer and Smith, "*Agape*."

20. *Encarta Dictionary English*, "Agape."

21. Dictionary.com, "*Eros*."

22. Thayer and Smith, "*Phileo*."

A Greek study Bible will be your best friend! If you start looking at how a word got translated in various versions, you'll see that translators—King James Version, NIV, RSV, for example—translated certain words differently.

__Jean Milliken, Executive Ministry Team Pastor, Grace Community Church (Auburn, WA)

I (Natalie) would add that a Hebrew study Bible will also serve you well! Many are available, including Hebrew-Greek key word study Bibles and interlinear Bibles. (See "Table 8. Recommended Resources…" for several suggestions.)

in the word, in that one aspect of it can mean "every person in the world." Yet, it can also mean something quite different, as in, "I am not of this *kosmos*." There's an "other-ness" involved in that usage. John's gospel is chock full of such nuanced words.

We certainly must strive to comprehend the meanings of the original words, then understand their uses in their contexts, because we obviously want the best possible translation. But, admittedly, sometimes it's just plain hard to do.

Translators' Fourth Challenge: Biases

The translation process involves interpretation, which can be influenced by biases.

A bias differs from an interpretive view in that a bias involves a predisposition for or against things being a certain way. It is often undisclosed, although possibly obvious. A translator may not even realize his or her bias, because it is so ingrained or culturally normative.

Definition: Bias

"A preference or an inclination, especially one that inhibits impartial judgment."

–"Bias." *The American Heritage Dictionary*. Online.

Even though people preserved many faithfully copied manuscripts for the New Testament, the problem of translating still exists—and translating involves a large degree of interpretation. A translator must decide which English word (or whichever language it's being translated into) fits best for the word in the original language.

A translator's choice of which word to use may be influenced by a number of things—perhaps their culture's attitude toward something or possibly their own attitude. Sometimes, translators throughout history have held preconceived notions about certain biblical and cultural issues.

Sandra Glahn related some difficulties she experienced as she was learning to interpret the Bible for herself:

> As I was taking Greek, I would read various Bible translations and think, "Um, wait a minute. Some of these translations aren't very accurate."
>
> For example, I had always heard that *anthropos* should always be translated "man." So I get to 1 Peter 3:4, where it is talking about a woman's gentle, quiet spirit. The Greek says, "Let it be the hidden *anthropos* of the heart" and the King James translation I was reading said, "Let it be the hidden *man* of the heart." But, this was written directly to *women*.
>
> I realized, "Obviously we need to be using the word 'person' here, not 'male person.'"
>
> Then, later on, I found myself—in the middle of this conservative atmosphere—looking at the original language, thinking, "You know, the New International Version is *really* biased. It's not reflecting that the text itself is gender neutral, or even gender friendly."

One major difficulty that can arise for translators is if the word only appears one time in the whole Bible. That creates a tough situation, because there's nothing to compare it to within the text.[23]

Another tough situation arises when those words that only appear once in Scripture appear differently in the oldest original manuscripts. Then what do you do?

The problem with translation bias, of course, is that the reader of the translation, without expertise in the original languages, is at the mercy of the translator to an extent. Sandra's experience shows this.

Yet, is the reader helpless? No. The situation creates a challenge, but not an impossibility. The "English-language-only-please" woman's most basic, yet powerful, tool is that of a side-by-side translation comparison of several versions of the Bible. It's easy to do and can be incredibly enlightening. Beyond that basic technique, you will find more tools in this book and other resources to strengthen your interpretation skills and help you become quite discerning—savvy, even—in your interpretation.

23. See discussion on "*hapax legomenon*," page 131.

✍📖Your Turn:

Consider this: What do you think you would do if you were a translator faced with a word that only appears once in the Bible?

Summary: Bible Translation Challenges

Remember, every translation of every word involves interpretation and what we could call "judgment calls" by the translator. This is particularly true for the major words, but small words are also often debated. Next, remember that the limitations of the English language greatly challenge the translation process of accurately conveying the meaning of the Greek or Hebrew word.

We have to realize that translators are people, too; they're not God. For this reason, the major translations have been undertaken by teams of people, rather than one person alone. This serves as a safeguard and balance. We certainly hope that translators, be they individuals or teams, seek the guidance of the Holy Spirit. We also trust that they give their best effort in their work. Still, in some cases they have to *choose* a translation based on their best efforts at studying the word and the context, even though they may not be entirely sure.

Choosing A Translation

All of this talk about translation begs the questions,

- How do I choose a Bible translation?
- Which are the most "trustworthy"?
- Which reflect the original languages the best?
- Which convey the *meaning* of the original languages the best for me, if I don't know those languages?

Excellent questions.

Something to know is that when a team of translators (solo translators, too) decide how they will translate the Bible into *any* language, one of the first decisions they need to make is whether to make their translation a "functional equivalent" or a "formal equivalent."

A ***functional equivalent*** translation, also called "dynamic equivalent," strives to convey the *meaning* of the original text, rather than provide a word-for-word translation of it. The translation team may actually go phrase by phrase in some instances, rather than word by word, to make sure the *meaning* is translated in an understandable way in English (or whatever the object language is).

Examples: Good News Bible, The Message, The Living Bible (1971, this is actually a true paraphrase), and others.

A ***formal equivalent*** provides a word-for-word translation, although it also tries to make it readable in the object language.

Examples: the King James Version, New King James Version, English Standard Version, Revised Standard Version, New American Standard Bible, and others.

Some translations attempt to produce a "happy medium," more formally called a ***mediating translation***. This type strives toward the accuracy of a literal translation while still using equivalent phrases in the object language. They've tried to find a balance.

Examples: New International Version, the New American Bible, the New Living Translation Bible, the New English Bible, and others.

Which one to choose?

When it comes to interpreting the Bible, the best thing to do is to choose several and use them side-by-side. Many publishers have made it easy with parallel Bibles, which present multiple versions verse-by-verse, side-by-side. Zondervan Publishing alone has at least ten, mixing and matching various versions. Other publishers offer a similar selection. If you are going to spend the money, get one that has several versions representing all three categories: formal, functional, and mediating. Free parallel comparisons also exist online. Biblos.com, for example, lists up to seventeen versions of a verse on a page, providing opportunity for very easy comparison.

Note that some translations are undertaken by a committee of scholars and some are by individual translators. Become familiar with who translated the versions you are consulting. A committee doesn't absolutely guarantee a superior translation; yet, the idea behind utilizing a committee is not only to put the best and brightest minds on the task to try to discern a faithful translation, but to reduce bias caused by only one translator's viewpoint.

For more on *How to Choose a Translation for All Its Worth*, read the book by that title! It's by Gordon D. Fee and Mark L. Strauss (Grand Rapids: Zondervan, 2007).

Because translators are not God, this leads to us needing to realize that the *translations* of the God-breathed Scriptures could *possibly* contain errors—errors in nuance, errors in original meaning, misunderstanding of original intent, errors in usage, and other errors. Yet, our hope and trust remains that God is overseeing these processes, and even these errors, by the power of his Spirit. Recall, too, our discussion about the original manuscripts (see page 77). Joyfully, this means our hope and trust is not blind.

SOME HIDDEN CHALLENGES TO INTERPRETATION?

"Keep your friends close and your enemies closer," said the Godfather in the movie by that title. This particular line from the Godfather movie has always struck me. It expresses the wisdom of keeping an enemy in plain view, no longer hidden, so you can watch his or her actions and predict how those actions might impact you.

Sometimes, the "enemies" to good interpretation are hidden. We need to get closer to them, so we can keep an eye on them. We have talked about a few already—interpretive view and biases. Yet, we need to keep three more "enemies" in plain sight: feelings, culture, and intimidation.

Not-So-Obvious Challenges to Interpretation:

- Feelings
- Culture
- Mental Intimidation

Hidden Challenge No. 1: Feelings! Wo-wo-wo, Feelings!

Warning! As you begin to learn more about Bible interpretation and begin to make your own attempts at it, be aware that for most people the issues involved go well beyond the academic. When it comes to deciding what the Bible means and what should apply to us today, presuppositions, opinions, assumptions, tradition, strongly held beliefs, and feelings all play with people's minds and hearts, challenging their objectivity.

These personal factors often lead to wrongly applying one's personal experiences as the primary factors in deciding what a Bible passage means, instead of letting the text speak first.

Hidden Challenge No. 2: Culture (Ours)

"Culture," said historian Anne Firor Scott, "teaches us what to see and what not to see."[24]

The mentors I interviewed had a lot to say about the influence of culture on our church theology in terms of beliefs and practices.

Mentor Elizabeth Conde-Frazier described her perspective on the importance of culture and its impact on our theology:

> As in any community, this [the question of women's roles] is a theological issue that stems from a cultural piece.
>
> I've always said that the original sin—and you will find it in *every* culture and *every* religion—is about the *confusion* and the *distortion* of the relationship between men and women. So, it should be of no surprise to us that theologically that's what's reflected back to us.
>
> In the Latino community, there are a lot of different Latino cultures, and the relationships between men and women have been influenced by different historical factors. So, I can't just tell you, "Oh, this is how it all is," because how women see themselves has a lot to do with how their culture taught them to see themselves.
>
> And then what has happened is that Christianity has found ways to use the Bible, and therefore the theology that comes from the biblical framework, to marry the culture in order to reinforce

24. Scott, "On Seeing," 19.

certain cultural pieces, forgetting that sometimes there are certain elements of the culture that Christ came to redeem and reform.

What does this mean for us, then? We must attempt to become more aware of our cultural biases when we read Scripture. We can start by looking closely at the overall makeup of our culture and why it is the way it is.

Elizabeth continued with an example from her home culture:

> In Puerto Rico, we start with the agrarian society, and in the agrarian society you have the sugar cane culture and the coffee culture. The sugar cane culture is more toward the eastern side; coffee culture is more the center to the western side.
>
> In the sugar cane culture, men have to move with the harvest, so women are used to taking hold of responsibilities in the home, which include financial responsibilities. Women also supplement the income of the home. When men return from the harvest, they rest from the harvest and allow women to continue to run the framework of the household, so they have more of a cooperative relationship.
>
> The coffee culture is different, because you don't have to move, and the husband is the king of the home and things revolve around the king.
>
> So there are two cultures and two different ways that women see themselves. The responsibilities and the roles women play help women shape who they are.
>
> One of the things that the coffee culture holds on to, then, is the role that families have always had. Since family works for them that way, that's how they continue to hold even more securely to those pieces here. Within that, the role of men and women in the more traditional sense is held onto very, very deeply, and the theology goes along with that. Remember that theology always goes according to the culture.

Recognizing these enormous cultural influences, such as the two primary cultures of Puerto Rico, is a very good place to start. Recognizing less sweeping, but no less important, influences produces even more understanding.

The African American church has also experienced theological shifts as a result of cultural shifts, all of which impacted women's and men's roles within the church.

LaVerne Tolbert told about her experience and what she observed about the greater black culture's influence on the black church.

> In a sermon series, our Pastor looked at Old and New Testament examples of women serving. He also looked at the traditional barriers in the church—in this case it was a Baptist church and there was a traditional, Baptist, male chauvinist culture. Added to that, he looked at the African church.
>
> We have a strong culture of "male leadership only." That really has to do with societal infringements on men participating fully in our culture. Black males have barriers to career, professional development, succeeding in corporate environments. . . . There are always limits to where a black man can go.
>
> Black women are less threatening in the culture at large; so for them there is more flexibility. They are more accepted. Black men, however, are considered to be very threatening. So, black males' making their way in society is more tentative.
>
> In the church, however, black men have a domain that is unchallenged. It is theirs. It is not dictated to them by any one, any culture or any gender, and they want to *keep* it that way.
>
> So, we have that issue—a cultural dynamic. Plus, we have the theological dynamic of, "What is a woman's role in the church?"
>
> If you *add* the familial challenges of fatherless homes, societal emphasis on women's rights and how that has influenced the black family; and how *welfare* has impacted the black family . . .
>
> I'm from a middle-class family economically. My father was a carpenter and a minister. We may have been poor, but I did not experience it that way. I guess in comparison to other black families, we had a lot of things other families didn't have.
>
> But in the black culture, poor families, especially black women, could not have a man in their home if they wanted to receive a welfare check. In those days, a social worker could look *everywhere* in the house—under the beds, in the closets, in the bathroom—looking for shoes, shaving stuff, for a man's clothes, and for any other signs of a man. If the social worker saw *any* signs of a man, she would cut the woman off from receiving her welfare check.

Meanwhile, the *man* is having challenges and difficulties finding work and providing money for his family. The families need the money, but they don't qualify to receive assistance if he is in the home.

This was long before women's rights and long before single parenting ever became "popular." So, we have *that* dynamic. We have women leading families, making it in the career world and professional world, and in a lot of areas in life.

So, in the *church*, black men rose up and said, "*We're* in charge. This is *our* domain." Black women acquiesced, understanding *all* of this—really without even discussing it. They intuitively understood the tensions and acquiesced.

Elizabeth Conde-Frazier said, "I have found that it is important not only to state the position of the person but to note the different factors that bring one to such a position." Obviously, the impact of our surrounding culture presents challenges. So how do we begin acknowledging culture while we do biblical interpretation?

Your Turn:

"Hispanic theology is very ecumenical because it arises out of issues of survivability and justice."

–Loida Martel-Otero, Professor of Constructive Theology, Palmer Theological Seminary (Wynnewood, PA)

Can you identify any issues (aside from Scripture) out of which your particular church culture's theology arises?

There's another layer to the cultural piece: that of the distance between our cultures today and those of the ancient world. When Dr. Michael Cosby teaches, he urges his students and readers to acknowledge that we are culturally outsiders to people in the Bible. We need to follow that advice!

Cosby advises that "the first step is to realize that the customs and beliefs of ancient civilizations can differ substantially from our own."[25]

Seems like a no-brainer, right? However, as some of us may have admitted by now, it is easier said than done. So we have to remember that

25. Cosby, *Interpreting*, 13.

our assumptions about how people should act and what is considered normal will be different from theirs.

Before we begin applying passages without understanding, we must appreciate the differences, be aware of the actual cultural facts and practices, and grasp the meaning of the actions depicted and the statements used in the Bible. If we allow our own cultural assumptions, be they civic, religious, or personal, to guide our interpretation, we will end up interpreting incorrectly.

Elizabeth Inrig gave some sage advice:

> As far as my background went, I had to sift the women's issue through Scripture. *Whatever* your background is, you still have to sift it through Scripture. And hopefully you come back to Scripture and not to culture.
>
> You may come from the "far left." You may come from an Assembly of God, charismatic "far left," where women have pastored for years. You *still* need to grapple with the Scripture.

Hidden Challenge No. 3: Mental Intimidation

You might also entitle this chapter, "Help! I'm Overwhelmed Now!" The most colossal challenge to overcome may be mental intimidation.

"Why start at all if I'm already behind in the game?"

Can you relate? To *really* know how to interpret the Bible—I mean, to truly *master* it—would mean absorbing instructions and information that could fill a bunch of seminary courses, maybe even an entire degree. My mother-in-law, Beulah, expressed frustration in this area one time, at the end of one of her many interview transcriptions for this book.

She wrote, "One of the interviewees said to seek the heart of God in these matters, and I am. But part of me wants to say, 'Yes, *but*. After all, I am old. I can't do much now.' Unfortunately, the biggest part of me is saying this, and I can't seem to hear what the rest of me is saying."

Scores of resistance techniques rear their heads when we experience intimidation. So, are we really dead-in-the-water before we even start if we're not going to seminary any time soon?

Admittedly, to really *master* Bible interpretation takes years of learning and training. Does that make me a complete optimist for suggesting that you try to learn how to do it?

I say no, I won't concede that, because of my own experience and the experiences of many other women who have been late starters. Please, don't let what *hasn't* happened yet in your life or "what might have been" intimidate you from starting. Allow yourself to begin. List your questions concerning women, leadership, and the Bible. Go ahead. Start with whatever comes to mind and work your way to deeper questions that have previously confused, intimidated, or even frustrated you.

Sure, many aspects of interpretation exist that we can't possibly cover in this book.

I *can*, however, give you an overview for making more informed observations and analyses on your own, whet your appetite for knowing more about interpretation, and show you some major steps and principles. I believe that in reading this book you can start your journey now and start it with strength. In starting your journey, you can

- Overcome fears and intimidation of learning to "do theology" or entering into "a seminarian's world."
- Deal with some of the challenges and obstacles we face as we learn to engage in Scripture interpretation.
- Recognize your own biases and the need to let the text speak for itself.
- Learn tools that will help you interpret and discern answers to your most profound questions.

What You Don't Get

In this book we won't—indeed we *can't*—cover things like:

- "Textual criticism."
- An in-depth introduction to "propositional analysis."
- How to do your own word study in the original languages from start to finish.
- In-depth training for interpreting various forms/types of literature found in the Bible. (We're limited here to recognizing the fact that the Bible contains a large diversity of literary forms and each must be considered in order to accurately interpret.)
- How to do formal exegesis from soup to nuts.

- See how other women did it: how they processed and analyzed as they interpreted and then applied their interpretations to their lives.

If I could reach out to you right now and give you an encouraging hug or smile, I would. Just remember the "cloud of witnesses" who have gone before you or those who sit elsewhere reading this book, too, holding similar thoughts to yours: "Can I do this? Should I bother? Is it too late?" Respond in your hearts to each other's hesitations, "Yes! Yes! Never!" Now go for it!

CAUTION: TEMPTATION AHEAD

Any of these challenges, be they hidden or obvious, can tempt a person trying to understand the Bible to try to make it say what they want it to say. That's certainly easier. This may apply even if a person doesn't know she's doing it.

We always need to check our inclinations against Scripture. This prevents us from acting first, then looking for Scripture passages to justify our actions. Chances are good you'll find Scripture verses to back up any idea you want to prove—but that's not biblical interpretation. The fancy word for this is "eisegesis," which means reading *into* the text, rather than letting the text speak for itself.

"Eisegesis" Spells Disaster

> **Definition: *Eisegesis***
>
> Eisegesis is the "interpretation of a text (as of the Bible) by reading into it one's own ideas—compare exegesis."
>
> –"Eisegesis." *The Merriam-Webster Dictionary*. Online.

Key phrases in this definition include

- "Reading into"
- "One's own ideas"

You get the idea. This is where we get into real trouble, because we're not letting the text speak to us. Effectively, when we eisegete a passage, we are putting *our* words into God's mouth, rather than letting *God* speak to us through his Word.

Think of a tea infuser. A tea infuser injects the tea's flavor into the water into which it is placed, changing the water's flavor and its very constitution. Like that, proof-texting infuses a meaning into the text that's different from what the text and the author intended.

You may have heard the term "proof-texting." Proof-texting as a practice falls under this category of eisegesis. When a reader proof-texts, she reads a verse or verses in the Bible without considering their immediate context, much less the greater context of all of Scripture.

Candie Blankman commented, "the evangelical community has a lot of biblical proof-texting going on and a lot of cultural support for that within its own system." I'm sure that could be said for most communities.

People sometimes eisegete unknowingly, like with the "point-and-shoot" approach to reading the Bible. When you point-and-shoot, you flip open the Bible anywhere it falls, circle your finger around in the air like an airplane, then "land the plane" on a verse and hope it gives you some message from God that you can apply to the situation at hand.

Others, of more dubious motivation, may eisegete knowingly when they are trying to prove a point. They "lift" a verse out of its context, then make it say what they want it to say. Conveniently, they ignore any verses that seem to counter or temper the point they're trying to make.

Another type of eisegesis prioritizes the reader's response to the text, more or less skipping the steps of letting the text speak for itself. In this case, the reader doesn't care or take into account who wrote it or what that author intended to mean. This reader only cares about what meaning she assigns to the text: a *big* no-no if you really want to let the Bible speak to you.

Eisegetical practices like these have led to many actions and beliefs throughout history that today we consider horrendous distortions of Scripture.

Like what?

Two examples can illustrate how eisegesis works, as well as its impact on our Christian understanding and practice.

The first of those examples is the idea of "the rapture," as popularly taught and understood in parts of the Christian culture. The term "rapture" is not found anywhere in the Bible. People teaching about this term often support it from a mixture of the 1 Thessalonians 4:13–17 passage regarding a description of believers being "caught up" in the air/clouds with those of Jesus' descriptions of the days of the Son of Man, judgment(s), passages in the Gospel texts (e.g., Matt 24:30–36, 40–41; Luke 17), and other passages.

Teachers commonly confuse Jesus's idea of being "left behind" with that of a rapture, based on the blending of these passages. However, consider this: Jesus clearly compares the situation of the coming judgment to the days of Noah (v. 37a). Just as many were taken in judgment and only a few left behind (Noah and his family), when the Son of Man comes many will be taken and others left behind (Matt 24:39b–42). Clearly, those who are taken are not "raptured" to heaven but are judged. And the ones who are "left behind" are not the unbelievers but those who are saved!

Had you caught that before now? Do you see how the two ideas may be conflated if you just miss the part about Noah? And, do you see how this can mess with the paradigm of much of popular Christian culture? Yet, in particular, reading Jesus's words on the judgment of the Son of Man as being about the rapture is a prime example of eisegesis.

Have you read the Jenkens/LaHaye novel series *Left Behind?* Exciting reads, certainly, but not strictly Scripture. You probably would agree with that immediately; but how many of us checked it out biblically before some of its end-times concepts infiltrated our belief system as fact?

The other example, more closely related to our current investigation, involves the idea of the husband as the "covering" of the wife. Some Christians teach a concept of a husband "covering," or protecting and shielding, his wife from physical and/or spiritual attacks in society and also a spiritual covering and protection for her committed or potential sins; as in, the male will be held accountable and the female forgiven. This teaching is based on ideas found in Ephesians 5:25–28 and 1 Corinthians 11:3–15, which are then often connected to the ideas of Christ as high priest (Heb 2:17), Old Testament practice (i.e., Num 30:1–16), and other concepts from other passages. Many implications for this understanding exist, some of which are good, some not so good; some true, some not.[26]

Let me be clear: the terms "the rapture," in relation to an event in which Christians ascend to heaven when Jesus returns, and "covering," in relationship to the husband "covering" his wife, do not exist anywhere in Scripture.

Does this mean that the supporting principles people understand and use to teach these concepts are all wrong? Not necessarily. What to do with those ideas, teachings, and terms, then? You guessed it: you must study, discover, and discern what is found in Scripture and differentiate that from what's not there. Then, you need to decide what those passages

26. I've also heard this term discussed as referring to a pastor as the "covering" to a congregation. Now, there's a heavy load for a mortal to bear.

mean in their immediate and greater contexts, as well as in comparison to other, similar, or related ideas found in Scripture.

I'll reiterate this book's refrain: I urge you not to assume that because someone has published their thoughts, or preaches them from the pulpit, that they have correctly understood them from Scripture, rather than placing their own ideas into the text. You need to detect where a teacher may be pulling texts together to support and insert their own idea (which could have been someone else's idea originally), whether or not they even recognize they're doing it, yet teaching them as fact and doctrine.

Eisegesis is the opposite of one of the key components to interpretation: exegesis. (See chapter 8, page 69.) How do we do exegesis, then, and not eisegesis? And can we *ever* hope to interpret well, given all of these challenges?

Indeed, we can. Indeed, we *must*. Now, to prepare for the task of interpreting well.

Chapter 10

Get into the Text! Fundamentals of Interpretation, Part 3

How Do We Prepare to Interpret Well?

BIBLE INTERPRETATION PRIMARILY INVOLVES discernment. Discernment brings all the skills, resources, sensitivities, senses, and wherewithal—everything we have—to the Scripture passage(s) in our quest to find answers to our questions. We examine the text from many angles and ultimately try to discern what it means.

Yet, before moving into interpretation, we need to *prepare* to interpret. In this chapter, we will cover two important preparatory topics: (1) checking our objectivity, and (2) doing some important "housekeeping."

TO PREPARE TO INTERPRET WELL, CHECK YOUR OBJECTIVITY

I teach voice to all levels and many types of singers. Students who come to me are often convinced that they are being objective with themselves. Sometimes, though, they have truly misled themselves and are honestly off-track. They need some objective input.

As their vocal instructor, my job is to tell them what they need to hear, whether they want to hear it or not. I try to do this as gently as I am able and find it easier to do when I have an "objective third party" who is right there in the room with us. Therefore, in each student's lessons, I employ two items that I tell them will be their new "best friends" as they study voice. Like a best friend, these items always tell and show the truth.

What are they? The first is a mirror; the second, a recording of the lesson, either video or audio. These third parties cannot only tell the student where the error is, but can *show* them. (And the mirror and recording don't have to be gentle about it!)

Of course, a student has the right to choose to ignore what they see in the mirror or on the video, but to their own peril. If they are unwilling to see what is staring them right in the face, then it's really time for us to call it a day.

Think about this in terms of trying to understand and interpret the Bible. We've seen a number of factors that can impact our objectivity (feelings, culture, and intimidation). We'd truly be fooling ourselves if we thought we were completely unbiased as we approach studying this issue—or any other issue, for that matter. As a result, wisdom would advise us to step back, take a deep breath, and ask ourselves what other factors affect our interpretation.

Being honest with ourselves when we want to learn about something may be painful at points, but will save us from tragic error in the long run. If we tell ourselves we're already objective about this issue, without really exploring our biases, we rob ourselves of a truly fresh and fair reading of the texts and the Bible overall.

This type of honesty about how much our beliefs are impacted by factors besides God's Word is difficult work. Therefore, allow me to introduce you to *your* two new "best friends"—friends that will help you prepare to face the challenges of biblical interpretation.

Your Two New "Best Friends"

As you begin your approach to this subject, two simple but crucial questions will be *your* best friends.

> **Best Friend #1.** "Do I already have ideas I believe about women's roles? If so, what are they?"

Karen Mains told about a time when she saw her church family's biases, along with her own, glare through, largely unrecognized.

Let me tell you one thing I learned at Circle Church when we were going through this entire discussion about a woman's role in the church and in the home.

At that time, there was a principle about being *objective* about what the Scripture says, which we *should* know is nearly impossible, but at that time (this was the sixties and seventies) we were still holding to this idea. We went around this group of elders—the women had been invited to this function to see if it would work—and everyone described what they believed Scripture was saying about this very issue of male headship as it related to marriage.

And I am sitting there listening, thinking, "They are *all* describing their own marriages! Their theological position has been pre-determined by what kind of marriage they have, and none of them are honest enough or objective enough to know or say that about ourselves."

Best Friend #2. "Where did these preconceived ideas come from?" (Try to be as specific as possible.)

Karen Moy said, "I like to get people to see, 'Okay, do you *really* know what you believe and why you believe it, or are you just repeating something you've heard?'"

Consider these two questions *before* you begin interpreting a verse or passage. They identify whatever biases or preconceived notions we may carry into our investigation, so it's critical to answer them *honestly*.

Barbara Fletcher spoke about the importance of acknowledging one's own viewpoint, saying,

When I began my biblical and theological exploration of the whole "women's issue" in the early 80s, I *assumed* that hierarchy was appropriate, because I had never been taught otherwise. When I began doing my own research while I was in seminary, though, the hierarchical view never resonated in my heart. But I hadn't done biblical studies on my own. I'd only read 1 Timothy 2 and so forth at face value.

To take a *big* stride toward thinking objectively and seriously about the question of women's roles, spend time now with your two new best friends.

> **✍📖Your Turn: Preconceptions**
>
> Spend some time dwelling on these questions before you begin any kind of interpretative work. Take a moment to jot down your answers.
>
> - "Do I already have ideas I believe about women's roles? If so, what are they?"
> - "Where did these ideas come from?" (Try to be as specific as possible.)

Remember, you can interpret with confidence because you have learned or are learning the tools of the trade for solid Bible interpretation. And you are not out there on your own; you are standing on logical and learned time-tested strategies. However, using good tools and time-tested strategies, alone, do not good interpretation make. The very best confidence you hold is that the Holy Spirit is guiding you as you seek God's wisdom and counsel. In *that* truth, you can walk forward in confidence.

TO PREPARE TO INTERPRET WELL, GET YOUR HOUSEKEEPING DONE

Before you clean your house, you have to *clean* it. Do you know what I mean? In order to get *to* the surfaces that need cleansing, you have to clear out and clean up the clutter, stacks, toys, work, and, well, junk, so that you can disinfect.

Each time, you have to make some decisions: "What am I going to do with this stack of bills? These toys on the carpet? This pile of unfolded laundry? These dirty dishes in the sink and all over the counter?" That is half of the work—and sometimes more than half. This step is critical, despite all efforts to avoid and deny it.

As with keeping a home, we must attend to certain housekeeping issues before interpreting the Bible. Only, for us, as we approach interpreting, it's not "housekeeping" but "mindkeeping." We need to identify, account for, and decide on a few "piles" that can get in our way if we don't take care of them first. We need to:

1. Explore our interpretive view.
2. Establish our interpretive principles.
3. Identify our starting points of agreement.

Mindkeeping 1: Explore Your Interpretive View

Two people can look at one event and see two completely opposite things. My former boss in ministry would sometimes joke, "Natalie, you and I could be standing on the same corner, seeing the same car wreck, but have two entirely different accounts of what happened." Why is it that something can seem plain to you, yet someone else can see it so differently?

Thomas Kuhn expressed in *The Structure of Scientific Revolutions*[27] how difficult it is merely to demonstrate a scientific law to two different groups of scientists. The difficulty arises because of something called a "paradigm"—also known as "worldview" or, simply, "view." These terms refer to how you fundamentally see something, as well as how you see a thing, or things, in relation to other things.

Kuhn basically said that two groups of people can see completely different things, even when they look from the same vantage point and in the same direction: ". . . that is not to say that they see anything they please. Both are looking at the world, and what they look at has not changed. But in some areas they see different things and see them in different relations one to the other."

This explains what happened between my former boss and me! It's nice to know this can also happen to scientists.

Kuhn continued, "A law that cannot even be demonstrated to one group of scientists may seem intuitively obvious to another."

Every person approaches Scripture from a certain perspective. Karen Moy spoke of the importance of acknowledging your own worldview and identifying the worldview of others with whom you're interacting:

> It really wasn't until I started getting asked to do some speaking and teaching that I started hearing that there were things I couldn't do

27. Kuhn, *Structure*, 150.

> as a woman. My own church was very supportive. It was churches outside of that that weren't.
>
> A Japanese church asked my husband, Ed, and me to come speak. There was a lot of confusion, because their assumption was that Ed would be speaking to the adults for the week and I would be speaking to the children. But that didn't come out until a week before the event. Ed and I had prepared all the adult stuff tag-team.
>
> I had to tell them, "Well, I don't work with kids, so you guys are on your own. We have used the written agreements as to who is doing what kind of speaking."
>
> To them, the worldview was, "Well, women never teach to adults."
>
> In my worldview, it never occurred to me that I couldn't.

Our views certainly present challenges to Bible interpretation. We always interpret from a particular view of the world. We see things relating to other things in certain ways for particular reasons. We may not even be able to explain in words exactly why we see it that way or what those relationships are.

Interestingly, a paradigm or viewpoint can also shift. As a person learns new facts, her paradigm can expand to accommodate the new pieces of information. As new developments occur, a person's knowledge base and perspective expands and the original paradigm can't accommodate the new information anymore. At a certain "tipping point," so to speak, that person can change her opinions and feelings about a subject or situation. This is called a paradigm "shift."

> Even though we think, "Oh, you *know*—it's *the Bible*," we're looking at the Bible with a whole lot of different lenses, and theology is related to worldview.
>
> —Elizabeth Conde-Frazier

This shift is nothing to be afraid of; it happens rather automatically. Occasionally, you might experience an "aha moment"; other times, you might not even realize it. Precisely because of that fact, it is important to introduce you to this concept. We all have paradigms and paradigm shifts, knowingly or unknowingly, and we experience their effects. We need to acknowledge this, because one's view affects one's interpretation. Our perspective impacts our decision making, even our theological decision-making (perhaps especially our theological decision-making), at a very fundamental level.[28]

Mindkeeping 2: Establish Your Interpretive Principles

Because we need to discern, we seek to understand both the particular passages that give us "trouble" and their place in the overarching story given to us in God's Word. Identifying and weighing interpretive principles we use to approach Scripture is an important step toward that understanding. We should use these same interpretive principles to make our determinations about Scripture *every* time we interpret.

What, then, are these interpretive principles? Let's familiarize ourselves with some examples.

Examples of Interpretive Principles

Many possible principles exist; here is a list of primary principles used by many Christians:

1. Respect for Scripture
2. Plain-text reading
3. Culture-appropriateness
4. Whole-Bible (or "harmonizing the Scriptures")
5. No contradictions
6. "Main features" versus "attendant features"
7. Moral imperatives
8. Redemptive-movement
9. Literary form
10. Principle: Christocentric
11. Controlling verse: Yes
12. Controlling verse: No

28. For more resources on exploring your worldview, see Appendix B, "Resources, A Strategy" (page 223).

Many other principles exist; we can't cover them all. Yet, it is important to become familiar with some of the core principles. Even within that core, you will see a variety. Of course, challenges come with that variety. Some of the principles people use contradict each other. This at least partly explains why this issue perplexes many and even causes conflict in the church.

Let's touch briefly on these twelve principles. These are not presented in a particular order in terms of priority; however, some are listed together for comparison purposes.[29]

1. Principle: Respect for Scripture

Respect for Scripture means that no text can be discarded as meaningless, because it is God's Word (2 Tim 3:16). However, a caution goes alongside this: a person or group's position may use a Scripture verse or passage to support it; yet that does not *guarantee* that position is correct, or even biblical overall. Remember, simply because something appears in the Bible does not mean God endorses it.

2. Principle: Plain-Text Reading

This principle states that a plain, or literal, reading of the text gives its most basic and normal meaning. Another way to state this is that whatever the Bible explicitly says, in most cases that is what it explicitly means—nothing more, nothing less. Originally, this practice was born out of a countering, or perhaps balancing, response to the historically accepted practice of determining textual meaning from "spiritual" readings of a text (e.g., the use of allegories, analogies, and figurative language to give a text meaning apart from its plain one.)[30]

29. You may have heard or read the terms "grammatical-historical" and "historical-critical" methods of interpretation. If these confuse or intimidate you, I highly recommend you take forty-five minutes and get a sense of exactly what they are. You can get a quick tutorial through two brief but extremely helpful answers on a wiki site called the "Biblical Hermeneutics Stack Exchange" (http://tinyurl.com/n3c6xbt) and the 1974 article by Raymond Surburg entitled "The Presuppositions of the Historical-Grammatical Method as Employed by Historic Lutheranism." See bibliography for complete information and both URLs.

30. Surburg, "Presuppositions," 281. Note that many of the early church fathers used these methods for interpretation; they weren't just one-offs, sectarians, or weirdos employing them. However, Protestant reformers countered these historically

In its most extreme form, a plain-text reading may involve a flat reading of the text and may not give any weight to historical or cultural context. Some scholars and Christians place much emphasis on a literal interpretation: "If there's a command in the Bible, it's meant for all believers at all times."

Notably, the emphasis on any reliability found in a plain-text reading depends upon reading the original languages, not translations.[31]

3. Principle: Culture-Appropriateness

This principle states that the message of the gospel remains consistent, even though its emphasis may change according to the needs of the culture it addresses. To flesh this out, for example, believers in the early church began to live out the good news of the gospel in a way appropriate to their culture. (Think once again of the meat sacrificed to idols situation in Acts 15, which was a burning issue in the first-century Roman world but not at all in the modern West.) We are also believers called to investigate the principles of Scripture and discern their relevance to our own culture.

4. Principle: Whole-Bible Approach

This approach, also called "Harmonizing the Scriptures" or "Scripture interprets Scripture," states that one should evaluate and compare all of Scripture to arrive at a proper position.[32] All scriptural evidence should be considered. This includes general principles, as seen through themes and other means, as well as any specific statements that seem to explain an idea or dictate a command.

Candie Blankman noted that you don't build doctrine on problem passages, but on the whole of Scripture.

> Regarding the "women's issue," you have four or five "problematic" passages, but any good theologian knows you don't build doctrine—you don't build evangelical *system*—off of problem passages. You

accepted practices in an effort to bring people back to the accessibility of the Bible to all its readers, not clergy alone.

31. For those of us who are not original-language experts, then this means we must be extra careful to compare and contrast translations, upon which we may depend.

32. Kroeger, "A Classicist's View," 3. Blomberg, "Response to Kroeger," 44.

> have a preponderance of Scripture that is the *other* way, that supports all sorts of egalitarian principles and theologically challenges both men and women to do all sorts of things; but you have these problem passages, that are almost always culturally bound in some way or another.

This means, in effect, that what Scripture seems to say literally in black and white in one verse may not be understood to say it quite so literally once you take all of Scripture into account. Candie clearly indicates an egalitarian position in her observation. However, know that complementarians use the same principle to interpret Scripture.

This principle might help us combine the principles of plain reading and cultural appropriateness by taking an overarching view of Scripture. It certainly helps us avoid the mistake of selecting verses that support something we want to say or believe, just because we want to say or believe it.

5. Principle: No Contradictions

This says that Scripture does not contradict itself. Wherever contradictions seem to emerge, Scripture is not at fault; instead, the fault lies with *our understanding* of what the author intended to convey. For instance, Paul does not say one thing in one place and its complete contradiction in another place. For example, consider the apparent contradiction between 1 Timothy 2:12 and 1 Corinthians 11:5. First Timothy 2:12 provides a prohibition of some kind to women teaching and 1 Corinthians 11:5—in the context of the issues of glory, honor, and authority—assumes women are prophesying in public worship gatherings. Comparing and contrasting these verses within their greater literary contexts involves a multistep study process. Among other things, to decide why women would be allowed by Paul to do something proclamatory in one situation and not in another, one must decide what "prophecy," "teaching," "honor," "glory," and "authority" each mean in each case, among other issues. And one must also analyze the specific and greater passages and then compare them.

This principle of "no contradictions," in the end, states that with close study we can find congruency between Paul's words and his actions in different places.

Another way to phrase this is that one will find that all relevant texts harmonize with each other once one understands them as the author(s) intended them.[33] This principle often goes hand-in-hand with the "Whole-Bible Approach" principle.

6. Principle: "Main Features" versus "Attendant Features"

Each major personality in the Bible has "main features" and "attending features." For example, God presents Abraham to us as a model of faith in God's promises. The fact he also lied about his wife (twice) and kept slaves are not the main features through which to view him and certainly not the elements we should emulate. The principle itself states that when we use the Bible, the texts we use should be used for their main emphasis, not their attendant features.

7. Principle: Moral Imperatives

This states that broad theological principles and themes in the Bible that carry basic moral imperatives should weigh most heavily when we address social issues, even more heavily than specific statements made about a certain topic in Scripture.

8. Principle: Redemptive Movement

A "redemptive" or "redemptive movement" interpretive view approaches Scripture believing the Bible reveals God's redemptive plan throughout Scripture, with a trajectory toward an "eschatological ideal"—meaning, what God's perfection might look like, as best we can understand it. It insists that the Bible points to what "ought to be," showing how God takes people from however they start out ethically and morally and moves them slowly to his own values. This principle states that readers today should and can analyze these trajectories to discern their logical ends.

33. Powell, "Stalemate," 18.

9. Principle: Literary Form

The Literary Form perspective thinks that understanding the literary form, also called "genre" (for example: letter, law, gospel, narrative, etc.; see page 178) of a passage plays a major role in adequate interpretation.[34]

Now, prepare yourself. If it hasn't been clear yet that the principles different people use can conflict with each other, it's about to become clear.

10. Principle: Christocentric

The Christocentric principle encompasses a number of practices and perspectives. However, it may be summarized as the belief that all overarching biblical themes and also many, if not most, specific figures and scenes show directly or indirectly the preeminence of Christ. This would include those found in the Old Testament. For example, Martin Luther said all promises found in the Old Testament find their fulfillment in the New Testament.[35] Its adherents approach Bible study seeking to answer the question, "What does this text tell me about the person, work, and teaching of Jesus?"[36]

11. Principle: Controlling Verse: "Yes."

The first principle in this category says it is important to identify a clear defining passage, which serves as a starting point through which to analyze other verses.[37]

The Controlling Verse principle is often used in partnership with the Whole-Bible Approach, because that principle calls for Scripture to interpret Scripture. Ideally, unclear texts should be interpreted in light of clear ones. However, the judgment of which passage is most clear lies, to an extent, in the eyes of the beholder. Dee Brestin and Mary Ann Hawkins, who hold different positions on the roles of women in church leadership, both use this principle. Interestingly, both pointed out the difficulties that

34. Fee, "Church Order," 146; Scholer, "1 Timothy 2:9–15," 200.

35. Surburg, "Presuppositions," 285.

36. Keller, "Introduction to the Christ-Centered Model."

37. Bruce, *Galatians*, 74–75; McClelland, "New Reality," 67; Powell, "Stalemate," 18; Scanzoni and Hardesty, "All We're Meant to Be," 18–19; Scholer, "1 Timothy 2:9–15," 213.

lie within the process of deciding which verses interpret which and how that decision greatly impacts the outcome:

> [Dee] As I matured in my understanding of Scripture, it has sometimes frustrated me that the *unclear* Scriptures, such as the end of 1 Timothy 2, are used as foundational, when difficult Scriptures *should* be interpreted in light of the clearer Scriptures. This is especially the case since we see there *were* women in leadership, like Deborah, Philip's daughters, Priscilla, etc., and since we discover that the word for "deacon" has a feminine and a masculine translation, but often is translated "servant," when it's the feminine. Also, the passage that is often used to defend the position that women can't be in leadership is that leaders must be the "husband of one wife" *probably* referred to polygamy, which wasn't a problem for women.
>
> [Mary Ann] I ask the question, "How do you interpret Scripture? Do you use Scripture to interpret Scripture?"
>
> Generally speaking, people say yes, because that is the most acceptable—Scripture needs to interpret Scripture. Otherwise, you don't have any validity to the whole body of canonized Scripture.
>
> Then I ask, "Will you explain to me why *this* passage in 1 Timothy is the 'window' [for interpreting other passages of Scripture] when this is the only place that particular [Greek] word for 'authority' is used? When the [other Greek] word 'authority' is used in numerous other places and women seem to be given all kinds of freedom in other places, why do you use *this* window to interpret all of Scripture, rather than using the rest of Scripture to interpret that passage?"
>
> Generally, I get a "Hmmm. Well . . . hmmm."
>
> And I go back to the Galatians 3:28—there is neither Jew nor Greek, male and female, slave or free—and ask the question, "If you have to choose a verse, why don't you use that one, because it actually resonates with the majority of the rest of Scripture?" That's the direction I go.

12. PRINCIPLE: CONTROLLING VERSE: "NO."

This principle states that it is *incorrect* to attempt to identify a controlling text through which to filter all other verses regarding women in the New Testament, because the New Testament does not identify such a controlling verse.[38] If all Scripture is inspired by God, then how can you set up one text as the interpretive grid through which everything else is filtered? This principle says you can't.[39]

These two obviously conflicting principles represent the clearest examples of how beginning with a certain interpretive principle can directly impact your understanding.

> ✍📖**Your Turn:**
> Which of these principles makes the most sense to you: controlling verse "yes" or controlling verse "no"? Why?

I could include more principles in this list. I have covered a lot of the basic ones, though, many of which are commonly used by evangelical interpreters. Let's look at some fictional examples of how these principles might apply when studying the issue of women's roles.

Applying Interpretive Principles: A Fictitious Example

We just saw that many possible interpretive assumptions exist, and some of them conflict. Consider the fictional cases of Theresa and Andrea. Theresa believes that she needs to consider both the context of a verse and the specific situation being addressed in it in order to determine why Paul says different things at different times. She thinks that one should evaluate and compare all Scripture to arrive at a proper position.

Andrea, however, believes that in order to understand what a Scripture means, you only need to read what it says. Whatever the Bible explicitly says, that is what it explicitly means—nothing more, nothing less. Andrea places minimal emphasis on considering a verse's historical and cultural context. She thinks that textual issues, such as grammar

38. Scholer, "Feminist and Evangelical," 417–18.

39. Blomberg, "Response to Kroeger," 44.

(sentence order) and etymology (what a specific word means), are more important when interpreting a verse's meaning.

In fact, the debate between how much emphasis should be placed on dissecting the specific text and on the cultural and historical context of the verse's situation is a major point of division between Christians studying women's roles.

Now let's look at a more specific example (still fictional) of whether a passage or group of passages that we might consider "difficult"—such as whether women should be ministry leaders or not—should be interpreted in light of how the Holy Spirit gives gifts for the benefit of the church.

Jennifer wants to understand what 1 Timothy 2:12 means. She starts her inquiry with an interpretive view in mind that the Holy Spirit freely gives spiritual gifts to both men and women for the benefit of the church. In terms of the principles we've seen, this would be a combination of Whole Bible Approach and Controlling Verse: Yes.

So, she might look at the 1 Timothy 2:12 verse and reason, "Well, I know the Holy Spirit has given women gifts for ministry—I've seen this in 1 Corinthians 11–14, Romans 12, and Ephesians 4. I don't see any indication there or in other 'gifts passages' that certain gifts are not given to women. I particularly understand that from Hebrews 2:4. So then, the apparent directive I read in 1 Timothy that women should not 'usurp authority' over men and should be 'silent' must be understood in some way that's not as directly limiting as it seems to be. So, I'll look at that verse, 1 Timothy 2: 12, along with its chapter and book, with a view toward understanding it in the light of women *not* being limited by the Holy Spirit."

Then, Jennifer must decide exactly what, in that light, those limitations would be or whether there would be any at all, and she would need to deal with why that verse is there.

Now, suppose a different woman, Sally, starts from a different perspective. Let's say Sally starts studying with the idea that what Scripture says, *it says*. So, whatever it says, we have to deal with it lock, stock, and barrel. In our terms, we would call this the Plain Text principle: a literal interpretation or a "flat reading"—word for word, so to speak. Read the black-and-white words on the page and they mean what they mean; nothing more, nothing less. It would also involve the view Controlling Verse: "No," at least in theory, due to her belief in the priority of the plain-text reading. Although, she might be considered Controlling Verse: "Yes," using 1 Timothy 2:12 and its surrounding passage as the control for interpreting other texts.

Therefore, when Sally reads 1 Timothy 2:12, she would probably understand it as a direct limitation on women. "There it is in black and white," she might think. "Paul is giving an order."

Then the first issue Sally would be faced with is having to decide exactly what kind of limitation on women it was making. Are women to be literally silent? At home? In a worship setting? Or, are women just not to teach men? (Let's put aside the question of what it means to "usurp authority" right now, just in case you're already familiar with the various discussions involved and that issue is on your mind.)

Once Sally decides what she thinks the parameters of the limitations are, then, in order to deal with the gifts of the Holy Spirit, she has to reconcile the lists of gifts elsewhere in Scripture with the decisions she made about 1 Timothy 2.

For example, if Sally decided that women are to be literally silent in the worship setting, one question she might need to consider is, "Does the Holy Spirit give only certain gifts for the church's benefit to women (anything *but* teaching, for example) and reserve certain types of gifts for men (such as teaching)?"[40]

Some people believe that the Holy Spirit would not gift women in ways that would apparently conflict with his Word elsewhere (such as in 1 Timothy 2:12). As such, women would not teach, preach, or perform similar functions in the church—at least not with men present. Some might further decide that women should never do these functions.

To sum it up, both the gifts passages and 1 Timothy 2 contain direct instructions from Paul. Yet, Jennifer interprets 1 Timothy 2 in light of the gifts of the Holy Spirit, believing that they take precedence. Sally, on the other hand, interprets the passages on the gifts of the Holy Spirit in light of 1 Timothy 2. She believes that whatever Paul means in the gifts passages, it cannot contradict what he means in 1 Timothy 2. To her, Paul's instruction in 1 Timothy 2 seems crystal clear and, so, she reads the gifts passages in its light. Each woman has brought her interpretive viewpoint—based on one passage or a series of passages—to bear on the passages in question at the moment.

40. Some people believe "prophecy" is a type of preaching; some, teaching; others, neither, maintaining that prophecy differs substantially from both. Therefore, Sally (and also Tamika, whom you will meet within a few paragraphs) would also, at some point, probably need to address the question of whether prophecy is a type of teaching or preaching and, subsequently, whether it is allowed or forbidden for women. She would probably examine 1 Corinthians 11:5 closely, as well as do word studies on both terms.

Yet there can be other, subtle interpretive twists. Let's say that a third woman, Tamika, takes a literal view of 1 Timothy 2, like Sally does. But Tamika understands the passages on gifts to read that the Holy Spirit freely gives gifts to both men and women, without reservation of any gifts.

In that case, Tamika might conclude that a woman could potentially receive the gift of prophecy, for example, from the Holy Spirit; so, she would need to decide what she believes Scripture says about how a woman might exercise the gift of prophecy. Can she use it in mixed groups of men and women or where only women are present? If she took a literal view of 1 Timothy 2:12, she might well decide that women *can* exercise the gifts of prophecy and teaching, if gifted with them, but only to women.

Problem: The "Real-Life" Conflict

By now, you probably see how approaching Scripture with differing interpretive views might cause conflict in the church. (Unfortunately, many of you may already know this from personal experience.) Let's revisit our fictional women, Sally, Tamika, and Jennifer, to see how conflict can develop from something as basic as these interpretive principles.

Sally, who's convinced that a literal interpretation of the apparently straightforward meaning of 1 Timothy 2:12 must be heeded, might quickly be at odds with Jennifer, who interprets that verse in light of an understanding that the Holy Spirit doesn't limit his gifts to women.

Sally and Tamika might be more easily able to work together, while it would be harder for them to agree with Jennifer in a ministry setting. Still, Sally and Tamika might rub on each other a bit as they work out how the gifts of prophecy and teaching would apply in a women's ministry.

All three women deeply love the Lord with their whole hearts and want to serve him fully, obey his Word, and serve his church faithfully. All three, at one point or another, might feel misunderstood, misrepresented, or even judged by the others when discussing the topic in either a personal or ministry setting.

Despite their common ground in Christ, Sally might believe Jennifer to be scripturally in error, leading women astray into error if she propagates the idea. She might also believe Jennifer to be damaging or undermining the men's rightful leadership role and possibly endangering marriages by erroneous teaching about men's and women's roles. She might even believe Jennifer is endangering the salvation of church members.

Jennifer, on the other hand, might believe Sally to be narrow in her interpretation and thinking, and judgmental of others' understanding of Scripture. She might think Sally to be limiting God by saying the Holy Spirit doesn't gift women in certain ways. She might think Sally is placing unhealthy restrictions on their local church as a whole, and perhaps even endangering the salvation of church members or potential Christians.

Messy, right? And all because of the different frameworks through which they interpret Scripture. Interpretation can be a hotbed for disagreement, because of the complexity of assumptions that individuals make, knowingly or unknowingly. In fact, the issue of differing interpretive views contributes enormously to confusion and conflict about the women's issue. You can see how that can also be the case for any given theological issue you might be exploring.

Yet, there is hope; so let's address that now.

Solutions: How We Work past (or through) Differences in Interpretive Viewpoints

Two actions will help us work with others despite differences in interpretive viewpoints.

- First, begin by recognizing your own interpretive viewpoint(s).

Whether we're going to start out studying alone or in the company of others, it's important to choose—or recognize—your own interpretive view.

"Is it better not to have an interpretive viewpoint at all?" you might wonder. "If I don't have an interpretive viewpoint, wouldn't I be more unbiased and have a better chance at letting the text speak for itself?"

Well, in theory, yes. The problem is that operating without an interpretive viewpoint is impossible to do. It's crucial to recognize that everyone (even scholars) begin with a framework that guides their thinking about Scripture—whether they realize it or not.

Therefore, the honest approach is to recognize what your particular interpretive view on Scripture is. Once you recognize the grid through which you're interpreting Scripture, you can try to account for that as you study. Additionally, when you honestly recognize your own interpretive view, you can compare your view and your conclusions with those of others whose views are identifiable.

- Second, decide some things for yourself.

You must first decide what *you* think about whether a person can truly approach Scripture objectively, then go from there. What makes the discussion of interpretation more difficult is that even the very question about whether a person can interpret Scripture completely objectively is subject to debate. Some say you can; some say you can't.

Obviously, I think we can't, because I just said so two paragraphs ago. Yet, take note: this situation exemplifies the critical thinking process. Don't accept my words as truth simply because I wrote them in a book or seem to know what I'm talking about. Take them into account, then make your own choice. This text box presents your next opportunity for doing precisely that:

Your Turn: Your Interpretive Principles

Which principles of interpretation make the most sense to you? What are your interpretive principles?

Make your list. Remember, whatever principle(s) you apply to one passage you will apply to all passages. When you get to chapter 11, you'll need to have this thinking done.

Summary: Weighing and Deciding upon Interpretive Principles

In brief, our task consists of thoughtful discernment and recognizing the interpretive principles by which we approach God's Word every time. Finding your bearings by deciding your own interpretive viewpoint helps you explore this topic in Christian community as well as during your personal study time.

When you explore this topic in community with other Christians, understanding your own and others' interpretive views helps everyone move forward. You can find starting points everyone agrees on. Conversely, you can acknowledge each other's differing perspectives and recognize that those differing perspectives will impact your understandings.

Mindkeeping 3: Identify Your Starting Points of Agreement

Through the last several pages, we have examined understanding your interpretive view. As a result, you have identified your interpretive principles or begun that process. If you have not already thought through interpretive view and done the exercises on interpretive principles (see page 99), you should do these steps now. Then, you can identify your starting points.

The term "starting points," as used here, means points of agreement among Christians concerning scriptural teaching. This step serves as your reminder that we need to identify all of the biblical and theological assumptions that we can—our own and others.' But it also reminds us that in the midst of the ongoing debate, "starting points" of agreement among many contemporary evangelical Christians *do* actually exist.

Lists of starting points vary somewhat between people, but here are several essential points in the discussion on women's roles in the church.[41]

- Genesis 1:27
  Women and men are both made in God's image (*imago dei*).

- Genesis 1:28
  Woman and man were both commissioned to the task of filling the earth and subduing it.

- Genesis 2:18; 1 Corinthians 11:9
  God created the woman to be a "helper" for the man, because it was not good for him to be alone. Also, the sexes were created to be complementary and interdependent. Be aware, though, that there are two caveats to this:

  1. The phrase typically translated as "helper fit for the man" or "helper suitable for," or even a "help meet," in Hebrew is two words: *ezer kenegdo*. The scholarly discussion concerning the best translation of this phrase not only continues, but has received renewed attention lately, especially among biblically conservative Christians.

41. Many of these starting points are combined and condensed from "Points of Agreement" in Henderson et al., *Ordination of Women Study Packet*, 4, and Lees and Baldwin, *The Role of Women*, 14–16.

2. While everyone agrees that "helper" is part of the phrase, interpreters see three related issues differently: (1) exactly what *kind* of helper the woman is, (2) what her identity is, and (3) what her roles are, particularly in relation to the man. Remember, the way a person interprets the meaning of the passage affects their translation, as well as their beliefs and practices.

Helper? Helpmate? *Ezer?*

Carolyn Custis James wrote three books that help us understand the phrase *ezer kenegdo*:

- *The Gospel of Ruth* (2008)
- *When Life & Beliefs Collide* (2001)
- *Half the Church* (2011)

These books (published by Zondervan) have brought attention to this phrase; but she's not the first Christian woman to do so. Over one hundred years ago, a woman named Katharine Bushnell created one hundred exegetical Bible studies, which were published in 1923 under the title *God's Word to Women*. You can read it in its entirety at www.GodsWordtoWomen.org/gwtw.htm

Bushnell wrote about *ezer kenegdo* in lesson four of *God's Word to Women*, "Beginning of Evil."

- Galatians 3:13–29
  God justifies both women and men through faith and, thus, both have equal spiritual standing before God.
- 1 Peter 3:7
  God calls both women and men to be in relationship with him.
- 1 Corinthians 12:4–31; Ephesians 4:11–13; Romans 12:3–8
  Via his holy Spirit, God gives a variety of gifts to both Christian men and women. These gifts are talents and abilities that are specifically granted to build up the church to maturity in Christ. Many Christians agree that the fellowship of the body of Christ should affirm and encourage these gifts and that the individual should develop his or her gifts within and for the context of the church, primarily. As these gifts appear in Scripture, they are not gender-specific.

- Ephesians 2:8–10
  God saves both women and men by grace alone.

On the topic of gender, other starting-point examples exist, but the list isn't extraordinarily long in terms of points on which Christians have complete agreement.

Assumptions

Interestingly, the assumptions Christians begin with in the twenty-first century are not the same assumptions with which church theologians would have begun with fifteen hundred, five hundred, or even one hundred years ago.

These starting points of agreement have morphed and changed throughout church history. Why? Because, often, they are based on assumptions and core beliefs people groups make about human life. In Christian life, the assumptions and core beliefs people hold relate to the purposes for living that God might have given us as male and female and to how we image God—or whether we image God at all. And these assumptions and core beliefs, believe it or not, change. We know this because they *have* changed a lot throughout church history.

This fact may surprise you, because today we hold certain assumptions about human life. Yet, our assumptions today would be completely foreign to the thinking of the general populous of most cultures two thousand years ago. One only needs to spend about fifteen minutes reading through the church fathers' quotes concerning women to get an idea. These types of changes are an observable fact of history.

Your Turn: Starting Points

Take some time to think through your own starting points and write them down.

RECAP: PREPARING TO INTERPRET WELL

Congratulations! You have officially begun the path of exegeting Scripture. Celebrate that beginning in some meaningful way today! Call a friend to share your progress. Go out for a fru-fru coffee. Dance around your living room to your favorite song. However you choose to commemorate the moment, know that you have made a commendable start. You've identified your starting points, established your interpretive principle(s), and done a good deal of thinking already to prepare your way toward your best effort at objectivity with God's Word.

All that being said and done, remember that we're not going to solve and settle this question with finality in this book. Recognize that this beginning is just that: a *beginning*. Still, it's a stellar beginning, so enjoy it.

When you've celebrated sufficiently, get your game face on, because the rubber is going to hit the road. We're moving on toward interpreting the Bible well.

Chapter 11

Get into the Text! Fundamentals of Interpretation, Part 4

How Do We Interpret Well? Use Basic Exegetical Skills

To INTERPRET WELL, WE need to give our discernment process a solid biblical foundation. Learning the practices outlined in this chapter and the next will help you gain that solid ground. In this chapter, we will learn how to study the passage using basic Bible exegesis. In chapter 12, we will learn to understand and discern categories of meaning.

Even merely reading through these two chapters to understand the concepts, without going further or consulting any of the resources, would put you a half-step ahead of basic Bible reading. However, if you will earnestly study these practices, try them out, and begin to apply them to your every day Bible study using some of the recommended resources and tips, expect an *explosion* in your understanding of God's Word!

This is where the fun *really* begins—the stuff of legend. If you will apply these practices and principles, I *guarantee* that at some point you will find yourself saying, "I never knew that! That is *so* cool! Thank you, God!"

Let's now focus on the three main steps that will put you on the road to thoughtful, responsible Bible exegesis:

Exegesis Step 1. Examine the Ancient Culture

Examining the ancient culture means considering the original writer's culture. Typically this meant the ancient Israelite culture, but it may even mean checking out the cultures that surrounded ancient Israel—Greek, Roman, Babylonian, and other Mediterranean and Near Eastern cultures, for example—depending on what the situation was at the time.

Exegesis Step 2. Examine the Literary Context

Examining the literary context means doing your best to understand the particular text you're examining in the context of the whole book in which it is contained, as well as what the author wrote elsewhere. For instance, we need to interpret the passage in 1 Corinthians 14 about silent women in the context of 1 Corinthians 11 in which women are not silent. And both need understanding in the wider context of 1 Corinthians, and then in the light of Paul's other writings.

Exegesis Step 3. Examine the Literary Content

Examining the literary content means scrutinizing the passage immediately under consideration, its words and its grammar. This includes comparing the specific passage, words, and grammar with others by the same author, as well as with related passages and situations in Scripture.

Let's be honest here: these three steps, obviously, by necessity will contain a number of sub-steps. For the exegetical process to be effective and for it to provide the insight—as well as the safeguards—you are looking for, it is a rather involved process. But I promise you that once you delve into Scripture using these steps, you will never see the Bible the same way again. Edging closer through this type of study to what God has revealed in the original languages, with all their marvels, will change your life.

These three main steps of exegesis provide categories that help shape your thinking. They help you discern whether something in the Bible applies to all Christians at all times or was meant only or primarily for the audience that received it.

Inherent in this process is the importance—and effectiveness—of asking questions. Engaging the Bible through these kinds of questions is healthy and helpful. When you want to have a conversation with a person you don't know very well, how might you get to know them? You ask questions, right? Asking questions of your friends is certainly wiser than making assumptions.

Often, perhaps most of the time, we make the wrong assumption and read the situation entirely incorrectly. And *that* is a pain, is it not? A heartache for both parties.

We do the same thing with the biblical text. In the case of reading our own interpretation into a biblical text, we set ourselves up for misunderstanding. Therefore, we must ask questions of the text. *This* is Bible interpretation in its most basic form.

EXEGESIS STEP 1: EXAMINE THE ANCIENT CULTURE

It's important to read Bible passages in their historical and cultural context, because (1) many beliefs commonly accepted and acted-upon today are not found in the Bible (and vice versa), *and* (2) many of our cultural practices today did not exist back then (and vice versa). We must be (or become) aware of these facts when interpreting.

Let's kick-start our thinking in this section with a provocative little exposé entitled . . .

Can You Believe This?

Where in the Bible does it say that Jesus was born in a barn?

Professor Michael Cosby in his book *Interpreting Biblical Literature* points out a number of reasons why we all think Jesus was born in a barn and his parents were turned away from the Bethlehem version of the Motel 12.[1] Read Luke 2 and think through this short series of questions.

How have the words in the passage been traditionally translated and presented popularly (as in, dramatic enactments and such)? And, what was your own understanding of this Word or passage before beginning to study it more closely?

For example, the word traditionally translated "inn" in this story is probably better rendered as "guest room," throwing a very different light on the scene.

Why might this be? In other words, why do so many insist on it as being an "inn"?

Answers: tradition and translators' choices. These traditionally chosen translations are embedded in religious tradition. People don't want to see it any other way and would not respond favorably if it was. Translators are aware of this preference.

1. Cosby, *Interpretation*, 6–11.

Another example: KJV (Luke 2:5) says Mary was "great with child." The Greek text gives no evidence of this at all. There's actually no indication of exactly how long they were in Bethlehem before Jesus was born. The text says: "*While they were there*, the time came for her to deliver her child."

What do you think so far? Befuddled? But, wait! There's more!

Archaeology shows us evidence that guest rooms were part of some Jewish homes of Jesus' time. Sociological studies of that period give us evidence of the extreme importance of family and the priority of elders as impactful, *assumed* realities in this story. This means that, given the extremely high value on family, including extended family, chances are slim that Joseph went back to his ancestral home and did not have anywhere to stay. In fact, Mary probably had kinswomen surrounding her before, during, and after the birth, because they more than likely would have been staying with Joseph's relatives. They probably weren't in the guest room itself, because with the influx of people for the census many extended family members would likely be staying there. Elders would have gotten the priority of the most comfortable room(s).

So then, why was Jesus in a manger and where was it (and what was it)?

Archaeology says that families in city homes kept their animals in the house *with* them (eew!), in attached rooms, not in a barn as our modern cultural assumptions and experience might lead us to think. The manger would have been an obvious place for putting the baby, because it wouldn't get stepped on by people or animals. Mangers sat in-between and accessible to both the family living space and the animals' space. Readers contemporary to the story would assume most, if not all, of these images and priorities, while they are mostly foreign to us. It would have been common understanding for them.

What images have been passed down through Western Christian tradition? Are these different from the original story as we now see and understand it from the cultural and historical evidences? Things commonly understood in the story's culture might be thought of as challenging new insights today, "turning things upside down for many readers."[1]

Then where do all of these ideas come from that we see in our "Christmas manger scenes"? Do any non-biblical texts contemporary to the Bible impact our reading today?

The *Protevangelium of James* (a.k.a. the *Infancy Gospel of James*, from *The New Testament Apocrypha*, vol. 1) contains many of the details that we think of as time-honored parts of the story of Jesus' birth but that are not in the biblical accounts, as well as many other, more fanciful ideas. Like what? Well, like Mary being nine months pregnant when traveling to Bethlehem; Joseph as an old man; Jesus born in a cave; Mary riding on a donkey to Bethlehem.

None of these are in Luke's account. Interesting.

1. Ibid., 9.

So, *can* you believe this? Well, obviously, you and I both can and did. We and millions of others swallowed the dramatic version over the biblical version—hook, line, and sinker! We have our work cut out for us as we learn to interpret the Bible for ourselves, because many influences can guide us away from an accurate understanding.

Let's now read a small portion of Sandra Glahn's story as she was sorting through some interpretive questions regarding her questions about women's roles. In this portion, we're capturing her mid-thought on the subject of, "what does 'headship' really mean and is it a valid concept?"

You will see she raised a slew of questions. To be sure, she had to do more research to answer her questions and, in this particular quote, she ponders some of the results she found. We should realize that she probably filled several notebooks in her office with more research material! Here she is *summarizing* some of her thoughts and findings.

Take note of the underlined items marked with superscripted letters. Perhaps place a bookmark on page 123, because we will be walking through this quote and picking it apart in the upcoming sections.

Table 2. A Mentor's Example: Sandra Glahn's Thinking

(Note the underlined items.)
Para. 1—I think that in Paul's culture[a] he was using the "head" metaphor in 1 Cor. 11:7 to teach us something about the firstborn being Christ, because the difference between man and woman as established *there* is whatever "glory" is.
Para. 2—But, because the primogenitor argument (that is, "the man was created first") is what Paul always refers to[b] when he pulls out the Genesis "trump card,"[c] I am not yet ready to say there is nothing about the man that is different in that sense. The "first-ness" of the male's creation happened before the Fall.[c] In other words, I have not figured out yet if that is cultural or if that is part of design.[a] As a point of comparison,[d] the Sabbath was also established before the Fall, but we don't always follow the Sabbath commands in the Church Age.
Para 3—My remaining element of doubt is in figuring out if, when Paul referred to creation order, was he "doing the Midrash thing" and/or using concepts that would have been familiar to a limited audience, or was he saying something that is true for all time and all cultures and situations?[a]
Para. 4—Specifically, do men have an honor before God by virtue of man's arriving in the garden before woman that women do not have? Do men have a glory before God that women do not have? If so, *that* seems to be the only legitimate basis[e] for limiting women—*not* all of the other reasons people have argued from the text but that Paul never used in his own arguments. Adam was *first—that* is what Paul always comes back to.
Para. 5—So if complementarians are going to argue for limiting women, I think they need to stick to the reason *Paul* gave. But, even then, it's tough to get a handle on how universal Paul's statements about first-ness were.

Now, let's apply our exegetical skills, as we track Sandra's path of thinking through the texts.

Most Important: Acknowledge Cultural Differences

Before you do anything else, acknowledge the differences between the cultures. Remember that the original writer was not writing to *us*. Thinking otherwise will lead us to a misinformed interpretation. The author communicated to an audience in a specific time and involved in a specific culture.

In paragraphs 1, 2, and 3 of Sandra's thinking, take a look at the items with the superscript "a." Notice that Sandra begins by wondering what would have been normal in Paul's culture.

Ladies, Start Your Questions

Now that we are not deluding ourselves by thinking that our cultures in today's world are similar to the ancient cultures of the Bible, we can start asking questions.

Begin with the overarching question, "What does the historical and cultural context tell us about these words and the scene?" Then, ask the text and yourself a bevy of questions. (Keep notes!) Use the following list to expand that overarching question into separate, specific questions.[42]

Table 3. Exegesis Step 1: Examine the Ancient Culture

Ask: What does the historical and cultural context tell us about these words and the scene?

- Consult a Bible **atlas**. What information can you gain regarding the location of the story? Is there any particular significance to that particular place? Its history? Its geography?
- Is there any **archaeological evidence** that can shed light on the culture contemporary to the story?
- Do any **sociological studies** of the time period give you insight into that culture? The author? The recipients of the document?
- Do any **non-biblical texts** (also called **"extra-biblical texts,"** meaning outside the Bible) that were contemporary to the Bible impact our reading today of this passage?
- What **images** from or of this scene or passage have been passed down through Western Christian tradition? Are these different from the original story as we now see and understand it from the cultural and historical evidences?

Notice any differences or interesting points you find, remembering that

- Readers contemporary to the story would assume all of these images and priorities, while they are mostly foreign to us. It would have been common understanding.
- Things commonly understood in the story's culture might be thought of as new insights today.

42. I condensed and simplified many of these questions and some of the information in this ancient-culture section from Michael Cosby's book, *Interpreting Biblical Literature*.

Resources for Ancient Culture Studies

At this point, you may be wondering where you can *find* the information that will help you examine the cultural context well. Fair enough. For each category of research, I have created some lists of recommended resources I hope will be helpful to you. Some even specifically address women in ancient texts and contexts. I'm sure you've heard of commentaries; but you may not have heard of some of these other resources. These lists should get you going; pick one and run!

Table 4. Recommended Resources for Examining the Ancient Culture

Ancient-Context Books on My Bookshelf	General Ancient-Context Information Books Recommended by Professor Cosby	Other Fantastic Helps
A Woman's Place: House Churches in Earliest Christianity by Carolyn Osiek, Margaret MacDonald and Janet Tulloch (Minneapolis: Fortress, 2006) *Daughters of the Church: Women and Ministry from New Testament Times to the Present* by Ruth A. Tucker and Walter Liefeld (Grand Rapids: Zondervan, 1987) *Gospel Women: Studies of the Named Women in the Gospels* by Richard Bauckham (Grand Rapids: Eerdmans, 2002) *Her Story: Women in Christian Tradition* by Barbara J. MacHaffie (2nd ed., Minneapolis: Fortress, 2006) *Maenads, Martyrs, Matrons, Monastics: A Sourcebook on Women's Religions in the Greco-Roman World* by Ross S. Kraemer (Philadelphia: Fortress, 1988) *The IVP Bible Background Commentaries* (any of them!). This series includes these titles (all published by InterVarsity): *Old Testament* by John H. Walton, Victor H. Matthews, and Mark W. Chavalas (2000) *Genesis–Deuteronomy* by John H. Walton and Victor H. Matthews (1997) *New Testament* by Craig S. Keener (1993) *Women's Life in Greece & Rome* by Mary R. Lefkowitz and Maureen B. Fant (Baltimore: The Johns Hopkins University Press, 1982)	*Daily Life in Biblical Times* by Oded Borowski (Atlanta: Society of Biblical Literature, 2003) *Discovering Eve: Ancient Israelite Women in Context* by Carol Myers (New York: Oxford University Press, 1988) *Handbook of Life in Bible Times* by J. A. Thompson (Downers Grove, IL: InterVarsity, 1986) *Life in Biblical Israel* by Philip J. King and Lawrence E. Stager (Louisville: Westminster John Knox, 2001) *The New Testament World: Insights from Cultural Anthropology* by Bruce J. Malina (Louisville: Westminster John Knox, 2001) *Palestine in the Time of Jesus: Social Structures and Social Conflicts* by Daniel Friedmann (Peabody, MA: Hendrickson, 2002)	*Dictionary of New Testament Background*, edited by Craig A. Evans and Stanley E. Porter (Downers Grove, IL: InterVarsity, 2000) *The IVP Atlas of Bible History* by Paul Lawrence (Downer's Grove, IL: InterVarsity, 2006) *The IVP Introduction to the Bible*, edited by Philip S. Johnston (Downers Grove, IL: InterVarsity, 2007) *Zondervan Illustrated Bible Backgrounds Commentary* (any of them!), edited by Clinton E. Arnold (Grand Rapids: Zondervan, 2002)

We've looked at the ancient setting; now, let's zoom in and look at the words.

EXEGESIS STEP 2: EXAMINE THE LITERARY CONTEXT

The literary context of the actual passage includes both what the author has written in the rest of the book in which the passage occurs and what the author has written elsewhere. This means asking yet another series of questions (see Table 5), like we did when examining the ancient culture; this time, however, we're looking directly at the text.[43]

Rule of Thumb: Ask Plenty of Questions of the Text

Essentially, you are thinking long, hard, and thoughtfully about the passage. You are asking attentive, probing questions of the text. All of these questions we ask can be summed up by thinking in terms of *context, context, context*.

Table 5. Exegesis Step 2: Examining the Literary Content

The Central Message and the Greater Context of the Passage
Ask: • What book contains the passage? Who wrote it? • What major themes do you find? What key issues? What key words (repeated, emphasized, defined, used elsewhere, etc.) do you find throughout the book? • What is the tone? Does the tone change during the course of the book? • When was it written or recorded? • Where was the author (or where were the authors) when he (or they) wrote that book or recorded this event? Under what circumstances did they write? • To whom did they write it (who was their audience)? What circumstances were those recipients in and why? • Why did the events occur?

43. Note: I consolidated, condensed, and simplified the questions, suggestions, and information in this Literary Context section from a number of resources: *God's Women Then and Now* (D. Gill and B. Cavaness), *Interpreting Biblical Literature* (M. Cosby), the mentors' interviews, and my own practice.

- Why did the writer include this narrative or these statements? How does it (or how do they) fit into the author's theme or purpose?
- How did it come to the original recipients? Another way of phrasing this question is, "What *type* of writing is it?" (The fancy word for the *type* of writing is "genre" or "form.") Was it arriving as a . . .
- Letter? Sermon? Book? Oral story/parable? A teaching by Jesus? Prophecy?
- Related to genre, consider what this passage (and the book overall) teaches or contains: History? Laws/legal writings/contracts? Parables? Proverbs (wisdom literature)? Psalms? Poetry? Songs? Prophecy? A teaching of Jesus? Interpretation of OT Scripture?
- Where did the events described in the passage (and in the book overall) take place?
- What comes before this particular passage of interest? What come after?
- What situation(s) are being addressed—or assertions being made—just before? Just after? Overall in the section? Overall in the book?
- What happened just after the passage as a result of what occurred in the passage you're studying?
- How does this narrative, statement, or section relate to other events in the same book?
- What is the *central message* of this paragraph? Surrounding section? Book?
- Consider why the author may have situated this particular passage where it is within the book. What if it was *not* situated at that place? What if it was somewhere else? What if it wasn't there at all? What difference might that make?

Studying the passage in light of its context fills in a lot of blanks as you go along. Remember, the idea is to let the text speak. The only way you can truly understand a passage is to understand its context.

Gill and Cavaness summarized all of this with the simple statement, "the individual verses must be seen against the background of the larger overall message of the section and book."[44]

44. Gill and Cavaness, *God's Women,* 24.

Table 6. Recommended Resources for Studying Literary Form (Genre)

Books	Online Article (Free!)
How to Read the Bible for All Its Worth by Gordon D. Fee & Douglas Stuart, 2nd ed. (Grand Rapids: Zondervan, 1993). *Interpreting Biblical Literature* by Michael R. Cosby (Grantham, PA: Stony Run, 2009).	"A Short Guide to Biblical Interpretation" by Andrew S. Kulikovsky (http://hermeneutics.kulikovskyonline.net/hermeneutics/introherm.htm). Kulikovsky has collected a lot of excellent links for free online resources that help people learn and do Bible interpretation. Most of them come from major universities, evangelical resources, institutions, and journals.

A note about online resources . . .
I'm sure you've noticed that I've included several online resources in this book. That's because a lot of you, like me, use the internet for many things, including basic research. Frankly, being able to look something up quickly and at no cost is an enormous help and blessing—that is, if I know it is from a trustworthy source. Discerning the trustworthiness of an online site sometimes presents challenges, however. Please know that wherever I have recommended a site, either I have used the site myself, have thoroughly reviewed it, or personally know the person or group running it and trust them.

We have looked around the passage we are studying; now, let's look at it directly.

EXEGESIS STEP 3: EXAMINE THE LITERARY CONTENT

Literary content includes the words and grammar found in the particular passage you are studying, as well as those found in other passages attributed to the author. It also includes making comparisons with related issues and situations throughout the whole of Scripture.

These steps will help you examine the literary content:

Literary Content Step 1. Examine the words in the passage you are studying.

Literary Content Step 2. Examine the grammar in the passage you are studying.

Literary Content Step 3. Examine the words and grammar in other passages attributed to the same author.

Literary Content Step 4. Read commentaries on the passage and the book as a whole.

Literary Content Step 5. Look for points of comparison in the Bible.

a. Find and compare similar theological issues.

b. Find and compare different theological issues that are argued similarly.

Important: Understand the *context* of your passage first. Then, scrutinize the *content* of your particular passage.

Literary Content Step 1: Words

"Sticks and stones may break my bones, but words will never hurt me!" That schoolyard phrase is hooey. Words are powerful. Words have potent effect. And because we trust God's Words to be even more powerful than our own, we look closely at the words in the Bible. As much as possible, we should look at the words in their original language, using all the word study tools to which we have access (more on that in a bit).

That being said, if we *only* look at the words and *only* do word studies—even super-*duper* word studies—and think we've done all we need to fully understand a passage's meaning, we would be making a serious mistake. It could actually be misleading; at the very least, it would be myopic.

For example, some people focus on trying to discern the meanings of specific words, especially the "controversial" words (like *authentein* in 1 Timothy 2:12—the one often translated as "authority"—or *kephale*, which means "head," in Ephesians 5), but fail to take everything else into consideration. We certainly need to include these studies in our pursuit, but keep them in perspective as part of a larger picture.

Bev Hislop addressed this very issue of people focusing, possibly too narrowly, on the most difficult words:

> The abuses of interpretation and misinterpretation from these Scriptures are more troublesome to me than *any*thing. I think trying to come to a clear decision on it is probably colored by the words that we use and the misunderstanding and misinterpretation of those *particular* words. You know, those are kind of "red-light" or "orange-light" words. To try to look at them objectively and rediscover them, I think, is very hard to motivate people to do. I think

there is just a lot of *junk* that is hard to get over and through, to get to the place of original intent.

This helps explain why we do the ancient historical context studies first and then we also do our very best to look at the literary context as well as the content. We need to get the big picture, as well as examine the particular words used.

Once you have done those steps, begin looking at the words in a passage using these four questions:

1. What words are actually used in the original text?

For those with no language training, an interlinear Bible will propel you into the wonderful world of original biblical languages. Even though I *learned* both Greek and Hebrew, I admit I find it fun (and easier) to use these at my proficiency level. I've already admitted I'm not a "language scholar," so I've nothing to hide.

For those with *some* language training, try something like *A Reader's Greek New Testament* published by Zondervan. They help you cheat as you read by giving you many of the word definitions at the bottom of each page; but you still get to feel like you're exercising your Greek muscles.

For anyone at any level, many online interlinear resources exist for both the Old and New Testaments. My most recent favorite is Biblos.com (see Table 8 for more information on it).

2. What are the possible meanings of the words in their sentences?

There may be several variations of meaning for a particular word or words. After researching them, what do you find are those possible meanings? Use a Bible dictionary or a theological wordbook to find definitions of critical words in the passage. Each of these types of resources is incredibly handy and typically very user-friendly for English speakers. Bible dictionaries also include significant places, people found in the Bible, noteworthy events, and helpful general information.

For the "sturdy of heart," and for those who have at least some experience with the biblical languages, you can also find this information in a type of resource called a lexicon. These exist for biblical Hebrew/Aramaic and Greek. When you are looking up definitions or doing word studies, a lexicon will provide ample meaty information on all of the words you'll ever encounter. Warning: using a lexicon may overwhelm you a bit, because they tend to be rather technical. You need to be comfortable looking up a word in the original language, because that is typically how they are formatted.

All of these definition resources provide a *range* of possible meanings for each word they define.

3. Which definition fits best in the context of your passage?

Questions to ask:

Is this word used several times in this passage or book?

How is it used each time?

Generally, an author will use one particular word the same way inside a passage and, usually, inside a book. Gather information on how he used that word throughout the book you're studying. Eventually, you'll also gather information on how he may have used that word in other books attributed to him. If this author didn't use the word again, did any other biblical authors use it? How?

How have the words used been translated? (Check several translations.) Then look at the English translations you have. Ask:

4. Have any other (different) original-language words been translated into English the same way this one has been translated?

Remember the "love," "*logos*," and "*kosmos*" examples? Complications arise if the word isn't used anywhere else in the Bible. In this kind of situation, the word is called a *hapax legomenon*, or *hapax* for short. A *hapax* creates difficulties in interpretation, because there are no other

Definition: Hapax Legomenon

"The term **hapax legomenon** is one of great use to linguists, especially those who study dead languages. A **hapax legomenon** is a word, phrase, grammatical form, or other usage that occurs only once in the written record of a language, in a particular text, or in the works of a single author." [Bold emphases original.]

–"Hapax Legomenon." *The Random House Dictionary*. Online.

instances in the Bible to which to compare it in order to find a range of its meanings or see its uses there.

Literary Content Step 2: Grammar and Sentences

Two important actions during this step will illuminate the passage for you:

- Check commentaries for understanding of the original language(s). What do two or three commentators say?

    Without mastery of the languages, the best approach for flagging and understanding any grammatical intricacies is using Bible commentaries—several of them. Using several commentaries gives you several perspectives. Remember, a *commentator* is a Bible *interpreter* with a lot of letters behind his or her name that indicate they've done a lot more study than we probably have; typically, they also have mastery of the languages. Then remember, as we have learned, that every interpreter has their own interpretive view and their own biases. Find a few good commentaries and keep them handy.

- Diagram the passage in the original language, if possible (or cheat with great grace and use a pre-diagrammed tool).

    Sentence diagramming provides you with a bird's-eye view of how all of the phrases and statements relate to each other. It sketches out, grammatically, the writer's thought process. You can learn how by using one of the nifty online resources listed in the resource box on page 142. Of course, this works best if you know Greek. However, you can also diagram an English translation with your English-grammar diagramming skills.

Literary Content Step 3: Examine Words and Grammar the Author Uses in Other Passages

Now, you're going to look at the words and grammar again, only this time throughout all of the author's writings.

Look back at Sandra's thought process in Table 2 on page 123. In paragraph two, she uses the phrase "what Paul always refers to."

In this simple phrase, Sandra has asked the question, "What does the author say in other writings attributed to him?"

"Hey, wait! Isn't that *context*? I thought this section was on *content*," you might be wondering.

And you would be right. Comparing what that author says in other places, as you may be thinking to yourself right now, is part of the larger process of looking at the literary conte***x***t. Yet, in order to know what words to compare, of course you needed to have looked at the literary conte**n**t by now, which you have done (kudos to you). From this point, you'll move back and forth between conte***x***t and conte***n***t. It's a beautiful dance.

Notice, also, that while Sandra thinks about the issue, she asks some simple but illuminating questions, such as:

- How does the author refer to or describe that same thing in other places?
- Does the author use the same word(s) each time?

This leads us to the rest of the process of examining the conte***n***t. Proceed by asking the same two questions Sandra asked. Remember to take notes! Then, ask even more questions, such as:

- If the author of the text used those particular words, or closely related words, elsewhere in that book or other books of the author's, *how* were they used? For example, remember the brief article called "Can You Believe This?" on page 120? Luke used the actual word for "inn" (*pandocheion*) in the parable of the Good Samaritan, but did *not* use it in the story of Jesus' birth. So, Luke used the word he used in Jesus' birth (*kataluma*) to mean *something*, but he did *not* mean it as "inn," even though it has been translated and interpreted that way. Note the words used in the passage you are studying, then look at other books written by the same author. Ask these questions:
    1. Can you find places where he uses the same words?
    2. Are they used the same way?
    3. Are they typically translated the same way? (Remember to use several translations to check on this.)
- What grammatical structures does the author use in various places?
- What emphases does the author choose to make throughout his writings?
- What themes does he employ in other places and perhaps even throughout his other books?
- How does the author support, or "ground," his statements in other writings? This one needs some explanation. Read on.

Ground

Sometimes, the biblical writers explained the reason for a particular command to their recipients. When we read a passage, especially one that seems to include a command, we look to see whether the writer gave a reason for the command. This *reason* is called a "ground," as in, "these are the grounds for this command."

Any time you see a word translated as "because" or "for" or "since," the author was probably giving a reason for whatever he was stating. Note that here "since" is used to mean "because," not an element of time. For example, "Since *you're* so smart, *you* get the keys out of the locked car."

What's This "Trump Card" Sandra Mentioned?

You may have been wondering what Sandra meant by "the Genesis 'trump card'" and whether it has anything to do with a "ground." Put your finger here for a minute and look back at the items labeled with a superscripted "c" in paragraph two of Sandra's thought process on page 123. This is an excellent question.

Essentially, her phrase "the Genesis 'trump card'" refers to whenever "things that happened before the Fall" are given as a ground for a statement. This kind of statement basically "trumps" other arguments, as in a card game when one card is more powerful than all the others and always wins. Why is it significant if something happened "before the Fall" and why would that be a "trump card"?

In the debate about women's roles in the church, one group or another will argue a point based on something that occurred in Genesis, typically in chapters 1 through 3, because that's what Paul does.

The basic thinking is that if it happened at the beginning of Genesis, when God was creating and establishing human presence, it establishes a precedent for interpreting the rest of Scripture.

When trying to discern what a New Testament writer like Paul is saying, or understand why he's giving a command, interpreters will (and should) look for whether the author referred to Genesis or another Old Testament passage. When the author refers to an Old Testament passage, he is interpreting the Old Testament for his own readers.

Once that's determined, then interpreters look to see if it happened *before* the fall as recorded in Genesis 3. Interpreters most typically view those things as the way God meant them to be. If the situation happened *after* the fall, interpreters generally regard them as part of a "fallen" or imperfect world, needing to be redeemed by the Messiah/Christ.

So where does Paul do this? Well, in terms of the debate over women's roles in the church, Paul makes some statements that must be reckoned with by any reader/interpreter, because he "grounds" his statements in "before the fall trump-material."

For example, in 1 Timothy 2:13 he says, ". . . *for* Adam was formed first, then Eve." (Or, as he says in 1 Corinthians 11:8, "*For* man was not made from woman, but woman from man"). The use of the word "for" shows that he is using the phrase as a reason, or ground, for what he is saying. Every interpreter examining this passage must address that ground, attempt to discern Paul's motivation for giving it, and, subsequently, determine its implications.

Notice that, essentially, Paul did to the Old Testament what we're trying to do to his writings: interpret the Scriptures for the believers in his day!

Literary Content Step 4: Read Commentaries on the Passage and the Book as a Whole

It's time to get some theological "expert opinion" on your passage. Choose several commentaries. Use a few one-volume versions, but also try to obtain access to a few complete sets, where one book of the Bible equals one whole commentary volume. You may even want to get some of the books in Appendix B that are not specifically commentaries, but which walk through your specific passage or through all of the "controversial" passages on women.

If it's possible for you, I highly recommend acquiring, by purchasing or borrowing, the two resources that represent the current loudest voices in evangelicalism on the issue of women's roles: *Recovering Biblical Manhood and Womanhood* and *Discovering Biblical Equality.*

As you read what commentators have to say, try to answer these questions:

- What theories do you find?
- What theological insights can you gain about the passage? Each verse? The book?
- How do the interpretations differ? How are they similar?

Literary Content Step 5: Look for Points of Comparison in the Bible

In this step, you will compare the same topic in different passages, along with different topics that are treated similarly. This comparison will shed light on your particular text.

Find and Compare Similar Theological Issues

When you study an issue, you can ask whether any other, *similar* theological issues are argued similarly in Scripture. Referring back to Sandra's thought process on page 123, look at the item in paragraph two labeled with a superscript "d." Sandra used the phrase "as a point of comparison."

In other words, when thinking over a question about a passage and wondering whether or how it applies today, Sandra was asking,

- Where else has this same topic been discussed in Scripture?
- Has this situation arisen anywhere else?
- Who raised it?
- What did they say?
- How did they say it?
- How did they argue their point?

Study and consider those passages and how they do or don't relate to the passage you're studying.

Elizabeth Conde-Frazier talked about going to the Word and trying to look at all the relevant texts, even those that aren't directly teaching about actions and roles:

The authority of the Bible is in the ability of the Word to change our lives for the better, to make better people of us, to mature us as persons, and to mature us spiritually. That's where the real authority of the Word lies. So, rather than going around and having heated discussions with one another, we go to the Word.

We say, "Well, here's what we find *in the Word*."

And in looking at "here's what we find in the Word," we have the usual scriptures that people who don't believe in women in ministry like to pull out. But then we have the "silent scriptures" that people don't usually pull out that talk about women in ministry.

And so, we're looking at the scriptures that deal with the women in Luke 8 that says that here were some women who were disciples along with Jesus. We're looking at Philip's daughter's in the book of Acts. We're looking at women who were prophets in the Old Testament, Huldah and Deborah. We're looking at the women who helped Paul and we're doing some serious exegesis about who these women are.

And so, you have a pastor who says, "Well, here in Timothy, he's speaking to the church at Ephesus, and here you have a particular situation." And he begins to describe the cultural context of that particular situation.

Now, the way that other people have been taught is that you look at the Word superficially: what it says, it says, right? Women should be silent in the church. And, you look at the original languages, but you're not looking too much at cultural context, such as "Why is Timothy saying this in *this* place? Why is this book saying this at this *particular* church? And why is it *not* being said in other churches, as well?" But when you do begin to look at it that way, it changes it.

And the pastor says that the reason he has to say, in this case, that women should be silent is because it's an exception. It's not the rule. And it's an exception because they were having a problem here. And he begins to describe what that problem is. And so now, women being silent in the church is not the rule, it's the exception, because you're looking at it in terms of the well-roundedness of the other letters and the example of the Acts community and so on and so forth.

Similarly, we try to fairly examine every relevant passage. Keep in mind that you might do your own examination and not come to the same conclusion Elizabeth did. That's part of standing on your own two "theological feet," so to speak. We do our own work. We take responsibility for our beliefs. As Karen Moy says, we chew our own food.

At this point, look at your passage in the light of everything else the Bible seems to say about women. Ideally, you will eventually apply all these steps of biblical interpretation to all of the major "controversial" passages about women in the church setting (i.e., 1 Cor 11:3–16; 1 Cor 14:34–35; Eph 5:21–33; and others).

These "tough passages" may serve as your starting points, but you also need to consider the other, "silent" passages that talk about women. For example, look at any feminine imagery used (for example, look at Luke 13:34) or words used to describe God that are also used to describe women (i.e., *ezer* in Genesis 2:18). Think through any other passages that shed light on the issue, whether they specifically mention women or not.

Find and Compare Theological Issues that are Different, But Argued Similarly

In terms of comparisons, when you study an issue, you can also ask whether any other, *different* theological issues are similarly argued in Scripture. As in the case Sandra was pondering in paragraph two, for example (page 123), one might ask, "Are any other theological issues argued 'from creation'?"

If you can find any other issues argued the same way in Scripture, compare the situations to see how they are similar and different. Similarities may mean that you can use the same logic for the situation you're studying. For example, in Sandra's quote she refers to looking at God's example during creation when considering questions about the Sabbath. God rested on the seventh day. This presents us with some follow-up questions we must address:

- Does God resting on that last day establish precedence for all people for all time, such that everyone, everywhere should observe a Sabbath rest?
- If so, on what day should that Sabbath rest occur?

Right now, we're simply using those questions as examples; so we won't address finding those answers in this book.

Next, ask, "What is the 'trajectory' of the issues in this passage?" For example, does the passage you are studying seem to be:

- Continuing something?
- Ending something?
- Fulfilling something from the Old Testament?

Dee Brestin, for example, notes how Jesus' treatment of women both went counter to the culture and, in one particular instance among others, fulfilled Old Testament prophecy:

> Looking at the way Jesus treated women, he was *such* a revolutionary. Looking at Mary of Bethany, for example, he wouldn't let Martha drag her into the kitchen.
>
> Something else interesting: in the passage in John where Jesus wrote in the sand and freed the adulteress, that's actually a *fulfillment* of a prophecy in Hosea where it says, "I will not punish your daughters who are caught in adultery, because the men themselves go apart with harlots."
>
> I mean, here she was, caught in adultery. Haven't you ever thought, "*Hello*, where's the *man*?"
>
> There's a debate over that passage and whether it should be there. But, my understanding, with the help of Darrell Bock, is not whether it's *authentic*, but *where* it should be in the Gospels.
>
> Jesus knew how unfair that was. And *that* was predicted in Hosea, because the character of God is to treat men and women equally—they are of equal value. It's not to discipline just the woman. I just *love* that. And I see that characteristic *again* and *again* in the Scriptures in a time when it was *not* culturally acceptable.
>
> I am *completely* convinced that God values me as much as he does a man; but it shook me at first. I think it was more the church's *perception*. And I think women still carry that. *And* I think that's why they have arts and crafts instead of serious Bible study, but that was *never* God's intent.

Table 7. Exegesis Step 3: Examine the Literary Content

Words, Grammar, and Points of Comparisons

Read slowly and purposefully through the passage.

What does the author say in *this* passage and how does he say it?

Literary Conte*n*t Step 1: Examine the words in the original language.

- What words are *actually* used in the original text?
- How have the words used been translated? (Check several translations.)
- Definitions: Understand the possible meanings of the major words in a sentence. There may be several variations of meaning for a particular word or words.
  - Use a Bible dictionary, theological wordbook, or lexicon to find definitions of critical words in the passage.
  - Once you find a range of possible meanings for the word you're wondering about, think about which definition fits best in the context of your passage. Questions to ask:
    - Is this word used several times in this passage? How is it used each time? Generally, an author will use one particular word the same way inside a passage and, usually, inside a book. Gather information on how he used that word throughout the book you're studying. Eventually, you'll also gather information on how he may have used that word in other books attributed to him.
    - Look at the English translations you have. Have any other (different) original-language words been translated into English the same way this one has been translated? (Remember the "love" example?)
    - If this author didn't use the word again, did any other biblical authors use it? How?
    - Remember: complications arise if the word isn't used anywhere else in the Bible ("*hapax legomenon*").

Literary Conte*n*t Step 2: Examine the grammar in the original language, if at all possible, in this particular passage. Understand the relationships of words in a sentence and how they relate to each other.

- Check commentaries for understanding of the original language(s). What do two or three commentators say?
- Diagram the passage in the original language, if possible (or use a tool that has pre-diagrammed for you).

Literary Conte*n*t Step 3: Look at the words and grammar the author uses in other passages attributed to him.

- How does the author refer to or describe that same thing or idea in other places? Does he use the same word(s) each time?
- What words does he use in various other places and how does he use them?

- How does the author refer to or describe that same thing in other places?
- Does the author use the same word(s) each time? Does he use those particular words or closely related words elsewhere in that book or other books attributed to him?
- How does the author support, or "ground," his statements in other writings?
- Does he use the same grammatical structures in other places?
- What kinds of emphases does he choose to make throughout his writings?
- What themes does he employ in other places and perhaps even throughout his other books?

Literary Content Step 4: Read commentaries on the passage and the book as a whole.

- What theories do you find and what theological insights can you gain about the passage? Each verse? The book?
- How do the commentators' interpretations differ? How are they similar?

Literary Content Step 5: Look for points of comparison in the Bible, including the "silent" passages.

- Find and compare **similar** theological issues.
    - Where else has this same topic been discussed in Scripture?
    - Has this situation arisen anywhere else?
    - Who raised it?
    - What did they say? What was the argument? How was it grounded (what reasons were given for it)?
- Find and compare **different** theological issues that are argued similarly or that simply shed more light on the passage or issue.
    - Are any other, *different* theological issues in Scripture argued similarly?
    - How are the issues or situations alike? How are they different?
    - How does this shed light on your passage of interest?
    - What is the other passage's trajectory? Is it continuing something? Ending something? Fulfilling something?
    - Do any other, *different* theological issues in Scripture shed more light on your passage (i.e., "silent" passages, as in passages that don't speak directly to the women's issue)?

Table 8. Recommended Resources for Examining Literary Content

Interlinear Bibles	Helpful Reference Tools	Online Interlinear Resource (Free!)
Interlinear for the Rest of Us by William D. Mounce (Grand Rapids: Zondervan, 2006) *The Interlinear NIV Hebrew-English Old Testament* by John R. Kohlenberger III (Grand Rapids: Zondervan, 1993) *The Zondervan Greek and English Interlinear New Testament (NASB/NIV)* by William D. Mounce and Robert H. Mounce (Grand Rapids: Zondervan, 2008) *Hebrew-Greek Key Word Study Bible (NASB)* by Spiros Zodhiates (Chattanooga: AMG Publishers, 2008). It's also available in NIV and KJV.	*New Bible Dictionary*, 3rd ed., edited by I. Howard Marshall, A. R. Millard, J. I. Packer and D. J. Wiseman (Downer's Grove, IL: InterVarsity, 1996) *New International Dictionary of New Testament Theology* (4 vols.) by Colin Brown (Grand Rapids: Zondervan, 1986). Zondervan also offers this in an abridged form (by Verlyn Verbrugge, 2003) and on CD-ROM (2006). *The Complete Word Study Dictionary: New Testament* by Spiros Zodhiates (Chattanooga: AMG, 1992) or *Old Testament* by Warren Baker and Eugene Carpenter (2003). AMG also publishes *The Complete Word Study New Testament* (1991) and *Old Testament* (1994). *Theological Wordbook of the Old Testament* by R. Laird Harris, Gleason Archer, Jr., & Bruce K. Waltke (Chicago: Moody, 2003)	*Biblos.com* has everything from soup to nuts: parallel versions, word studies, encyclopedia, timelines, outlines, commentaries . . . even images and an atlas. This site is like one-stop shopping for doing in-depth Bible studies. Additionally, it's great for folks with no language training. (Bonus: You don't have to install any special fonts on your hard drive to view Biblos.com's interlinear Bible or other language tools.) *Sentence diagramming online:* • For purchase, already done for you (in Greek): http://www.in-thebeginning.org/e-diagrams/ • Free downloadable how-to Guide (for Greek; PDF): "An Intermediate Guide to Greek Diagramming" by Eric Howell (Lexell Software, LLC, 2002): http://www.lexelsoftware.com/Resources.htm • How-to (in English): http://grammar.ccc.commnet.edu/grammar/diagrams2/diagrams_frames.htm • Many users have uploaded helpful how-to videos (for English) on Youtube.com. Just search on "sentence diagramming."

Table 9. A Few Less-Known Commentaries

One-Volume	Women's Commentaries	Online
New Bible Commentary: 21st Century Edition, edited by G J. Wenham, J. A. Motyer, D. A. Carson and R. T. France (Downers Grove, IL: InterVarsity, 1994) *Matthew Henry's Commentary in One Volume* by Matthew Henry (Grand Rapids: Zondervan, 1960)	*The IVP Women's Bible Commentary* by Catherine C. Kroeger & Mary J. Evans (Downers Grove, IL: InterVarsity, 2002) *The Women's Evangelical Commentary: New Testament* edited by Dorothy Kelley Patterson and Rhonda Harrington Kelley (Nashville: Broadman & Holman, 2006)	*BibleGateway.com* has two commentaries online (and an *impressive* number of Bible versions). *BibleStudyTools.com* has twelve well-known commentaries online, one of which includes a harmony of the Gospels, which is a useful tool. This site offers many other helpful tools, in addition to these.
A Note about Multi-Volume Commentary Sets:	*Commentary sets can be extremely expensive, unless you can buy them used. I suggest you begin with online commentaries and sets you can use at your public libraries or in your church library, or perhaps that of a nearby seminary. If you find over time that your interest has been so piqued that your inquiry extends into more scholarly reaches, then buy a few commentary sets for your personal library.*	

Chapter 12

Get into the Text! Fundamentals of Interpretation, Part 5

How Do We Interpret Well? Understand Categories of Meaning

When statements or practices found in the Bible apply to us and when they don't is, of course, one of the primary questions we are trying to answer when we interpret. When it comes to the particular issue of women's roles in church leadership, it is *the* primary question.

We have already seen that not all passages apply equally to every contemporary situation. We specifically want to answer the question, "What, if anything, applied only 'then and there' and what, if not every little thing, applies in the 'here and now'?" In other words, what does this text mean for us today? Does this passage include anything that we need to apply obediently right now? Therefore, we use "categories of meaning" to help us discern answers.

> **Definition: Categories of Meaning**
>
> Categories of meaning are classifications of different types of verses, the purpose of which is to aid the interpreter in discerning the contemporary applicability of statements or practices found in the Bible.

THE CATEGORIES OF MEANING

Categories of meaning are groupings, or classifications, of different kinds of verses.[45] That would also mean it may apply to our "here and now" and "take priority in our values, our thinking, and the way we act."[46]

There are three of these categories. Knowing them will help the definition of "categories of meaning" make more sense:

1. Enduring Truths
2. Restricted Commands
3. Historical Records

Let's walk through each of the three categories, and then discuss some challenges to discerning them.

Category of Meaning 1: Enduring Truths

If the original author made a statement that appears to have been meant for *all* believers in God, it may be "enduring." That means it's possible that it should be applied as a command for all believers in all places for all time, not only to a specific audience. That would also mean it may apply to our "here and now."

How do we discover whether the author intended a particular statement to endure when he made it? According to whether it communicates "highest norms or standards taught in the Bible."[47] Here are some clues:

- Sometimes, the writers identify for us the principles that reflect highest norms and standards, such that it is nearly unmistakable. For instance, Matthew records Jesus' summary of the gold standard for behavior: "In everything, do to others as you would have them do to you . . . for this sums up the Law and the Prophets" (Matt 7:12).
- Bible writers (1) interpret Old Testament Scripture or (2) evaluate an event in such a way as to demonstrate their permanence (e.g., Pentecost, Acts 1:4–8; 2).
- A writer may summarize a truth at the end of a book. For example, in Hebrews 10:8–18 (and the following verses), the writer of Hebrews summarizes why the sacrifice of Christ on the cross preempts

45. Gill and Cavaness, *God's Women*, 25–28. The concept of categories of meaning as a tool for understanding the contemporary applicability of Scripture comes from Drs. Deborah M. Gill and Barbara Cavaness in *God's Women—Then and Now*. I have merely expanded upon their ideas.

46. Ibid., 26.

47. Ibid.

the sacrifices of the Old Testament Law, which the writer has been arguing throughout the book. This passage includes how that preemptive sacrificial act affects all believers in Christ, supported by the testifying proclamation of the Holy Spirit (vv. 15–17).

- Although we can't always assume that Jesus' teaching applies easily and directly to us, because his audience was first-century Jews and modern Gospel readers are not, most times we consider Jesus' teaching to be enduring truth. We must certainly pay attention when he calls people to or informs people of a higher standard than previously understood or historically taught from the Hebrew Bible (e.g., Matt 5:27–28 "You have heard it said . . . but I tell you . . ."). Other examples include:
    - Breaking with practices of the former life (Luke 22:20; Jer 31:31–34).
    - Reinforcing and sometimes strengthening Old Testament commands (Matt 5:27–28).
    - Replacing old laws (e.g., Mark 7:9, 15–23).
    - Gill and Cavaness make this bottom-line statement in their book *God's Women Then and Now*: "Any teachings that seem contrary to the high norms taught by Christ must be weighed and examined carefully."[48]

Category of Meaning 2: Restricted Commands

Restricted commands are commands or regulations for a specific people, where they were in place and time. That is, they were "temporary." In other words, if a biblical author spoke or wrote something meant only for the readers or hearers in their culture at that time, then those statements were for "then and there."

We infer, by looking at a variety of factors, that the original author never meant for these statements to apply outside that specific situation and they certainly didn't mean for them to apply for all time. We call this kind of statement a temporary or "restricted" command, because it was "restricted" to that time and place.

48. Ibid., 28.

- Make a list of the references you find difficult to understand because so much time and culture have elapsed between "then and now."

Some are difficult to understand, *because* so much time and culture have elapsed (Lev 19:19; Deut 22:8). Some are obviously specific to the situation (e.g., Paul to Timothy: "bring my cloak and scrolls before winter" 2 Tim 4:13, 21; "take a little wine for your digestion" 1 Tim 5:23).

- Does anything, at least on first pass, seem obviously specific to the situation?

Category of Meaning 3: Historical Records

Not all historical events are meant to shape our lives today. Remember, the Bible records stories of people, their actions, their words, and their relationships, often without clear commentary. Just because the Bible records something doesn't necessarily mean God approves of it.

For practices the Bible recorded but you think may be questionable, you can investigate from several perspectives:

- Did New Testament authors comment on it? If so, what did they say? How did they interpret it for the church(es) to which they wrote or ministered?
- Can you discern a pattern throughout the Bible that shows some kind of redemption of the original actions?
- On the other hand, can you discern a pattern that shows it is actually unapproved by God and eventually was or will be ended?

Of course, discerning categories of meaning brings with it difficulties. And here we run up against a challenge.

CHALLENGES TO DISCERNING CATEGORIES OF MEANING

Answering the question whether something in the Bible applies today provides the fodder for church practices today, both in terms of what *is* practiced and what *isn't*. In fact, this may well be the biggie in terms of what fundamentally separates Christians and creates denominational divisions.

For example, do we greet each other with a holy kiss, as appears to be commanded in Romans 16:16, 1 Corinthians 16:20, 2 Corinthians

13:12, and several other places in the New Testament? It's not only included by Paul, but by Peter. So, should we be greeting one another with a kiss? Or, is that somehow limited to that time period, perhaps because it was part of their culture?

In the case of the question of women's practices in the church, should we all be wearing head coverings? Obviously, some denominations and sects practice this today in one form or another. Among the Mennonites, the Amish, and some Brethren gatherings, the women wear at least a small scarf or possibly a hat. They do this because, somewhere along the line, their leaders interpreted 1 Corinthians 11:3–10 to mean that all women should cover their heads in some way during worship. Exactly how they thought women should cover their heads has varied. Even though they all interpreted Scripture to say women should cover their heads today, they differed on how that should happen.

In many African American churches today, women commonly wear hats, although this is probably more often a cultural practice. Forty to sixty years ago and earlier, most women wore hats in church as a general rule. But, again, that was often a cultural practice, typically based on the styles of the day or what was considered proper. It wasn't necessarily a practice that was biblically discerned and believed spiritually essential for all women for all time.

Try this fun (and somewhat frustrating) exercise, which I have adapted from a 1975 magazine article by Mont Smith, a missionary in Ethiopia.[49] My professor, Dr. Alice Mathews, first introduced me to this little quiz. The complexities involved in thinking through it astounded me. Smith put this quiz together to help missionaries face the fact that they have to interpret the Bible concerning many issues on the mission field, so they'd better learn how to do it.

The same responsibility falls on us. Missionary or not, we are on the "field" of life—for life. Our own spiritual lives and our ability to help others understand God's Word depend on our grasp of these skills.

On the line before each statement, write a "P" for "Permanent," meaning it still applies to us today and should apply to all people in all times and all places. Write a "T" for "Temporary," if you think the practice was appropriate for the first-century church or for the ancient Hebrews, but isn't relevant to us today.

49. Smith, "Temporary Gospel," 36–37.

Table 10. The Temporary Gospel? A Critical Thinking Exercise

____	Greet one another with a holy kiss (Rom 16:16)
____	Wash one another's feet (John 13:14)
____	Sing songs, hymns, and spiritual songs (Col 3:16)
____	Abstain from . . . sexual immorality (Acts 15:29)
____	Call the elders of the church to pray over the sick and anoint them with oil (Jas 5:14)
____	If your right eye causes you to sin, gouge it out and throw it away (Matt 5:29)
____	I want men everywhere to lift up holy hands in prayer . . . (1 Tim 2:8)
____	Give to the one who asks you, and do not turn away from the one who wants to borrow from you (Matt 5:42)
____	When you pray, go into your room and close the door (Matt 6:6)
____	Look out for the interests of others (Phil 2:4)
____	Whoever believes and receives Jesus, to him is given the right to become the child of God (John 1:12)
____	I would like every one of you to speak in tongues (1 Cor 14:5)
____	Sell your possessions and give to the poor (Luke 12:33)
____	Do this [the Lord's Supper] in remembrance of me (1 Cor 11:24)
____	Divorce is not permissible under any circumstance (Mal 2:16)

Painful enough? Sorry, but you haven't seen anything yet. Believe it or not, Dr. Mathews pointed out that the original article cites fifty scriptures! Ouch!

The real fun begins when you ask yourself what **principle** you used to determine your decision for each between temporary and permanent. If you put a "P" in front of some statements and a "T" in front of others, what standard did you use to make that judgment? Whatever standard or principle you used for one must be able to apply to *all* of the statements on the list.

Gulp.

✍📖 *Your Turn:* Journal

How do you feel knowing that every time you put a "P" or a "T" next to one of those statements, you put yourself in an "interpretive box," so to speak?

Go back to the quiz above and think through the standard you used to determine your answers. Then, for a real party, complete these statements:

All commands or practices that ______________________ are permanent.

All commands or practices that ______________________ are temporary.

Candie Blankman expressed frustration about times she had observed people applying one principle to one portion of a passage and a different principle to another portion *within the same passage:*

> I don't know how many times I have asked people who have quoted the 1 Timothy 2 passage (where it says a woman ought not have authority over men), "What about a few verses down where it says a woman is saved through child bearing? Do we go along with that, too—that only women who have children are going to be saved?"
>
> Of course not. It's ludicrous to say that. So what do you *do*? Obviously, in the same text as verses 11 and 12, later on in verse 15, we have something weird, somehow culturally bound.
>
> I have not yet found a scholar or text that says definitively what this means. They know it's really odd. But four verses before? No, verses 11 and 12 are *wooden literal.*

You could certainly say, "I think all commands in the Bible should be taken literally and are permanently applicable to everyone." You could certainly do that.

Or, you could also say, "Well, *I* think that all commands, because they happened in a certain place and time well-removed from us, don't necessarily apply to us. They *all* have to be reinterpreted for us today." You could certainly say that.

However, you could also say, "Well, it seems that some are more obviously tied to that culture and time than others are. I'd have to look at it more closely to determine whether it applies today or not."

Which is the hardest option of those three?

Right, the third one. That option requires having to weigh and balance lots of factors and make a decision about it based on everything you've learned and observed.

Which one do you think I'm going to tell you is the best approach of the three?

Right, the third one.

Welcome to the rest of your Christian life.

All of these important issues and questions need to be discerned, or interpreted. This calls for "critical thinking."

Definition: Critical Thinking

- **Thinking** thoroughly and thoughtfully about the practices in which your church or culture engage,
- **Comparing** those practices and beliefs-held-dear against what you find in the Bible, like the Bereans did, and
- **Sifting** through what is biblical and what is cultural, or simply assumed in the culture.

Critical thinking means not merely "swallowing" what you see, hear, or experience hook, line, and sinker merely because that's what has been taught or practiced there "for a hundred years."

Allow me to assure you: this is what we are *supposed* to do—critically discern.

Overcoming These Challenges

To discern the categories of meaning for a passage, essentially, continue your research. We need to use a variety of approaches and tools to decide whether something was simply recorded or actually had God's approval and, subsequently, whether it still applies today. This includes thinking about the passage in a number of ways, but also examining it closely through the process of exegesis.

Wouldn't it be nice if someone (preferably God) wrote up a tidy handbook of rules for understanding the Word? What a relief it would be if we didn't have to discern anything. Just tell me what to do and I'll do it; tell me what to think and I'll think it. Unfortunately, or not, he chose not to operate that way. And, although many methods exist, which you're tasting in this book, there are no hard-and-fast rules that, if we follow them, will "*give* us the answers" on a silver platter. We must discern. Sigh.

I particularly like how Scot McKnight summarizes this predicament in his book *The Blue Parakeet*:

> Many of us, in fact, claim we do apply Jesus' teachings, literally to some degree, to everything we do. Why talk about this? Because it is the *claim* that we follow Jesus alongside the obvious reality *that we don't follow Jesus completely* that leads us to *ponder how we are actually reading the Bible*. . . . It is my belief that *we—the church—have always read the Bible in a picking-and-choosing way. Somehow, someway we have formed patterns of discernment that guide us.*
>
> Picking and choosing is how the church has always read the Bible! It is no doubt safer to call this "adapt and adopt." Whichever expression we use, it all comes down to one word: *discernment*.[50] (Emphases are McKnight's.)

I have found McKnight's methods helpful as an approach to answering the categories of meaning questions. He says,

- View and read the Bible as story, and
- Follow a historic pattern of discernment.

Regarding reading the Bible as story, mind you, he does *not* mean reading it as myth or fiction. He means read it as one long narrative that contains a bunch of smaller narratives/stories within it. All of these smaller narratives, together with the overarching storyline, show—in story form—the relationship between God and his people and his creation.

And what *is* the historic pattern of discernment?[51]

- Read the Bible as one big story containing a lot of little stories.
- In reading a specific passage and trying to discern a particular issue, you locate its place as a story in the overall story.
- As we read, we listen for how God is speaking to our world through his ancient Word.
- And, as we listen, "we *discern—through God's Spirit and in the context of our community of faith—a pattern of how to live* ***in our world***. The church of every age is summoned by God to the Bible to listen so we can discern a pattern for living the gospel that is appropriate for our age. *Discernment* is part of the process we are called to live."[52] (All of those emphases in the quote are McKnight's.)

50. McKnight, *Blue Parakeet*, 122–23.

51. Ibid. I have summarized this list from McKnight's book.

52. Ibid., 129.

So far, we have a lot of good guidelines for discerning the answer to the questions, "Does this verse apply to us today? If so, how? What obedience does it require?" By applying our critical thinking skills to our basic exegetical skills and these principles regarding categories of meaning, we will be able to go deeper in the Word and discern more fully. Additionally, we trust our discernment will move us closer to God's heart and desires for his people.

Chapter 13

Get into the Text!

Why We Can Yet Hope to Interpret with Confidence (Despite Daunting Challenges)

In "Step 3: Study" thus far, we have discussed various techniques for and challenges to interpretation. Alongside those discussions, we have gained insight into the comments and thought processes of many mentors who studied this issue. In many cases, we've seen the way in which many of them faced and moved past their hesitations and challenges.

You have also had opportunity to read other reminders and motivators, both biblical and extra-biblical, for moving past challenges that you may face. This begs another question that might be nagging you: given all these challenges, both obvious and hidden, how can we possibly hope to interpret with any level of confidence?

Three important factors give us hope that we can indeed interpret with confidence:

- The Holy Spirit guides us.
- We are learning to use tools of the trade.
- We stand on time-tested strategies.

HOPE FACTOR 1: THE HOLY SPIRIT GUIDES US

Here is some extraordinary news: the Holy Spirit guides our interpretation and teaches us!

In fact, the naked truth is that without the Holy Spirit's guidance, we're lost on a number of levels. Specifically as regards interpretation, we naturally don't understand things that are spiritually discerned (1 Cor 2:14). In fact, things of God are foolishness to those not guided by the Holy Spirit. Literally, we can't understand the Bible without the Spirit giving us understanding of it.

But if we are in Christ, we have the mind of Christ. Read 1 Corinthians 2 and be encouraged!

HOPE FACTOR 2: WE ARE LEARNING TO USE TOOLS OF THE TRADE

We've already acknowledged, realistically, that not everyone will have an opportunity to take Greek or Hebrew. The good news, though, after the Holy Spirit's help and guidance, is that many resources exist that shed light on words in the original language, even if we don't know those languages. And many of those tools are *fun*.

You have already seen many resources throughout Step 3. But, there's more! "Appendix B: Resources, A Strategy" (see page 223) offers an annotated list describing tools, books, and other media the mentors and I found to be most helpful in our development and studies. Admittedly, so many resources exist that it can easily become overwhelming. Therefore, in that appendix, I present the resources strategically, suggesting a place to start with general resources, so you can gain a handle on the whole issue. Then, additional approaches and resources are listed that will help you work more deeply into the issue's specifics.

HOPE FACTOR 3: WE STAND ON TIME-TESTED STRATEGIES

Woven throughout this five-step discernment process, you will find many standardized, widely used approaches that can help you progress.

To accomplish this in a way honoring to the Lord and faithful to Scripture, we follow a number of steps that are both **logical** and **learned**. The steps are *logical*, in the sense that they simply make sense. For example:

- In this approach, we try to examine, systematically and thoroughly, all the words and passages involved directly with the issue in question, as well as those that are related indirectly.
- We also closely examine the whole of Scripture to see how the subject and related subjects flow throughout.
- We try to discern patterns and progressions, as well as whether things seem to end or not.
- We look at every piece of knowledge we can bring to bear on an issue found in the Bible: archaeology, sociology, non-biblical literature of that era and as many other pieces we can get our hands on.

You can see it's logical: we start with words and sentences, progress to passages, and widen to the entirety of the Bible. Alongside that progression, we study the historical and cultural context of the Bible.

But these steps are also *learned*, because some steps in the process may involve knowledge we don't yet have. For example,

- Knowing Greek or Hebrew well enough to use it in the discernment process,
- Knowing enough about grammar (specifically, grammar in the original languages) to understand how it might shed light on what the author was trying to say or emphasize, or
- Knowing about and then locating resources that will help us move forward.

By following these time-honored guidelines and principles, you can grow closer to the heart of God through the hearts of the biblical writers.

Summary of Step 3: Study

LET'S SUMMARIZE THIS OVERALL study process.

A. Remember, with *great* thanksgiving and loud amens, that the Holy Spirit will guide us into all truth (John 16:13). We depend on him in all of this. Because of this, there is hope for all of us as interpreters!

B. Check your objectivity by meeting with your two "new best friends."

   a. Determine what assumptions you're already making.

   b. Determine (admit) where those assumptions came from.

   c. Do your "housekeeping":

      1. Recognize and acknowledge your interpretive view.

      2. Determine your interpretive principles.

      3. Identify your starting points of agreement with other Christians.

   d. Do your exegetical Bible study:

      1. Examine the ancient culture. Do your very best to take the original writer's culture, along with that of the recipients of the document, into consideration. Carefully observe context, both historical and cultural. They help explain the text.

      2. Examine the literary context and content. Do your very best to understand the text by examining both words and grammar from every perspective and every level of context you can. This includes looking for and comparing passages of similar theological issues, along with different issues that are argued similarly.

e. Consider the category of meaning of the passage and book.[53]

MOVING ON

Hopefully you've gained some ideas in "Step 3: Study" regarding how to begin studying on your own. We have examined the basic nuts and bolts of how to interpret well. Our primary goal in our pursuit of understanding women's roles is to move forward with strength and confidence in our understanding of God's Word, rather than with uncertainty or fear. I hope I've demystified the process for you. It's not rocket science; but Bible study that will really give you answers does take time and effort.

If you find the solo-study isn't cutting it for you, try out one of the group-study ideas mentioned in these pages. Enjoy the process—you're plumbing the depths of God's Word!

> ✍📖 **Your Turn:**
>
> Once you have studied this issue and are more familiar with why certain groups have strongly held, specific ideas about women's roles, you can tweak the spectrum-list you made in "Step Two: Identify." Make any adjustments you see as necessary. Add new positions you've identified based on major shifts in ideas and ideals. Subtract positions that are redundant. Change the order if a nuance has come to your attention about which you were previously unaware.

In step 2, I asked you not to evaluate the positions you identified just yet. The time has now come to sort through what you have thus far, evaluate each one, and start the elimination process in an informed, systematic way. It is time to begin filtering.

53. You might wonder, "How do I apply these interpretive steps to an actual passage of Scripture involved in the debate on women's roles in the church? Also, how do I put it all together and make a decision for myself?" We ultimately want to determine whether there is a legitimate basis for our beliefs and practices and then formulate a plan for where to go from there. We tackle these and other questions in Appendix C: "Where Do I Start? A Case Study in Biblical Exegesis: 1 Timothy 2:9–15" (page 246). Those ready to tackle the case study may feel free to jump to that place in the book.

STEP 4

Filter

The Plan

1. Prepare
2. Identify
3. Study
4. **Filter**
5. Choose

Studying certainly consumes a fair amount of time and occasionally challenges our emotions. However, the filtering step you're now approaching can rightfully be called the most difficult. Up to this point, you might have identified a few positions about which you felt strongly one way or another, but I've urged you to wait to eliminate any possibilities.

Guess what? It's elimination time.

Chapters 14–16 lead you through a series of considerations, assisting you in your own analysis of each position. In chapter 14, "Your Job Now: Analyze and Critique," you will don your white curly wig and black robes as you shift into the role of judge. Chapter 15, "External Filters," will walk you through externally oriented, more objective filters; chapter 16, "Internal Filters," through internally oriented, more subjective filters.

You will notice a bit of doubling back to many elements of your Bible study. This is because you will plug those discoveries into your overall assessments of each position and overall discernment of the issue.

Now, buckle up. You start a new job today: powder your wig and be on time, because "*you de judge!*"

Chapter 14

Your Job Now

Analyze and Critique

PIGMEAT MARKHAM, WHOM MANY consider to be the real father of rap music, made his mark on the American "chitlin' circuit" of night clubs with his comic vaudeville act and rhythmic song, "Here Comes the Judge." Sammy Davis, Jr. later spoofed it and made it famous on the TV show Laugh-In, and that is what I remember seeing as a girl. Sammy strutted in wearing his long black robe and parliamentary white-curly wig, repeating, "Here come de judge! Here come de judge!"

Now, *you* are "de judge." You are the judge in this court of quality —the quality of the arguments undergirding each position. At this stage of the process, you can begin assessing in earnest the strengths and weaknesses of each position on your spectrum. You will analyze the main positions and all of their supporting presuppositions, looking for strong points as well as flaws in logic. Obviously, you will eventually choose from these options, so examine them closely.

Like a judge, you will ultimately decide the fate of each position on the spectrum, in terms of whether you're able to embrace it biblically, after you've listened to all of the external and internal counsel.

This stage could take you a fairly long time. Even if you've clearly identified the questions you're trying to answer (see "Study Guideline 4: Know When to Say When" page 65), this stage could take you a few days, weeks, or months. If it's taking you more than two or three years (depending on everything else you have going on in your life, of course), you might want to talk to a friend or a small group that can help you process it enough to find the sense of closure you need to move forward. Yet, don't rush yourself.

PREPARING TO FILTER

To understand this type of evaluative thinking, here are a "prep talk" and a "pep talk."

Prep Talk

Judging, analyzing, and critiquing others' ideas takes critical thinking of your own. Here we run up against a problem I've seen in the church at large, which is that women have a difficult time knowing *how* to think about theological questions, largely because they haven't been *taught* how. So, let's address this now. Thinking critically involves these elements:

- Examining an issue or idea carefully and thoughtfully
- Identifying strengths and weaknesses of arguments
- Asking thoughtful questions about different lines of thinking surrounding the issue, along with the issue itself
- Making judgments and assessments about the information
- Listening to your own voice while still listening to the voices of others
- Weighing the teachings of various authorities or sources, often conflicting, against each other and against what you believe to be true.

Critical Thinking Example: My "Thinking Cap" Friend

Friends, especially friends who serve as examples of good thinking, can be important for this process. In addition to providing emotional support and laughter, friends can teach us, sharpen us, and help us to learn better. I've learned a lot about thinking by watching my good friend Hannah Wong. To Hannah, thinking on a topic is an activity in which to purposefully engage.

Hannah is ten years and one week younger than I am, and I met her when she began attending the youth group I ministered to in Maryland.

But I admired her thoughtfulness from the very first time we met. For nearly twenty years now, I've enjoyed a relationship with her that truly sharpens me. I learned from her that thinking can be an occupation for a duration—sometimes long, sometimes short—but a duration to which one should concertedly attend.

When she encounters a topic that interests her or upon which she is unsettled, she'll say, "I really need to think more about this." What separates her from me (although I am getting better at it) is that then she dedicates blocks of time to think about whatever it is. She analyzes it, analyzes her own relationship to the topic, prays about it, and tries to come to a thoughtful conclusion about it.

I haven't perfected her personal method for systematically thinking about something, but I have improved in that area and have found my own groove, so to speak. I find that a combination of intense research and study; sitting in front of a computer screen and writing stream-of-consciously; journaling in a prayerful mode; discussions with friends; and, yes, writing papers all help me form my own analyses and opinions about things. You can experiment with some of these approaches—and any others you can devise—and find *your* own groove for thinking.

When it comes to thinking critically about Scripture, you must pass others' ideas and your own ideas through what I call a "sieve." Your sieve includes all you know to be true about the Word, the Lord, his people, people in general, church history and history in general, and "your" world. It eventually includes forming a thoughtful opinion about the issue, having considered it in the context of all of these other inputs.

My brother, John, once described this well to me. Some years ago, a good friend of his, who was divorced, wished to remarry. For the first time in his adult Christian life, John decided to study in depth the biblical arguments surrounding a controversial issue that came close to his heart. Of course, he had thought about divorce and remarriage before; but he had never actually studied it biblically for himself. Because this matter now involved a close personal friend, he decided he needed to think it through thoroughly and clearly, instead of simply going along with what he assumed other Christians thought, or what he heard other Christians around him saying about it.

He told me, "I have been like a funnel, with no discriminatory sieve on the end to discern or filter the flow of words and information that have been poured into me. If a Christian speaker, preacher, or other type of authority, such as an author, seemed reasonably educated and had a plausible argument, then I just accepted it as true and factual."

What someone else says may well *be* plausible (and *may* even be accurate), but *your* goal is to be a "sieved funnel," not an un-sieved one. And you *can* do it!

So, a primary lesson for critical thinking is this: take what Natalie says (or anyone else in this book says—or anyone at all, for that matter) into consideration, but don't just swallow it all lock, stock, and barrel as if she knew everything.

Even if it sounds plausible.

Even though you're reading it in a printed publication.

Even if it eventually ends up on TV—or *even* on the Internet! In considering your questions concerning women's roles in the church, compare the comments you find in this book, or that you read or hear elsewhere, with what you know from your own research and study. Evaluate. Form an educated opinion. Test it against some other resources and opinions. Re-evaluate. Repeat. Move on. *Listen to your own voice and listen to the Holy Spirit.*

Each woman interviewed for this book had to learn this, as well. Everyone does. Some learn it earlier in life; others learn it later.

Pep Talk

I didn't learn to sift, sort, and evaluate theologically ideas *formally* until I was in my thirties. Prior to that, for theological issues I depended almost exclusively on others' opinions and interpretations. So listen, if you're feeling frustrated about your own critical thinking skills, take heart in my own story: I was in full-time ministry for most of my twenties! And prior to that, I was a student leader in high school and college ministries.

Is this to say that I was a completely brainless Christian? No. I've loved Bible study for a long time. I just didn't have most of the skills we discuss in this book for evaluating people's ideas about what the Bible says. I knew small bits and slivers of the exegetical process, but didn't know the whole of it. Of course, I didn't know Greek or Hebrew either and I do now; but the original languages aren't required for exegesis. Plenty of tools exist to help you in that area, once you know what they are and how to use them.

Some people have the privilege of being taught how to think critically; for others, it's mainly caught. Either way, it's the exercising of the ability that's the important thing. See how Sue Edwards and Karen Moy applied their analysis skills. First Sue:

> I think for some of us it was a real eye-opener when we were exposed for the first time to the possibility that there were different interpretations concerning women's roles—that there *were* those who held the Scriptures in a high place, who viewed the Scriptures as inerrant and true in every way, and yet they came out with a different end result.
>
> I have to say that I think some of those views are weak and their exegetical process is flawed at times. That's why I am careful and try to look at all those things very cautiously and say, "Yes, this really holds; no, this doesn't."
>
> Some of the views have some really good points and some of them I think are a stretch. So I want to be very honest about those kinds of things, because all of us want to do what we believe the Bible says; and I don't want to get out there and do *anything* that God would not want me to do.

Well said. We also want to be *doing* everything God has called, equipped, and allowed us to do. This calls for an equal application of discernment.

Karen Moy, as part of her analysis process, talked with people holding positions different from her own, in addition to doing her own study. She listened and discussed until she understood their thinking and their arguments: "I spent probably about ten years reading books and then seeking out people that I knew had different positions from me: sitting down, listening to theirs, *walking* through theirs, fleshing it out, looking for weaknesses, and hearing the strengths. Then, I kinda 'smorgasbord' drew on different ways of looking at it, so that when I had to articulate it to somebody else, I might use a good turn of phrase that somebody else had already developed."

Note a key element here: *discernment involves a process over time.* You might not know exactly what you think about the issue of women's roles in the church for a while as you, metaphorically speaking, pick up different ideas, try them on, and take them off again. You might even be confused at times. Give yourself the time and space to explore it thoroughly to your heart and mind's satisfaction before the Lord.

It's possible that this process will run counter to your church culture, which may emphasize knowing exactly what you believe (especially knowing whether you agree with the prevailing position or not, so they know how to categorize you). Don't be intimidated, whether the intimidation is real or perceived. Be strong and courageous in the Lord. Press on reading, thinking, talking, listening, looking, judging, hearing, analyzing—all of these actions contribute to your thinking on an issue.

Bring *everything* you've got in your thinking arsenal to bear on a subject and take the time you need to do it. Ready? Let's filter.

THE FILTRATION PROCESS

At this point, you have before you a spectrum of possible positions concerning the issue of women's roles in the church. You have studied each position and know its major points and the substantive tweaks of each. It's time to think critically about them.

If you've read this far, and certainly if you've done your *own* homework, you've already realized there's no cut-and-dried, definitive, ever-after, only-one-right answer to this issue.[54]

Most theological situations aren't cut-and-dried. They involve subtle nuances. Acquiring a biblical perspective on an issue that we can then live out isn't only about collecting empirical data. You have to find answers you can live out. It's not theory alone.

Interpreting the Bible isn't always as simple as merely reading it and then doing what it says. You probably wouldn't be reading this book if that were the case when it comes to questions about women's roles in the church. There wouldn't be as many denominations (and non-denominations and parachurch organizations) as there currently are if the situation

54. Now I've just gone and tipped my hand a bit. This doesn't state my exact position (if you read the Introduction and chapter 1, you already realize I don't intend to do that in this book), but it does show I believe that my own position is subservient to the belief that this theological issue is not cut-and-dried, but must be discerned. I do not believe this is a "well-it-says-so-right-here-in-the-Bible" situation.

wasn't complex biblically, not to mention interpersonally. You can, however, learn to use filters to sort through the options.

Here's the basic idea. You will examine each position in turn, using the filters described in this chapter. As you assess, you begin eliminating positions or their sub-positions and variations. Don't feel pressured to choose one particular position during this step. You're still in examination mode.

As I've mentioned, this filtration process can take some time—hours, days, months, even years. It's your decision to make before God. You will live with it and ultimately account for it to God. Don't let anyone rush you.

A Working Decision

When I proposed this book, I had to come up with a working title for it. I quickly learned that any title I assigned to it probably wouldn't be the book's ultimate title when published. Yet, deciding on a working title served three purposes:

1. A title immediately gave this book a name and an identity.
2. It communicated what the book was about, whenever interested people would ask.
3. It gave some form to an otherwise formless idea while I wrote the content.

In a similar way, at this point in your discernment process you may want to make a preliminary working decision about which position seems best to you. With a working decision in mind, you still have liberty to sort through issues you feel are still up for discussion, but you have a conclusion with which you can work and in which you can begin living, even if tentatively, right away.

Essentially, you are saying, "This is my decision based on all that I understand at present."

Kathy Keller described it this way:

> I can't say that this particular issue at this moment—and this could change tomorrow or this afternoon—has any submerged mines of which I am unaware. Maybe someone will come up with a new one and I'll welcome it if they do! I do not want to spend my life barking up the wrong tree!

With Apostles' Creed issues, you hold your convictions with a grasp of iron. On secondary issues, you hold your convictions strongly, but you're willing to have your mind changed if someone shows you a better way.

I'm always willing to have someone say, "I think this may be a mistake; please, can we talk about it?" Okay, let's talk about it. And we'll go through it again. I think I'm fairly *au courant* with where the discussion is at the moment.

> **✍📖Your Turn: Your Working Decision**
>
> What is your working conclusion, based on all that you know thus far?

Your decision is in place; but give it and yourself grace, realizing it might flex over time as new ingredients are added to your knowledge-base. This gives you a basis on which to live, work, and minister, even as you continue seeking to understand it more deeply, study more passages, or get a more whole-Bible view of it.

To address complex theological issues, just like cooking a delicious stew, we need to

- Bring together ingredients (information) from a variety of realms and sources,
- Evaluate a variety of possible answers, ideas, and situations,
- Let it simmer all together, and
- Produce a meal we can eat (your working conclusion).

You now know that you must discern what is biblical, defendable, and workable from among the possible options. You know you're the judge in this court of quality. You also know it's going to take you some time, so you've got a flexible working decision in place for the time being.

Moving forward in this process, you'll carefully eliminate different positions. In order to eliminate positions, you can use both external and internal filters. Let's look at the external filters first.

Chapter 15

External Filters

START THE ELIMINATION PROCESS by examining each position using external filters: Scripture, Christ, Conversations, Community, and Church. Of the filters, these tend to be the most objective, depending the least on our emotions and other subjective factors. Let's look at each one.

EXTERNAL FILTERS:

1. Scripture
2. Christ
3. Conversations
4. Community
5. Church

EXTERNAL FILTER 1: SCRIPTURE

As we have discussed Scripture study within the bigger picture of Bible interpretation and discernment, it hasn't necessarily been with the idea that you were going to drop everything and do it right then. But to go forward, you should begin now.

Scripture Is Your Primary Filter

If you find a position or interpretation to be discordant with the whole of Scripture, then, of course, you will eliminate it. The great thing about it is you won't be eliminating it because of how you feel about it or because of what somebody told you about it or because you don't like the person who espoused the idea.

Those particular feelings and factors may ultimately end up being true, but they won't be your primary reasons for eliminating an idea about what the Bible says about women's roles in the church. You'll be eliminating it because you did your own Bible study and, in the process, you learned important factors that influenced your decision, factors like

- Where the position came from in the Bible (typically, ideas for positions started with a Bible verse).
- The strengths of that position's argument from Scripture. Does the argument/position flow logically from Scripture?
- The weaknesses of the position, in terms of whether the argument is not actually supported in Scripture. For example, the idea may not have originated from Scripture; rather, someone started with an idea and then tried to piece together enough Scripture to make it appear to be a scriptural idea. People do this both knowingly and unknowingly; your job is to search that out. You can't judge the originator's motives; but you can catch whether or not their idea truly comes from Scripture.
- What variations (or "tweaks") on the main idea exist.
- How the idea fits into and interacts with the entire story and message of the Bible.

All in all, you're asking, "Is this idea plausible and does it come from Scripture? Does it resonate with the whole of the Bible?" After seeking those answers, if you don't think the idea holds up *biblically*, you eliminate it. Good job. That's a big step and an important distinction.

As you examine the positions in Scripture's light, consider this suggestion: it's possible that a number of ideas—even ideas that have different conclusions—are argued well and logically from Scripture. Have you ever wondered why men and women who love Jesus, love and respect God's Word with all their hearts, and walk in step with the Holy Spirit can come to different conclusions about what Scripture says? *This is why.*

If a position holds up scripturally, it makes the first cut. Keep it for further evaluation using the rest of the filters.

Get Going with Scripture

If possible, gather into one place any notes you might have from your previous studies on this issue and on the relevant passages. Read and think through your notes. If you have already done any exegetical studies, reflect on your notes and evaluate the discoveries you made. Ask questions about what you found. Make lists. Make personal notes.

For example, every time you read a new article, book, or commentary, write down (on a notepad, in the margins, or in a word processing file) your gut reactions as you read, connections you notice, and your personal assessments about the author's conclusions.

Two tools you can use for analyzing ideas in light of Scripture are (1) summarizing and (2) asking questions.

Tool 1: Summarize

Stopping frequently during your reading to summarize ideas can help you keep track of where the author is headed, as well as simply keep your own thoughts straight. Summarize and list what you believe are the most important or most relevant scriptural factors for each position.

Tool 2: Ask Questions

Ask some specific questions about how each position stands scripturally:

- Does Scripture lead to this position, or is it imposed on Scripture? Can you defend it from Scripture?
- How well is the argument built? Think about the *quality* of the exegesis and the quality of the reasons given for the interpretation as well as the flow of the logic.

Judge whether you think the exegesis and the reasons for the interpretation and its resulting position are good or poor.

For example, look at how Sandra Glahn reasoned, compared, and assessed several sources, including her own research, as she was seeking to understand how the word "head" was used in the New Testament (for example, in Ephesians 5:23 and 1 Corinthians 11:3):

> I came up with all of this [information about the word *kephale*, the word used for "head" in the Bible,] during my research; and then Sarah Sumner discussed the head metaphor beautifully in her book, *Men and Women in the Church*, and convinced every last one of my students. Some of them are still staunch in their complementarianism, but they *will* concur that she made a mighty fine argument

> for head being part of the body, not an authority figure. She didn't discuss preeminence, but it's all part of the package.
>
> I thought she messed up when she went on to deal with 1 Corinthians 11, because she makes the body the more *vulnerable* part and the head the less vulnerable part. This is fine, except that the key words in that passage—that show up *over and over*—are glory, glory, glory, honor, honor, honor. Some of my thinking came out of my Principles of Biblical Interpretation class on Bible study methods.
>
> I just asked, "What are the key words in that passage?"

Sandra literally judged the quality of Sarah Sumner's conclusions, including both the items she agreed with and where she thought Sarah "messed up." Is Sarah going to lose any sleep over this? I doubt it! Sandra's comment represents a healthy expression of an educated opinion. Whenever Sarah gets around to reading this, she'll probably appreciate the feedback and the slightly different way of thinking about the metaphor. As a scholar, she's accustomed to reading a lot more critical opinions about her work than Sandra expressed! Sandra actually *liked* Sarah's exploration!

In your case, don't worry about hurting someone's feelings when you're assessing their work. No one ever has to see the questions and comments you write, although you may find it helpful to discuss them with a few others who are working through this.

With that in mind, do you find the position or tweak to be based *directly* on Scripture or is it dependent on one or more assumptions first?

At times, a scholar builds an argument or position without realizing that she has made certain assumptions about the Bible on which she has built her position. Let me give you two examples from my own experience when I was in the thick of research for my doctoral thesis.

One important book I read was *Recovering Biblical Manhood and Womanhood*. I was surprised by a rather enormous assumption Ray Ortlund, Jr., made in his chapter on the interpretation of Genesis 1–3, "Male-Female Equality and Male Headship." After a few pages interacting with Genesis 1, he makes the statement,

> Moses does not explicitly teach male headship in chapter 1; but, for that matter, neither does he explicitly teach male-female equality. . . . What Moses does provide is a series of more or less obvious hints as to his doctrine of manhood and womanhood.

> The burden of Genesis 1:26–28 is male-female equality. That seems obvious—wonderfully obvious! But God's naming of the race "man" whispers male headship, which Moses will bring forward boldly in chapter two.[55]

My problem with this statement is not so much the statement that God named the race "man," as in male, although that is not my understanding of the Hebrew word *adam*, but the "whisper." After I had interacted with the entire chapter, I realized that "whisper" was more than a description of Moses' "more or less obvious hints," it was an assumption he had knowingly or unknowingly made and built his entire argument around. I call this kind of thing a "leap" in logic.

This particular proposition creates a critical weakness in the book, because it is foundational not only for the argument in his own chapter, but essentially for the entire book. Genesis 1, 2, and 3 serve as cornerstone chapters for the entire issue; but also, several of the other contributors refer to his chapter and his particular interpretation of Genesis 1–3 as a basis for points they were making and for their own overall interpretations. As such, a number of chapters in the book rest on a "whisper." I found that significant.

However, I didn't throw out the entire book over this leap and the domino effect it created in other chapters. I can't do that. Why? Because, here's the honest truth: many scholars on all sides of the issue have made their fair share of assumptions and leaps in logic!

As a second example, in *I Suffer Not A Woman*, Richard and Catherine Kroeger construct a possible scenario for 1 Timothy 2:9–15 based on ancient evidence by which it may be clearly viewed in an egalitarian light. They are persuasive in many ways, but receive several disapproving reviews of their work from fellow scholars. For example, the Kroegers find support for viewing this passage as "a launching pad for service and study and the development of Christian character" for both women and men. They discern this interpretation from material culture and textual evidence of the city of ancient Ephesus, with much emphasis placed on the influence and impact of Gnostic culture upon the Christians of the time (e.g., genealogies, female hierarchies, sexual prohibitions, asceticism, forbiddance to marry, and other Gnostic ideas).[56]

55. Ortlund, "Equality and Headship," 98.

56. Kroeger, *I Suffer Not a Woman*, 180.

Yet, at least one history scholar, S. M. Baugh, disagrees. Baugh asserts that the Kroegers have misunderstood, and even mishandled and misinterpreted, both the ancient evidence nearly entirely and Scripture in certain cases.[57] He stresses that Ephesus was not at all a matriarchy.[58] This would, of course, undermine the Kroegers' entire argument at its core.

Do we throw out the Kroegers' book, then? No. Not being a trained historian, archaeologist, or classicist myself, if I'm going to make a good decision it is my responsibility to read the propositions in it for myself, which I did, and compare and contrast them to several of the respondents' rebuttals, which I also did. If you are not a scholar of history, this is your duty, as well.

To make a fully informed decision, this is how we must approach these types of situations whenever we possibly can, even if it takes us a while to accomplish. In the end, we must weigh the interpretations and understandings of both text and history of various scholarly viewpoints. Then, we make our own decision as we go along in our studies.

In either of these cases, we can't simply throw the baby out with the bathwater when we find a leap in logic, something that confuses us, or something we disagree with.

Aside from the logic of reading thoroughly on the subject and understanding various viewpoints, we can't throw out either of these contributions for another, very important reason: both Ortlund and the Kroegers, as well as Baugh, love the Lord, regard his Word as inerrant, and worked hard to understand that Word. They faithfully brought all their scholarly knowledge and experience to bear on it; then, they attempted to bring it to light for the rest of us. Each party brought many details and points, both subtle and striking, to the overall discussion that we must consider. The fact that they disagree as believers on its meaning produces one of our challenges for discernment. Yet, it's a challenge we must meet and can meet well, in thoughtfulness as well as love.

Believe me, you will find leaps of logic *everywhere*, on every "side." You'll find them while you're in the thick of your own studies and assessments. With every work you read, read critically, taking nothing for

57. Baugh, Review of *I Suffer Not a Woman*, no pages. Despite the lack of page numbering in the online article, note that Baugh asserts this and gives his evidence and conclusions for his assertions throughout the paper. For some examples, see the sections "The Bottom Line," "Teaching and Exercising Authority," "Errors of Fact," and "Key Errors of Fact."

58. Ibid.

granted. Each contribution to the published debate is given by a fallible human being. Scripture should be your primary guide; all of the additional resources you read serve to shed light on particulars and peculiarities of Scripture, as well as historical and cultural contexts.

If you observe that a position does begin with an assumption, it *might* be okay; but you should be clear that it is beginning with one. Tread lightly.

> **Encouragement:**
>
> You may not be an expert on exegesis or Bible interpretation in general. You may be learning it as you read this book. That's okay. You have to begin somewhere. I'll echo the refrain I've said before: take your time, but do start somewhere.

Analyze the Big Scriptural Picture

Kay Daigle describes herself as a "big-picture person," who looks for connectivity within the overall storyline of Scripture. She found,

> As I read a lot of the egalitarian books for our Doctor of Ministry classes, it almost seemed that *every* argument wasn't quite convincing.
>
> It seemed to me a lot of the arguments were piecemeal and situation-specific: "Here's a passage. Let's work our way out of this one. Now, let's go over here and do something else with this other verse."
>
> I always wanted to say, "But what about '*this*'?!"
>
> I'm a very "big-picture person." That's probably why it seemed to me that Genesis 3 and Romans 5 fit together with everything else better than some of the piecemeal arguments did.

Each of us needs to develop that same internal radar for connectivity. This helps with interpretation.

Now that you've done some scriptural fine-tooth combing, step back a few feet from your books and notebooks and think through two big-picture items:

Big Picture Item 1: Use Your "Grid"

Sue Edwards talked about how, as she has gone along in her studies, she has developed in her biblical and theological understanding, as well as her exegetical capability. With every bit of intellectual and spiritual growth, her "grid" for investigating issues grows deeper and wider, so that she can consider issues more fully:

> In seminary, you get a thorough biblical and theological education. That education/theological grid has impacted every piece of study since. And I brought that to my work at Gordon-Conwell, certainly, as we went in and read the different literature on women's issues. Of course, I am going to be processing that reading through that biblical and theological grid that I have.

You may not have gone to seminary. No problem. What is *your* grid? Everything you know and understand thus far biblically and theologically, everything you believe to be true about God, and everything you understand of and from the Bible—this is your grid. Now that you have looked at a number of the relevant passages exegetically, process each position through that grid.

As I implied above and have stated firmly throughout the book, you do not need to go to seminary to do this. You've been studying this on your own or with a group. You've been developing yourself biblically and theologically as you've done so. Aside from that, you probably already had more biblical and theological knowledge and understanding than you realized. Use what grid you've got!

Big Picture Item 2: Look at the Fit

How does each position fit into the overarching themes and stories of all of Scripture? How does each position seem to fit into the big scriptural picture of God's plan for his creation?

In other words, how do the ideas contained in the position you are examining fit with what you know thus far about *all* of Scripture? You may not have read the entire Bible yet. That's okay for the moment, although I encourage you to embark on that adventure as soon as you possibly can. As you analyze each position, however, you can still stop to ask how it all seems to fit with what Scripture you do know, such as Mary Ann Hawkins described when considering whether 1 Timothy 2:12–15 should be used as a controlling verse for interpreting other Scripture passages:

> I ask the question, "How do you interpret Scripture? Do you use Scripture to interpret Scripture?" . . . If you have to choose a verse [through which to interpret other passages], why don't you use [one that] resonates with the majority of the rest of Scripture?" That's the direction I go.
>
> That certainly makes more sense to me than saying, "A woman should be absolutely silent in the church." If we are going to take "silent" to its extreme in that passage, then she should come in the door and zip her lips. She should not teach children. She should not greet people at the door. She should not sing. She should not say anything to anyone when she is serving coffee and donuts.
>
> She's to be *silent* when she's within those doors. But there doesn't seem to be a definition of "how silent?" We have applied whatever limits are used. We have *interpreted* it. *We* have determined it over the centuries.
>
> And then you come down to the whole thing about being saved through childbirth. Well, my sister, who can't have children, can't be saved then. You can't take verses like that in a literal interpretation and make it stick. It will not walk with Scripture, with the whole body of the Word. It just won't.

Mary Ann used the method of taking a passage or word to its literal extreme to challenge others' and her own thinking, interpretations, and perceptions. Of course, she speaks somewhat tongue-in-cheek about this passage, with interpretive examples we would all probably consider ridiculous, as would she. However, it can serve as a helpful device.

In following an interpretation to its most extreme, it becomes something of a caricature of the original. By examining the caricature, you can more easily see how a passage might possibly be interpreted incorrectly; conversely, it can also show that a verse indeed "walks" with Scripture. As Mary Ann pointed out, if an interpretation really walks with the whole of Scripture, even its caricature will walk with it. You can employ this type of device, too, in your own analysis.

EXTERNAL FILTER 2: CHRIST

Some people look at Jesus' teaching, relationships, and actions first when discerning theological issues. Those considerations serve as their primary filter within Scripture. Other people lean more toward the epistles as a primary filter; others, the wisdom literature, such as the Psalms and Proverbs; others, historical documents or other portions of Scripture.

The portions of Scripture most typically studied as a way of filtering ideas about women's roles in the church are Jesus' teaching and Paul's letters or the other epistles in combination with the first three chapters of Genesis. You may sense a conviction or leaning toward one "genre," which is a term used to mean literary form, of biblical literature over the others as a primary filter. This does not mean that you ignore the other genres; it just means that you might weigh one form more heavily than others in your consideration.

> **Definition: Genre**
>
> A category of artistic, musical, or literary composition characterized by a particular style, form, or content.
>
> –"Genre." *The Mirriam-Webster Dictionary*. Online.

Whether it is your primary filter or not, you will need to scrutinize each potential position under the light of Jesus' teaching and actions. As God incarnate, how Jesus interacted with, talked about, talked to, and taught women should be critical factors in determining whether a position or idea is biblical. Jesus spoke about people's relation to God and to the kingdom of God; he spoke about how people related to God and to other people; he spoke about people's character; and he spoke about love, fear, power, status, and leadership, as well. These general teaching points, and any others that Jesus addressed that you find to be pertinent and important, also need to be considered.

EXTERNAL FILTER 3: CONVERSATIONS

Several mentors mentioned that they talked with a lot of people while discerning this issue, especially people who held different perspectives from their own. When it comes to this kind of conversation, the goal is always to understand, not to argue or win a point. It's not even necessarily to gain more certainty of your own view, although that may happen in the end. The goal is to understand the other person's view of Scripture and how that view of Scripture impacts their life and ministry. From that understanding, you can then compare and contrast that view with what you understand from Scripture. Until you truly understand it for yourself, however, you're not really in a position to comment on it much, and certainly not in a position to discount it.

To have a posture of understanding toward a conversation partner, then, and particularly one with whom you may not necessarily agree on an issue, requires a key ingredient: listening.

Adela Carter said, simply, "I listened to a *lot* of people."

Start some conversations of your own. Don't be afraid of them. Remember, you're purely the learner at this point. Don't think or worry about arguing with your conversation partner or feel like you need to defend some other position to them. Of course, because you've done some serious study already, you know a fair bit about all of the positions, including the ones your conversation partner doesn't hold, and you can assess and raise good questions during your conversation. You may even know more about those other positions than he or she does. Right now, though, just focus on listening and understanding. As you listen, or afterward, you can assess the arguments and logic in light of Scripture and everything else you know.

Tips and Possible Concerns

One tip: ask people who are themselves informed. If you want to improve your tennis game, play tennis with someone who's better than you are. If you want to become more informed theologically, have conversations with people who are reading widely, asking good questions, and praying a lot.

Another, related tip: ask people who are "safe" emotionally and spiritually. If you know a person to be knowledgeable, yet harsh, abrasive, and always wanting to be right, then find someone else to ask who holds the same view. It's also best to ask someone who has objectivity enough to admit his or her own uncertainties about it and/or what's at stake for them in the issue.

You may wonder whether listening to a viewpoint you've always been told was unbiblical might in some way lead you down a path toward heresy—"the slippery slope," some call it—or give the appearance of agreeing with it. Remember and be assured of the Holy Spirit's guidance and strength. He is leading you throughout this discernment process. Also, be confident of your own mind. You have been studying the Word all this time and you've become much more knowledgeable about it. In these conversations, you're trying to understand how and why someone might see it differently from the way you've come to view it.

Think about Jesus' heart for his church to live in unity in John 17. Listening to understand helps us grow toward unity and maturity as individuals and as part of the body of Christ. Listening to understand also helps us grow in grace toward brothers and sisters in Christ.

Finally, listening to understand is not the same as embracing. If you avoid listening for fear of appearing to agree with it, or perhaps because you fear you might even secretly agree with it, then you are operating out of fear, rather than out of the strength of the Lord and soundness of mind. Remember, "Trust in the Lord with all of your heart and do not lean on your own understanding. In all your ways acknowledge him and he will make your paths straight"(Prov 3:5).

If, after *much* listening and conversing to understand, along with a lot of prayer, you believe a person's view to be soundly unbiblical, then you may want to ask to continue the conversation and ask to share your own perspective on this issue with them from Scripture. As you do, you can either allow the differences to reveal themselves or directly point out where and why you differ from them scripturally. Pray for understanding and pray for peace. Pray for growth and maturity for you both. Always be open to the possibility that you may, in the end, be wrong. This is called humility.

Always allow grace to lead and fill these conversations.

EXTERNAL FILTER 4: COMMUNITY

Consider the impact of your theological choices on your interpersonal relationships. As a part of her course curriculum, Elizabeth Conde-Frazier requires this of her students:

> As a professor, one of the courses that I teach is "Latinas and Latinos Doing Theology: Men and Women in Ministry in Partnership." The course examines their theological positions on women in ministry and where they come from. It looks at the different views and asks participants to critique the arguments by looking at the way the Scriptures are treated by different scholars, both men and women. They then must construct their own theological and

ministerial position. And lastly, they must look at how that position influences their personal and family relationships.

In the discernment process, we listen to our community for clues. Are people you respect as ones who know the Word and listen to the Holy Spirit affirming or contradicting the opinions or ideas you are considering? Almost every mentor spoke of this as integral to her process. It's not the foundation of the quest—it shouldn't form the basis of your beliefs and practice—but it serves as a healthy check.

EXTERNAL FILTER 5: CHURCH

Paul repeatedly uses the metaphor "body" to mean the church (Col 1:24), which is made up of all believers in Jesus as Christ. "Body" is an "everyday" word, when you think about it. It's our most basic experience of life. And it's a wonderful image for how, as Christians, we live together, work together, grow together, and depend upon each other.

We live with our physical bodies every day. Each member and part of our body has a unique contribution to our life and experience of the world and people around us. Even parts of which we have two or more contribute uniquely, because each contributes to either function or form; and each communicates with the brain from its own specific location concerning the input and stimuli it receives. As such, we need every part.

Paul uses and emphasizes these facts about the physical in his metaphor of the "body"—the church as the body of Christ:

- 1 Cor 12:12, 27—All of the parts, including you, me, and every other believer, make up one body.
- Rom 12:5—We belong to each other in Christ.
- Eph 3:6—We all share together in the promise of Christ Jesus.
- Eph 4 & 5—We function together as a body with Christ as our head, and all effect maturity in each other. Either we contribute to each other's maturity and to our collective maturity, using the gifts the Spirit has given us and the way we relate to each other, or we get in the way of it. That collective maturity is expressed in unity of faith and unity of the knowledge of Christ (4:13).
- Col 3:15—We are (supposed) to be ruled by the peace of Christ.

In short, we need each other, because God has purposed us for each other.

The body of Christ, in theory, should be one of the first places we go for sorting through this issue. Yet, many find this difficult. It's possible that your local church experiences quite a bit of conflict over the issue of women in leadership roles. It may be out in the open or swept under the rug. Even the historic church has not always agreed on this issue, with godly people taking different sides of interpretation and practice.[59]

Still, you can look in your church and in other churches for people and resources as a place to begin letting the body help you grow and mature in your understanding of this issue. You've prepared yourself by thinking through your plan for ambiguities (see chapter 5, Prep Method 3, page 34). You've steeled yourself in preparation for finding variety for your research. There's certainly no reason why your own church, even your pastors, might not serve as beginning fodder for your variety! In fact, there's a lot of reason to suspect you will find a fair amount of variety right there.

You definitely want to get the church's "collective take" on this, *especially* so you can see the variety that exists within the church, including both individuals and groups. A lot of people have done a lot of good thinking about it, so use those resources. Remember, you're gathering this information as part of your continuing effort to add to your understanding of the issue.

Ask your pastors for your denomination's official position, if applicable. Ask them for some of their favorite resources and books on the topic. Talk with them about their thoughts. Ask them if there's anyone else in your local congregation, or in the region, who they know to be somewhat expert on this issue. Call those people and interview them, either on the phone or in person over coffee.

Your Turn: Assess

As you talk to people, read resources, and gather more information, take notes. Try to assess each person's level of biblical knowledge and their understanding of the "ins and outs" of this issue. Evaluate the quality of each person's and resource's reasoning. List what you find to be the pros and cons of their reasoning and positions.

59. On the book's site, www.womenleadershipbible.com, you will find resources addressing and examining several of the many fears and hesitations women can face when they think about this issue. The mentors share how they faced their own fears and moved past them.

Other questions to ask are, "What are my church leaders saying to *me*? What is my church asking me to do? What are they giving me opportunity for?" Of course, the answer to all three of these questions may be "nothing," but you still need to ask the questions.

Think beyond the words, too. "Nothing" might be your answer at first blush; but perhaps your powers of observation will shed more light on this for you. Is the official position of your church that no women are ordained to a pastoral role, but women are active in every other way, role, and position available in the church?

If your answer was "nothing," and was accompanied by a negative or sarcastic tone, think about your part in the church-person relationship. Here are some not-so-comfortable words for you to consider: think about the vibes you send. Have you been asked to lead a small group, but said no because you felt you didn't have time? Or felt a small role was below your capabilities or training? Just remember that people need to be able to see your gifts in order to know how they can best be used, even in a church that limits the roles of women in one way or another. If you say yes to some requests and, over time, sense that there is an attitude that continues to make you uncomfortable, you can ask the Lord what to do at that point.

As we've clearly seen, what your church is or isn't doing should not *define* your understanding of the issue. Impact your understanding, yes; but not define. What your church practices may or may not be scriptural.

Another possibility is that your church's practices may have a biblical basis, but may depart from your understanding of how that biblical basis should work out in the life of the church. The bottom line, always, is that your primary filter is Scripture—studying it for yourself first, and then filtering other input through it. However, we also need to consider our community, because God has placed us in those contexts. Sometimes, a community may surprise you.

As LaVerne Tolbert described, a community may take time and Scripture study of its own to determine its beliefs:

> Added to my own theological understanding of women's role in the church was that I had just gotten married. I married late (I

> was forty-two), and when he married me, I was not a "Pastor." We began to talk about women's role in the church, asking the questions together.
>
> We were dealing with, "Well, wait a minute . . . you do all of this, but on Sunday mornings, you sit on the floor"; but neither of us was sure. We decided to meet with the pastor and talk to him about it.
>
> The pastor got very alarmed, asked us, "Why are you asking me about this?!"
>
> Well, it was just something we'd been dealing with. It turned out, the reason he was so alarmed was because he'd been dealing with the *same* issue! He had actually been working on a sermon series he ended up calling "Reverend Sister."

Now let's turn for help to the "cloud of witnesses" that has gone before us in the body of Christ.

Church History

It is imperative to remember that, as the church, we do not exist in the vacuum of the here and now of the twenty-first century. People have been seeking the Lord for two thousand years—and a good many of them sought the Lord on this very issue. Therefore, at this point in the process, look for documents from church history that deal with the question of women's roles and identity. These are "primary source references," meaning that they are the actual documents from history. They're not documents *about* those documents from history, written by someone living now or who lived in recent years. They are the actual documents. You may have seen some already when reading through some books and commentaries. Some excellent collections exist, such as Professor Elizabeth Clark's *Women in the Early Church*.[60]

Reading these documents, for better and for worse, gives you perspective on the varieties of interpretations, beliefs, and practices concerning women held by church leaders and theologians throughout church history. These leaders' thinking, teaching, and writings greatly influenced the church.

60. See Appendix B for suggested books and other media.

✍📖Your Turn:

Whether you keep your Bible study notes in your journal or not, keep them in one place. Make any special reflections and notes on your Scripture studies in your journal or create a notebook journal specifically for this purpose.

- What observations can you make about Jesus' teaching about and actions toward women?
- What thoughts do you have regarding the beliefs of the historic church in regard to women's roles?
- What key conversations have you had that can help you toward your discernment?
- What sense do you get from your personal community at large?
- What are your church body and leaders saying?
- What opportunities exist for women in your community?

Chapter 16

Internal Filters

> **INTERNAL FILTERS**
>
> 1. Personal Convictions
> 2. Internal Harmony
> 3. The Holy Spirit

AFTER FILTERING EACH POSITION through your external filters, it's time to look inward. Think of times when you've read through something or listened to a speaker and thought to yourself, "Huh? That doesn't seem quite right to me."

In another situation, you're reading along and something clicks; you immediately resonate with the idea you're reading about. Your brain goes on, either consciously or subconsciously, to consider that idea further, comparing it to and contrasting it against everything else you know or believe to be true.

Much of the process of filtering through internal inputs occurs internally, without our initially being aware of the process. Our intuition, gut, feelings, and such are unavoidable and we shouldn't try to avoid their influence. These internal functions are God-given, implanted within us to serve as guides.

Yet, we don't *start* here. And we need to avoid depending on these internal responses as our foundation or primary guide. It's wise to consider big issues internally in a more formal manner. We aim for objectivity—at least, as much objectivity as we can get.

In this chapter, we will look at three useful internal filters: personal convictions, internal harmony, and the Holy Spirit.

INTERNAL FILTER 1: PERSONAL CONVICTIONS

What firmly held beliefs and opinions, which we Christians commonly call "convictions," do you hold already regarding

- Women in church leadership?
- Human relationships?
- God's character?
- Church relationships?
- Church structures?
- Authority?
- Spiritual gifts?
- A call on a person's life to a certain ministry or type of ministry?
- A call on *your* life?

Whatever these firmly held beliefs are, you entered this discernment process with them. Be aware that they influence your thinking and your interpretation. Take some time to hold them out at arm's length, trying to get some perspective on them. This may seem like a revisitation of checking your objectivity, because it is. We performed similar exercises in chapter 10 ("How Do We Prepare to Interpret Well?") to self-check for biases before we exegeted our passages. We're doing it again because we want to make sure we're not barking up the wrong tree based on incorrectly held convictions.

As a first step, since you've been developing your biblical, theological, and interpretive muscles, can you tell with any amount of objectivity whether the convictions you hold come from Scripture? In other words, what biblical support do you have for them?

Your Turn:

Examine each of the possible positions on the spectrum you've made against and in light of the personal convictions you've identified.

Hold your own firmly held beliefs up to the fire: have they come from an overall understanding of Scripture and an understanding of specific passages in the Bible or are they ideas you or someone else placed onto Scripture? These are tough questions, certainly, but necessary for making sure we're not trying to make God's Word say something it's not. We always want to extract ideas *from* the biblical text, not impose our own ideas *onto* the biblical text.

As Christians who believe the Bible to be our guide for life, we tend to lean *hard* toward receiving guidance from Scripture. Along that same line, many actively lean away from the sensory and emotional experience of our relationship with the Lord. However, even the most revered theologians of history paid attention to the experiential aspects of our relationships with God. Indeed, spend thirty minutes reading about early and medieval Christianity and you will read story after story of Christians who experienced the Lord in many ways. But you could also start by reading Paul's conversion account in Acts 9:1–19.

Experience should never usurp what we know from the Word, but we still need to pay attention to it. For Mary Ann Hawkins, who studied the question of women's roles biblically and theologically, inside and out, experience still figured prominently in her call to ministry:

> The fact that my salvation experience had been based on the word "all"—"for all have sinned"—dumped all of humanity in the same boat. When I began to see the gifts given and the fact that God called me very dramatically and confirmed very dramatically my call to the ministry, I had an "OK, so women *can*," but now I have to figure out how to articulate it to others.
>
> If you just talk about your *experience*, people who think they are biblically astute and theologically sound think, "Oh, well that's just your *experience* and that's *wrong*." Experience alone can be washed out.

✍📖Your Turn:

What firmly held beliefs and opinions can you identify?

- Why do you hold these ideas?
- What biblical support do you have for them?

You might eliminate a position or two at this step as being incompatible with your understanding of Scripture as a whole at this time.[61]

61. If you have already read *Interpreting Courageously*, which is one of the e-books

INTERNAL FILTER 2: INTERNAL HARMONY

During one of my early post-college years, I worked for a man who coached me a few times in making decisions that honor the Lord. He used the term "settled peace" to describe the sensation of arriving at a decision.

This is more than just "settling" for something because it's the path of least resistance. As I've come to learn, that settled peace results from harmonizing everything you understand from God's Word with all of the personal, social, and situational factors you experience. You might think of this as an "interior harmony and integration (that is, a profound sense of being content)."[62] In short, you're looking for that in this process.

From what I understand in Scripture, we will each give account to the Lord for the choices we make and actions we take during our mortal lives (Rom 14:12). I believe this includes accounting for our theological choices and how those choices impacted how or whether we used our gifts and how we interacted with other people. In other words, we'll account for how our theological choices furthered or hindered our participation in building up the church toward maturity.

I further believe that this type of responsibility before the Lord applies to deciding about women's roles in church leadership. We need to seek a settled peace or an internal harmony, or whatever you want to call it, that takes seriously our accountability to God on the matter.

Several of the mentors refer to a similar understanding: looking for this kind of settled peace. This particular desire prompted more than one of them to get to the bottom of this issue scripturally. Susan McCormick, for example, checks her inclinations toward leadership involvements with the question, "Is this my calling and the Holy Spirit prompting me, or is it my inner impulse?"

So, how would we know the answer to that question, and how do we find this settled peace?

When you find a position, or perhaps a set of decisions, that gives you a working conclusion that

---

found on the WomenLeadershipBible.com website, and participated in the journaling exercises found in its pages, you may want to gather and reread those notes. In reflecting on your thoughts and observations in your notes regarding conflict, fears, and authoritative influences, has anything changed for you? Improved? Gotten worse? Take note and make notes.

62. Panicola, "Good Decisions," 75.

- Sits well in your soul in terms of your Scripture study,
- Furthers using your gifts to bring the church toward maturity in your own way, and
- You have run through all of the internal and external filters,

then you can look to the Lord for a settledness in your heart and soul. If he doesn't bring a settledness and a peace with that working conclusion, then you might want to revisit it. Perhaps you can seek counsel from trusted, wise people who know you or run your working conclusions through each of the filters one more time.

Depending on your personality, you might have difficulty finding a settled peace about it for reasons that have nothing to do with biblical and theological veracity. This might well be the case for someone who tends toward perfectionism, someone who prefers for things to be black-and-white, cut-and-dried, or for someone who generally has a hard time making decisions. It might be hard for these women, because, as we've repeated often in this book, theology is rarely cut and dried and rarely-to-never is there one perfect answer. Try to give yourself and others—and God—grace if you tend toward either of these personality and learning traits.

✍📖Your Turn:

The key to all this is that it has to sit well in *your* soul, before the Lord. So, try these steps at this point:

- List your working conclusions thus far.
- List whatever questions still remain for you to answer satisfactorily.
- Summarize what you think Scripture says.
- Spend time dwelling on this in prayer, seeking the illumination of the Holy Spirit.

Remember, the Spirit is your guide and you can depend on that.

One additional thought on the subject of internal harmony bears mentioning. Although we may be seeking God's peace, sometimes *fear* can cause something not to sit well in our soul. You might think, "Maybe fear is good, in that it helps keep me in check in case I might make a bad decision about this." That might be true; that could be one beneficial outcome of fear. However, check that impulse against this: the only fear that's appropriate is the biblical fear of God's glory, because fear, otherwise, is incompatible with faith (no major study here, just 1 John 4:18 and Luke 12:5).

INTERNAL FILTER 3: LISTENING TO THE HOLY SPIRIT

Assess each position through the big picture of the Holy Spirit's aims (see "Theology of This Plan" on page 15) through prayer and listening. As the Comforter and Advocate who indwells you, the Spirit speaks to your spirit, soul, conscience, heart, and mind. In other words, he speaks to all that you are and to all of the internal sense of God's truths that he has given you. Trust him to lead you in this process and keep an attitude of prayer as you evaluate each position.

As you consider each position, ask, "Do I sense in my spirit that this position supports the Holy Spirit's work of uniting believers, love, diligence, and leading us toward growth and maturity?"

As with every step in this process, using the internal filters to discern answers from the Lord does not exist in isolation. Use this process of reflective, prayerful Spirit-directed analysis alongside and hand-in-hand with your Scripture study and the external filters. Pray, meditate, and "chew" on *all* these things and listen to the Holy Spirit. This takes place best in the context of your personal prayer time, Bible study, and an overall discernment process like this one.

ASSESSMENT TIME

You have filtered and filtered, then filtered some more. It's time to assess what you've got thus far. At this point, you should have narrowed your spectrum list considerably. If not, seek the Lord's insight and direction on your discernment process as you go back through the positions again. Really hold each one to the fire:

- Does it hold up scripturally?
- Does it withstand the tests of your external filters?
- Does it withstand the tests of your internal filters?

And so on. Really stick-it-to-'em. Begin to hone in on what sits well with the whole of Scripture, what rests well in your heart and soul, and what is affirmed in the church at large that holds Scripture high.

Now, make your short list of those positions you are still considering; then, move to "Step 5: Choose."

✍📖Your Turn: Your "Short List"

STEP 5

Choose

By now, you have filtered each position through both your internal and external inputs, including doing your own respectable, relevant, in-depth Scripture study. At some point, when you've done all the inputting and filtering you can do by some time that you designate for yourself, it's time to choose a position.

The Plan

1. Prepare
2. List
3. Study
4. Filter
5. **Choose**

In chapter 17, you will have opportunity to decide upon and write down your choice, and describe the basic elements of your current understanding/position. In essence, it gives you the opportunity not only to "believe in your heart," but to "confess with your mouth"[63] what you believe about this issue.

Several times throughout the book we have observed that this process, its issues, and its results do not occur inside a vacuum. We live in relationship to God, to ourselves, to a nuclear and extended family, to the community of Christ in which God has placed us, and to the world at large. Therefore, in chapter 18 you will take time to consider what impact this choice will have in your life, relationships, and ministry.

63. Nod to Romans 10:9. Note: By referring to this verse, I do not mean to imply that I believe a person's beliefs concerning women's roles indicate whether or not he or she is saved. I do not believe it is an issue directly related to salvation and redemption—eternally *significant* and important, yes; but salvific, no.

Chapter 17

Just Do It

Making a choice can be difficult for "Meyers-Briggs type-P's" like me, who love to think up options, but hate choosing from them with finality. In the end, though, you have to choose and you have to choose for yourself. Jesus walked that lonesome valley by himself; so you are able to walk this valley by yourself.

You've got to take the leap at some point. When Sandra Glahn taught her first course on women's roles in ministry at her seminary, she encouraged the same priority of taking responsibility and action. Each woman in the class had to assimilate all of the information she had studied, then decide for herself:

> When I finally started teaching the class, the way I set it up was that the students had to do a boatload of reading prior to each class. When they arrived for class, we could then spend three hours assessing how the authors came to their conclusion, what their strengths and weaknesses were, and their arguments.
>
> The last day of class one time, one of the women said, in complete shock, "*What?! You mean you're not going to put this all together for us?!*"
>
> Noooo! You've got to do it yourself!

The good news is, because you've done your homework, your choice will be defensible, educated, and flexible enough to withstand your own and others' scrutiny, should that occur. Let's look at those three qualities:

DEFENSIBLE

The choice you make will be a choice that you understand, because you have done the work on it. Because you understand it, you will be able to articulate it. In other words, you will know why you believe what you do—the *why* behind the *what*. It's like Karen Moy said:

> I did enough reading to be able to say, "I see that there are different 'camps.' But, it seems to me that at some points the data are insufficiently clear and you are going to *have* to *choose* a position. . . . I choose 'this.'"
>
> And I can defend why I chose what I did.

EDUCATED

An educated decision, remember, comes not only from cerebral pursuits and studies, but also the study of many other considerations, both internal and external. Alongside and in the light of your intentional biblical and theological study, your choice emerges through your deliberate discernment of your community, your faith tradition or denomination, church history, your observations of how the global church views the issue, and your own heart.

Karen Mains lives and serves based on scriptural study alongside an ongoing dialogue of learning in the body of Christ:

> First, I'm living and serving based on my biblical understanding. But I am also informed by dialogue, within both the contemporary church and the church historic. I love Orthodox theology—Eastern Orthodox theology—because their roots are so much in the early church fathers and their early discussions, as they were attempting to find words appropriate to God and to love. I think we've never stopped that.

FLEXIBLE

Think through some potential ambiguities that might arise in real life when it comes to women in church leadership roles. Without being wishy-washy in terms of biblical truth, your position needs to be flexible enough to withstand the ambiguities that arise in particular contexts.

For example, the way you live out your understanding of Scripture may change or evolve, depending on the situation at hand.

It is *very* important to note: this does *not* mean you are "waffling" in your understanding of or your belief in the Bible. It means that you maintain your understanding of Scripture, but are able to flex a bit either to the "right" or to the "left" on your spectrum as a situation shows need.

Karen Mains gave an example of this. Let's say a church was experiencing a lot of chaos, like the Corinthians and Ephesians did, both of which Paul had to address. "If there was a lot of chaos in a situation," Karen said, "I would lean far into headship, because that is the recommendation that Scripture makes for bringing order from chaos." She later added, "Another negotiation needs to be established when harmony has been established. The instructions to Philemon regarding Onesimus—another power deferential used in Scripture—set up the same principles that should be used in empowering women: 'treat him as a brother.' Once folk on top start doing that, the dynamic changes."

To clarify, by "lean[ing] far into headship," Karen was referring to leaning more toward allowing the men in a situation or group to have a stronger presence if that offered the potential to provide more stability in a chaotic situation.

Most of Paul's letters have large sections devoted to addressing chaotic or confusing situations within the local, growing churches. Paul often faced coaching churches that experienced the thrilling "problem" of an abundance of new believers in Christ, including many from non-Jewish heritages. So did the leaders of the other earliest churches. So, the counsel he gave had to work in an old-come-new situation: maintaining the solidarity of the gospel while welcoming new ideas unfamiliar to the "old guard" of Jews who had come to believe in Jesus as Messiah while still in the context of Jewish worship. There were times Paul counseled fervent, yet holy, expression in prayer (1 Tim 2:8) and displayed and declared his own joy outright with a sudden eruption of praise ("Rejoice!" Phil 4:4); then, there were times he counseled withholding oneself for the sake of orderliness so that worship could continue for the whole group (e.g., 1 Cor 14:26–28).

Is your position flexible enough to operate within varying situations? In her own example about flexing in different situations within the church, Karen Mains continued, "If the situation were the privileged misusing the underprivileged, I'd lean much more into egalitarianism, or to lifting up the non-privileged into places of development and function."

Karen Moy described the flexibility needed for any perspective in terms of how well the gospel is advancing:

> It isn't always about "role," as in saying, "I believe women should be allowed to lead; therefore, I should *always* be allowed to lead."
>
> No, that's not what it's about and that's not ever what God gives leadership abilities to people *for*—for *you* to self-actualize or to maximize.
>
> It *is*, however, "How does it achieve the bigger purpose?"
>
> For me, it's always like a football game. There are all these players on the field. They have *one purpose*: advance the ball. You don't *do* things on the field that cause you to lose yardage.
>
> Your purpose on the field is to work in a coordinated fashion to advance the ball, with people clearly having leadership roles. And if you do enough screw-ups that not only don't advance the ball but lose yardage, you get yanked from the game! And that, to me, looks like a pretty reasonable way to do some things in the body of Christ.
>
> There are times where women might say, "Right now, I'll just shut up, be quiet, and let the guys lead, because anything else isn't going to advance the ball."
>
> But, that's a willful choice and it's an obedient and surrendering choice, not because somebody has said, "You *can't* do this and you can't *ever* do that."

IT'S TIME

Your Turn:

What is *your* choice, your position?

Write down your chosen position, with its various tweaks and shades.

Why?

Write about the major Scripture passages, thoughts, ideas, and feelings that led to your choosing that position.

I recommend you journal about this, because "declaring yourself," so to speak, even if you are your only audience, is a fairly big deal. The question concerning what women's roles should or should not be in the church is a big issue in the church. It probably has been a relatively big issue in your life, or you wouldn't have bothered to go through all of this work. And you *have* done a lot of work to get to the point of making an informed, thoughtful, biblical decision. Journaling reflectively will aid your understanding of not only your choice, but the process you took to get to that choice.

✍📖Your Turn:

Write about how you feel about having just made that decision.

You may want to go one step further and write about the positions you *didn't* choose.

- Was one position or tweak a close second?
- Why, in the end, did you not choose that variation?
- Write about why certain other positions were easy for you to eliminate.

Of course, write about anything else related that comes to mind. These remarks will serve as a benchmark you can refer to in the future, if you so desire.

This is the point at which you can and should do a "happy dance." By God's grace, you have undertaken extensive, substantial work, study, research, and soul-searching to arrive at this juncture. Based on that hard work, you have intelligently, thoughtfully, and prayerfully made a critically respectable decision about women's roles in the church. Well done! Really, this is *monumental*. So, dance that dance!

Now . . . what's next? The rubber really hits the road.

Chapter 18

What's Next?

Live Out Your Choice in Your Own Context

CONGRATULATIONS: YOU'VE MADE AN informed decision! Once you choose, you face integrating your choice into your daily life and ministry. In this chapter, we'll look at seven tips for the integration process.

INTEGRATION TIP 1: YOU DON'T HAVE TO "COME OUT," BUT DO TELL SOMEONE

You certainly don't need to "come out of the closet" and make some big statement to your church or organization or whomever: "Guess what, everybody! I'm complementarian with a side-tweak of biblical egalitarian tendencies!"

I do suggest, however, that you tell one person or tell the group of people with whom you've been walking through this. Share how and why you reached your conclusion. Welcome their questions; don't fear them. Consider that conversation as further filtering and/or clarifying your choice.

Be honest with yourself as you converse: if your choice doesn't hold up under their questions, then perhaps you didn't ask enough questions of your own during your discernment process. Remember, you're not fooling anyone but yourself if you've set up "strawman arguments" for the positions you didn't like, only to knock them down.

INTEGRATION TIP 2: BE PREPARED FOR FRICTION

It's only fair to warn you that thinking critically, in and of itself, might very well alienate you from your current group, *whatever group you're in*. Many groups are at least initially resistant to outside thought, no matter their position.

My friend Jane Hendrickson spent several years studying the Bible, researching to find answers to her questions about women's roles. In a series of email exchanges with me, she shared eloquently how her own development brought some tensions, even within some dear friendships. She also shared how she handled that internally, and allowed me to include her experience.

> By far, the most difficult part of the process of reaching my conclusions was coming to terms with disappointing people, particularly women that I really loved and admired. I found very quickly that my shifting views were taken personally by people around me. Also, because they had experienced a lot of hurt, oppression, and disempowerment around this issue, I was contributing to their sense of hurt.
>
> At times, I felt a little annoyed that I was being pigeon-holed as a "conservative" or something, because I just wanted to understand what the Bible was saying. I think on some level I needed to do enough thinking, praying, and reading on the issue to come to a personal conviction that, even if I were the only person in a particular context to think this way, I was able to say, "I have faithfully discerned this position and am okay being the only one here thinking this way right now."

Several of the mentors interviewed, *both* complementarians and egalitarians, spoke about a similar feeling, that of swimming upstream, so to speak. With just about anything, you'll have some people who cheer you on and some who challenge you. It's just life. But you're ready for it now, at least mentally. You know where you stand and why you stand there.

With long-time, close relationships, it's often not a matter of bringing another around to the same convictions as yours about the issue of women in leadership. Sometimes, it's about living alongside and relating with respect, kindness, and support to your dear ones who have also studied the issue intensively, yet don't agree with you and perhaps take very different paths within orthodox Christendom. In the 1970s when Kathy Keller attended seminary at Gordon-Conwell, this topic was all anyone ever talked about. Everyone wanted to sort out the matter, professors and students alike. Yet, in the end, not everyone came to the same conclusion, including her closest friends:

> Everything in seminary—*everything*—was about women's ordination. Every class was about it. Now the professor might not have taught it that way, but it was taken into the cafeteria and it was applied and it was discussed and parsed out for application to the ordination of women, because that was the issue *du jour*. There was no escaping it. And no one *wanted* to escape it; everyone wanted to figure it out. You didn't have to have a particular interest in it. In fact, if the topic bored you to tears, it didn't help! You *still* were involved in the conversations. [*Laughs.*] It was the only thing anyone talked about.
>
> [Yet] at seminary, there were six women who got to be *really* close friends. We met for dinner every Sunday and brought along our husband or boyfriend *du jour*. We have stayed friends for four decades. We started a round-robin letter and we call each other; we've been to each other's weddings; we all have grandchildren; but we keep this round-robin letter going. We email each other almost daily, but the letter is still a big event.
>
> One of the women amongst us has become a Catholic. One of us has become ordained. One has got her D.Min.
>
> We have gone in many directions, and yet we remain very, very, very good friends. These are subjects we sometimes talk about, and sometimes don't.

One aspect of this journey is holding your conclusions firmly yet, perhaps ironically, holding them humbly and with an open hand in potentially difficult conversations. Kathy expressed this well:

> I can't say that I have any outstanding questions remaining about women in church leadership. I hope that doesn't sound egregiously self-congratulatory, but I've been through it sooo often. I can't go a

month, I certainly can't go two months, without somebody bringing it up again in some fashion.

In some crowds, I was thought of as the raving liberal and in some crowds as the raving conservative. It gave me whiplash from time to time. It's not been bad for me—I don't regret this.

I've from time to time all along had someone begging me to reconsider and reread and go through all of *their* research. A woman from our church went off to Gordon-Conwell and took a year off and got a Lilly Grant to study this whole subject and came to a different conclusion. She wanted me to go through every single thing that she had written, and I always feel like it's my obligation to do so.

We had a woman leave our church staff five or six years ago. She went out to California and got ordained. She and I had lots of conversations. Any time a woman comes to Redeemer and learns in the membership class that we don't ordain women as elders . . .

I mean, we don't *hide* it: the elders are listed in the bulletin every Sunday and men are up front whenever we ordain someone. So, it's not hidden, although women are so prominently in ministry at Redeemer that it takes a while for people to put two and two together. It usually doesn't happen until the membership class and there's another woman on my doorstep saying, "I can not believe you don't ordain women in your church," and then I go through it again.

So, I've gone through whatever is the argument *du jour*. I cannot tell you how many times I've gone through it. I've listened to the arguments and read the research in the new books and etcetera. So, it's not been one time or two times, it's been something like a hundred times or more. I stopped counting a long time ago.

I always say, "I hold my convictions strongly, but with an open hand. I don't *want* to be wrong. I don't want my life to be based on the *wrong* thing, so hit me with your best shot."

I'll be glad to be convinced, to find, gosh, I've made a mistake. It sure would make life easier in New York City!

Mary Ann Hawkins explained how she handles conflict if it rolls around:

> I try to avoid confrontation over interpretation—not because I am not comfortable with it, but because I find it really produces very little positive results. If I can encourage someone to go back and study and if I can raise enough question in their mind, usually the Lord brings them around and I don't have to.

Karen Moy shared a very helpful insight into learning how to communicate with a person who disagrees with you.

> Along the way, if there was anything that really helped me, it was that category of books that helped me get *good* at having the kinds of conversations I needed to have with other people who had tensions about this. Often, those conversations had *nothing* to do with women in leadership directly.
>
> The foremost resource was called *Caring Enough to Confront*.[64] I read this and gave away so many copies that I had to keep buying new ones. The author gives a very specific biblical framework—specific tactics—for how you go to somebody you *disagree* with, reasons as to *why* we get angry with each other, what you *do* with the anger, and how you actually try to *resolve* conflict with someone whenever you'd actually confront them with, "You *did* 'this' to me and it was painful."
>
> That book, more than any other book, I would highlight and give a copy to a person and say, "I won't *have* this conversation with you until you've read such-and-such portion of this book. When you've finished it, then we can talk."
>
> Sometimes women have difficulty with somebody who's putting them down or diminishing them. In my experience, women tend to just curl up into a little ball and pout. I have zero tolerance for that.
>
> So, I'd tell them, "Well, you're going to have to acquire the facility to have a conversation with somebody who's not treating you well without (a) curling up in a little ball and pouting, or (b) bursting into tears. There has to be a way for you to have enough self-control to stay in the conversation and actually achieve some kind of resolution about this. I don't want to hear, 'I can't.' So, do your homework. Read this and give it a try."

64. By David Augsburger. See bibliography for complete information.

> I don't think *I* could have sustained some of the conversations I've had with people over the years if I didn't *also* have the skills to have a difficult conversation with somebody (who may even have authority over me) on one of the most contentious subjects in the Christian church, which is whether or not women can lead.

We can boil our preparedness for friction down to two principles: know why you believe what you believe (do your homework) and learn to communicate in emotionally charged, difficult, or tense situations without losing it. If you haven't learned this already in your life, begin to learn it as soon as you can. It's never too late. This will help you, no matter where you begin your journey on this issue and no matter where you end up. In fact, the confidence to communicate evenly, thoughtfully, and graciously in a charged situation helps you become more effective in *every* area of your life. I'm a constant student in this area and still have a long way to go.

In the end, knowledge and conviction combined with prayer, grace, love, and humility may serve as your best strategy.

✍📖Your Turn:

Think through your own personal style and imagine how you might discuss the issue with someone you know disagrees with you.

INTEGRATION TIP 3: YOU DON'T HAVE TO HAVE IT ALL MEMORIZED

Don't worry about being ready every second of every day to defend, or even simply talk about, your decision.

Grace May said, "I am so immersed in the subject, and yet if you would ask me for a really good explanation of 1 Timothy—if I had to do this in front of a large audience—I would still want to take some time to study it so I made sure I had all the nuances set."

It's normal to need a refresher every once in a while.

INTEGRATION TIP 4: ACKNOWLEDGE YOUR REMAINING QUESTIONS AND THE REALITY OF ANY REMAINING PROBLEMS

Sarah Sumner said what had impacted her decision process most of all was seeking to arrive at a place at which the fewest or no contradictions remained. She explained her reasoning: "Mortimer Adler says that when there is a contradiction, you know you haven't landed on truth yet. And just philosophically speaking, it's clear to me we haven't landed on truth yet in the all-male leadership paradigm, because there are so many contradictions. And *that's* where I hung my hat, really. That was the biggest thing of all."

Although Sarah believes that not all the contradictions have been knocked out, she has a working decision in place.

So does Bev Hislop:

> I think probably the issue of "headship" and what that actually means (and I don't buy that *kephale* means "source") is key to where we go from here. I feel like I am probably closer to understanding it than I have ever been, but I am not finished. I'm still processing it and all the implications of what it means. I think that has a bearing on 1 Timothy 2.
>
> Then, there's the idea of whether there is significance in the creation order—the fact that Adam was created first. I know the animals were created before him and there are some of the arguments from the other side, but that is still one issue that I just . . . How can I express this? When it's repeated in Scripture, there is just a little bit of question in my mind about what that means.
>
> . . . So, you can see that I'm still on the journey. There are still a couple of issues I haven't fully resolved yet.

INTEGRATION TIP 5: ENJOY THE FUN

Karen Mains' excitement begins *after* the study has been done and the choice has been made. She loves engaging culture with theological issues and vice versa, how theological issues impact culture.

> I'm not interested in creating a nice little happy community. I think that's important and has a lot to offer; and people *are* looking for

genuine community. But I want to be among people who are tangling with "How do we make the gospel interface in such a way that the culture is changed?" I think we've done that with the movie *The Passion.*

There are some other interesting things that have happened, too. *Searching for Debra Winger* is a *really* interesting documentary about actresses who are "of a certain age" and what the Hollywood system does to them. When we get into these "How bad the church is" conversations, let us remember how de-humanizing some of those other systems are. That's a structure I would be very eager to see broken.

And the gal who is the director of *What Women Want* and *Something's Gotta Give*, Nancy Meyers; that's a woman who's breaking that "old boys" culture (well, really it's a "young boy's culture") in Hollywood. I mean, here you have the Baby Boomers who are all aging, and we still have this *youth* ethic? *Please!* Then you have this woman who is making a film about a woman who's in her fifties, and it's had box office success.

That's the sort of stuff that I would love to have the church *grapple* with—not just on the popular-culture level, and *particularly* in relationship to women's voice.

That's when it *begins* for me. The theological discussions are not as interesting to me as the application of them. That's when my buttons start to turn on, when I hear about a group that begins to really say, "Okay, we understand this; it is satisfactory to us and is scriptural. Now, how does it *work*?" And then they begin to tackle the environmental implications and systems implications of this. *That* is when I get excited.

And you can get excited, too: you can contribute significantly to many more conversations now, because you know more about the whole issue.

INTEGRATION TIP 6: HELP SOMEONE ELSE

Chances are good that the opportunity will arise to help someone else along in their journey to understand this issue. You now have the ability to recommend resources that were helpful to you, assist someone with their exegesis, or even mentor an individual or group along these lines. I first met Karen Moy because she was mentoring my friends. It's a part of her life. She often encounters women searching out this subject and can show them how she studied it.

Like Sandra Glahn wouldn't give "the right answer" to her students, Karen is not the type to merely hand out answers; she leads people through the process of thinking about issues for themselves.

She said, "Passages in many books I own are marked with a post-it or a highlighter because I frequently go back to them. Also, I frequently engage with younger women who are figuring this out for themselves. When I am engaged with one, to be economical, I can just hand her a stack of books and say, 'Look for all the stuff I have highlighted in yellow. You'll understand how I've reached my conclusion.'"

INTEGRATION TIP 7: REPEAT. MANY TIMES

The icing on the cake is that this discernment process is *repeatable*. You can apply the principles we've discussed here to just about any set of theological questions and ideas. Any person or group can use them. You can repeat this plan whenever you want to assess whether the practices of a person, church, or group are biblical or not.

You can discern your own thoughts, feelings, and, ultimately, beliefs about women's roles in the church or any other theological issue using every tool you can bring to bear on it. Use this same plan for your next theological question. For example, after I finish this book, I am considering writing a similar one about the Trinity, so I can learn more about the whole concept of the Godhead, as three in one. (That ought to keep me busy for a while.)

Conclusion

In terms of women's roles in the church, Sandra Glahn gave excellent expression to our concerns when she asked,

> *Do* men have an honor before God by virtue of man's arriving in the garden before woman that women do not have? *Do* men have a glory before God that women do not have? If so**, *that* seems to be the *only* legitimate basis for** limiting women—*not* all of the other reasons people have argued from the text but that Paul never used in his own arguments. [Bold emphasis mine.]

Rather than looking for Bible verses that seem to support what we're already doing or what we think, the question we should be asking is, "Is there a *biblically legitimate reason* for what we're doing, the way we're acting, the efforts and projects on which we're expending our energy?"

Of course, in a perfect church-world, our actions would be *preceded by* our study and questions, such as, "What is the Lord leading us to? What do we know from the Word that we should be pursuing? How should we live together? Whom should we ask to do this job or begin this ministry? [Or, better yet] What gifts and skills does so-and-so display and where can they best be developed and used for the church's maturity in Christ?"

Remember: our goal through this plan is to learn to think critically about any given issue. We want to precede our actions with biblical and theological awareness or correct existing practices that aren't biblically based.

Real-life learning and decision-making isn't about listening to someone's interpretation and then regurgitating it. Real-life learning and decision-making is about discernment. It's about prayerfully sifting through a variety of other people's opinions and interpretations about facts and situations. It's about prayerfully analyzing, comparing, and contrasting those varied opinions against each other and against what you already know or are currently learning. It's about prayerfully exegeting God's Word. It's about prayerfully forming your *own* conclusions and opinions, then weighing them alongside expert and historical interpretations and opinions.

It's about being responsible before God for your own thinking. And *you* are choosing this path of responsibility before God.

Well done, you!

Appendix A

Meet the Mentors

ONE BEAUTIFUL THING ABOUT women is that we want to help each other.

If you read the introduction of this book, you already know that in my own search for answers regarding women's roles I interviewed a number of women over the course of several years. I found thirty-seven women who had gone before me when it came to this issue, many of whose stories I share in this book. These women had already asked good questions, studied hard, made discoveries, developed biblically centered and theologically sound conclusions, and then lived into their decisions in spiritually healthy ways.

They warmly opened their hearts and lives to me, including their own fears and how they moved past them with God's help and the Spirit's empowerment. Frankly, they held back very little.

What's in this for you? The women I interviewed eagerly desired to share their experiences with other women. Even the women who found themselves in delicate positions desired that their research, resources, and experiences might inform, empower, and encourage other women searching out this issue biblically. That is a beautiful thing.

I wish I could tell you all of the admirable personal details of these women's lives in addition to the bullet-points of their résumés. I wish I had the space. Several are cancer survivors. Several are grandmothers or great-grandmothers. Several are single. Several are widows. Several are adoptive moms. Several have ministered in the farthest reaches of the Earth. Several are professors. Several are pastors or ministers. Several are stay-at-home moms. Several are businesswomen. Most, if not all, of them speak and lead retreats of all types, in between family, work, ministry, and other responsibilities. Several have, in addition to their primary ministries, worked tirelessly throughout their lives to defend defenseless populations and promote justice in our world in noble, godly ways.

I wish I could recreate for you the settings I was able to enjoy with them:

- Conversing intensely with Karen Burton Mains while lingering over a seafood dinner in Provincetown, MA;
- Chatting with Sarah Sumner in her office in Azusa, CA, just before she headed off to teach aerobics;
- Relaxing and talking with Sandra Glahn beneath the welcome shade of a wide umbrella next to a sun-drenched hotel swimming pool in Orlando, Florida, where we were attending a women's conference;
- Facing Beverly Hislop across a booth in the "Holy Hill Café" on the Gordon-Conwell seminary campus as we munched and talked about her life and ministry;
- Sipping coffee with Sue Edwards in a friend's sunny kitchen on Cape Cod.

We met as sisters in Christ. We met as mentor-mentee and teacher-learner. We met as women. Several of us met as friends and colleagues. Some of us met as friends of friends. Each is delightful and I do wish you could have been there for every conversation.

I want to give you enough context to allow you to know them, even if only in a limited way, and enjoy the women as I was able to enjoy them—to let their personalities and passions shine through. With all of this in mind, and to give you more of a "feel" for the women instead of just using a sentence or two to make a point, I have hoped to give you more than mere snippets of helpful quips from them. Where their quotes are included as examples, I attempted to include the largest portions of conversations I could manage without the book becoming unwieldy.

As you read excerpts from these interviews, you will see words emphasized via the use of italics. I used that formatting to indicate that the mentor verbally emphasized that word or phrase in her speech pattern.

You may know, or know of, some of the women. If so, you can envision them sitting across from you on a comfortable couch, sharing their experiences and discoveries with you. As you read their brief biographies (listed alphabetically), you can get to know them a bit and see what a fantastic and diverse group of women they are. You will see that they come from varied theological, denominational, geographical, social, and cultural backgrounds, with the common denominator of holding the Lord and his Word highest in their lives.

For women with whom I had opportunity to spend a bit of time, either in person or on the phone, or who I already knew, I have listed a few words that come to mind when I think of them, just to give you a quick connection with my impression of their personalities.

Ready to meet the mentors?

MEET PHYLLIS BENNETT

Currently: Director, Women's Center for Ministry (2011–present) and Adjunct Professor in Pastoral Care to Women, Western Seminary (WA, 2002–present). ***Author:*** *Our Wise Counselor: Trusting God's Guidance* (NavPress, 2008); *Discovering Your Spiritual Gifts* (Zondervan, 1998); and *Our Perfect Example, Following God's Ways* (NavPress, 1994). Board member of By Design Ministries (www.bydesignministry.org; 2009–present). ***Formerly:*** Past Director of Women's Ministries, Grace Baptist Church (Hudson, MA, 2002–9) and Mountain Park Church (Lake Oswego, OR, 1990–99). MDiv, Western Seminary (Portland, OR), D.Min. in Effective Ministries to Women, Gordon-Conwell Theological Seminary (South Hamilton, MA). http://www.westernseminary.edu/women/Resources/Speakers_info/Bennett_Phyllis.htm

Words for Phyllis: Motivated. Kind. Focused.

MEET CANDIE BLANKMAN

Currently: Pastor/Head of Staff, First Presbyterian Church (Downey, CA, 2003–present). Instructor/Coach, SCORRE Conference (formerly the Dynamic Communicator's Workshop, Inc.; Franklin, TN, 1985–present). ***Author:*** *Forged by War* (CreateSpace, 2011). ***Formerly:*** Pastor, Palos Park Presbyterian Community Church (Chicago, IL, 1996–2003); Social Studies teacher, Richfield Public Schools (Richfield, MN, 1988–93); Director of Children's Ministries, Eastminster Presbyterian Church (Wichita, KS, 1985–88). MDiv, Gordon-Conwell Theological Seminary (Boston, MA). Websites: www.candieblankman.blogspot.com and www.FPCDowney.com.

Words for Candie: Calm. Confident. Encouraging.

MEET DEE BRESTIN

Currently: Speaker. ***Author:*** *Idol Lies* (Worthy, 2012); *The God of All Comfort* (Zondervan, 2009); *We Are Sisters* (David C. Cook, 2006); *The Friendships of Women* (David C. Cook, 2005); *Living in Love with Jesus* (co-author with K. Troccoli, Thomas Nelson, 2003); *Falling in Love with Jesus* (co-author with K. Troccoli, Thomas Nelson, 2002); and numerous other titles and Bible studies. Website: www.deebrestin.com.

Words for Dee: Warm. Incisive.

MEET ADELA RIOS CARTER[1]

Adela Carter, a fabulous, feisty Latina, grew up in South America and emigrated to the U.S. as a girl. She comments on culture in her books, lectures, and speaking ministry and helps women engage faith and culture more fully and more authentically.

MEET ELIZABETH CONDE-FRAZIER

Currently: Dean and Vice President of Education, Esperanza College of Eastern University (Philadelphia, PA, 2009–present). ***Author:*** *Listen to the Children* (Judson Press, 2011); *Hispanic Bible Institutes* (University of Scranton Press, 2005). Co-author: *A Many-Colored Kingdom* (with S. S. Kang and G. A. Parrett, Baker Academic, 2004). ***Editor:*** *Multicultural Models of Religious Education* (SCP/Third World Literature Publishing House, 2001). ***Formerly:*** Lecturer, Center for Latino Church Studies, Brite Divinity School (Ft. Worth, TX, summers 2006–11). Professor of Religious Education, Claremont School of Theology and Lecturer of Hispanic/Latino theology, the Latin American Bible Institute (La Puente, CA, 1999–2008). Founder and Director, the Orlando E. Costas Hispanic and Latin American Ministries Program, Andover Newton Theological School (Boston, MA, 1988–99). MDiv, Eastern Baptist Theological Seminary (Wynnewood, PA); PhD in Theology and Religious Education, Boston College (MA).

1. Name changed at her request, due to the nature of her ministry.

Words for Elizabeth: Straightforward. Joyful.

MEET KAY DAIGLE

Currently: Founder and Executive Director of Beyond Ordinary Women Ministries (Plano, TX, 2013–present). ***Author:*** *From Ordinary Woman to Spiritual Leader* (West Bow Press, 2012) and the *Wise Women Bible Study Series* (Bible.org). ***Formerly:*** Minister of Women and Marriage, Northwest Bible Church (Dallas, TX, 2003–10); Director of Women's Ministry, Prestonwood Baptist Church (Plano, TX, 2000–2003). M.A.C.E., Dallas Theological Seminary (TX); DMin in Effective Ministries to Women, Gordon-Conwell Theological Seminary (South Hamilton, MA). Website: www.kaydaigle.com.

Words for Kay: Intent. Engaging. Thoughtful.

MEET SUE EDWARDS

Currently: Associate Professor of Educational Ministries and Leadership and Mentor Professor for the Women in Ministry DMin concentration, Dallas Theological Seminary (Dallas, TX, 2005–present). ***Author:*** *The Discovery Series* (seven inductive Bible study volumes, relaunch, second release 2012); *Leading Women Who Wound* (Moody, 2009); *Mixed Ministry* (Kregel, 2008); *Women's Retreats: A Creative Planning Guide* (Kregel, 2004); and *New Doors in Ministry to Women* (Kregel, 2002). ***Formerly:*** Pastor to Women, Irving Bible Church (1998–2004, Irving, TX). MA Biblical Studies, Dallas Theological Seminary (TX). DMin in Effective Ministries to Women, Gordon-Conwell Theological Seminary (South Hamilton, MA). Website: www.newdoors.info.

Words for Sue: Dependable. Fun. Persistent.

MEET BARBARA FLETCHER

Currently: Associate Pastor of Group Life Ministries and Bible Study Curriculum Writer, Salem Alliance Church (Salem, OR, 2011–present); Board President, Salem Free Clinic (Salem, OR, 2009–present). ***Formerly:*** Pastor of Adult Ministries and preaching team member, Salem

Alliance Church (Salem, OR, 1991–2011); Adjunct Professor of Message Preparation, Multnomah Seminary (Portland, OR, 1991–95); Teaching Leader, Bible Study Fellowship (Salem, OR, 1978–83). MA Biblical Studies, Multnomah Seminary (Portland, OR).

Words for Barbara: Intense. Devoted. Delightful.

MEET SANDRA GLAHN

Currently: Adjunct Professor in Media Arts and Worship, and editor in chief, "Kindred Spirit" magazine (Dallas Theological Seminary, 1999–present). PhD candidate in Aesthetic Studies, University of Texas at Dallas. ***Author:*** *Informed Consent* (Cook, 2007). Co-author: *Sumatra with the Seven Churches* (with C. Keeth, AMG, 2011), part of The Coffee Cup Bible Series (AMG, 2006–11). Co-author with W. Cutrer: *When Empty Arms Become a Heavy Burden* (Kregel, 2010 rev.), *Sexual Intimacy in Marriage* (Kregel, 2007), *The Contraception Guidebook* (Zondervan, 2005), and *The Infertility Companion* (Zondervan, 2004), along with three acclaimed medical suspense novels. She serves on the boards of several associations and ministries. ThM, Dallas Theological Seminary (TX). Website: www.Aspire2.blogspot.com.

Words for Sandra: Creative. Critical thinker. Perceptive.

MEET MARY ANN HAWKINS

Currently: Professor of Intercultural Studies and Dean of the Chapel, Anderson University School of Theology (Anderson, IN, 2006–present). ***Author:*** *Women and Men in Ministry Partnership* (forthcoming); Editor, *A Thread of Hope: Church of God Women in Mission* (Evangel Press, 2009). ***Formerly:*** Associate Pastor of Adult Programs and Music Minister, South Bay Church of God (Torrance, CA, 2002–5); Assistant Professor of Inter-Cultural Studies, Hope International University (Fullerton, CA, 1998–2002); as a missionary (1990–98): Academic Dean of Kima International School of Theology (Kenya) and Acting Principal of Babati Bible School (Tanzania); Associate Pastor of Administration, East Tulsa Church of God (OK, 1984–86). MA, Azusa Pacific University (Azusa, CA); PhD in Intercultural Studies, Fuller Theological Seminary (Pasadena, CA).

Words for Mary Ann: Passionate. Dedicated. Helpful.

MEET BEVERLY HISLOP

Currently: Founder and Executive Director of the Women's Center for Ministry and Associate Professor of Pastoral Care to Women, Western Seminary (Portland, OR, 1996–present). Consultant for starting and staffing ministries to women (1987–present). Board member, Synergy Women's Network, Inc., and *Fullfill* leadership magazine (MOPS International). ***Author:*** *Shepherding Women in Pain* (Moody, 2010); *Shepherding a Woman's Heart* (Moody, 2003). Contributing Author: *Women's Ministry Handbook* (ed. C. Porter and M. Hamel, Victor Books, 1992). ***Formerly:*** Radio Host, "Western Connection for Women" (1996–98). Developer/Instructor of Women's Ministry Module, Moody Bible Institute (Chicago, IL); Founder/Director, Florida Intercessory Network (1992–96). Founder/Director of Ministries to Women in Florida, Oregon, and Germany (1971–96). Board member for several national ministries to and for women. MSM, Multnomah Bible Seminary (Portland, OR); DMin in Effective Ministries to Women, Gordon-Conwell Theological Seminary (South Hamilton, MA). Website: www.shepherdingwomen.com.

Words for Bev: Tender. Generous. Understated.

MEET ELIZABETH INRIG

Currently: Pastor of Women's Ministries, Trinity Evangelical Free Church (Redlands, CA, 1993–present). Adjunct Professor, Pastoral Ministries Department for Women's Ministries, Talbot School of Theology (La Mirada, CA, 2008–present). Director and Life Coach, "The Shelter" (Redlands, CA, 2012–present). ***Author:*** *Release Your Potential* (Moody, 2001). ***Formerly:*** National Director of Women's Ministries, Evangelical Free Church of America (1997–2007). MA Biblical Studies, Dallas Theological Seminary (TX); DMin in Biblical Interpretation and Communication, Trinity Evangelical Divinity School (Deerfield, IL). Website: www.women.trinityonline.org.

Words for Elizabeth: Focused. Open. Creative.

MEET KATHY KELLER

Current: Church Planter/Co-founder, Director of Communications, and Assistant Director of Communications and Media, Redeemer Presbyterian Church (New York, NY, 1989–present); Editor, Redeemer City to City (New York, NY, 2009–present). MA in Theological Studies, Gordon-Conwell Theological Seminary (South Hamilton, MA). Author: *Jesus, Justice and Gender Roles: A Case for Gender Roles in Ministry* (eBook, Zondervan, 2012). Co-author: *The Meaning of Marriage: Facing the Complexities of Marriage with the Wisdom of God* (with T. Keller, Dutton, 2011).

Words for Kathy: Forthright. Humorous. Articulate.

MEET KAREN BURTON MAINS

Currently: Co-director, Mainstay Ministries (Chicago, IL, 1993–present); Director, Hungry Souls (2002–present). ***Author:*** *The God Hunt* (InterVarsity, 2003); *Open Heart, Open Home* (InterVarsity, 2002 rev.); *Comforting One Another* (Thomas Nelson, 1997); *Making Sunday Special* (Star Song Communications Group, 1994); *Lonely No More* (W. Pub Group, 1993); *The Fragile Curtain* (David C. Cook, 1983); and has authored and co-authored numerous other titles (more than twenty-seven) for both adults and children. ***Formerly:*** Pastor's Wife, Circle Church (Chicago, IL, 1967–77). Co-host: "The Chapel of the Air Ministries" nationally syndicated radio show (1978–93) and "You Need to Know" television program (1990–96). Chair of the Board of Trustees, InterVarsity Christian Fellowship (1991–93). Website: www.karenmains.com.

Words for Karen: Candid. Intuitive. Current.

MEET GRACE MAY

Currently: President, Women of Wonder, Inc. (New York, NY, 2011–present). Faculty, City Seminary of New York (New York, NY, 2011–present). Adjunct Professor of World Christianity, Gordon-Conwell Theological Seminary (Boston, MA, 2005–present). ***Contributing author:*** *Honoring the Generations* (S. M. Park, S. C. Rah, and A. Tizon, Judson Press, 2012); *Proclaiming the Scandal of the Cross* (M. Baker, Baker Academic, 2006);

Growing Healthy Asian-American Churches (P. Cha, S. Kang, and H. Lee, InterVarsity, 2006); and *The Global God* (A. Spencer and W. Spencer, Baker Academic, 1998). ***Formerly:*** Pastor, Chinese Christian Church of New England (Boston, MA, 1999–2005); Associate Pastor, First Chinese Presbyterian Church (New York, NY, 2006–8); and English Ministry Pastor, Oversea Chinese Mission (New York, NY, 2009–11). MDiv, Gordon-Conwell Theological Seminary (MA); ThD in Systematic Theology and Missiology, Boston University School of Theology (MA). Website: www.womenofwonder.us.

Words for Grace: Cheerful. Intense. Gracious.

MEET SUSAN MCCORMICK

Currently: Co-director, Serve Austin Community Group at First Evangelical Free Church (Austin, TX, 2009–present). ***Formerly:*** Director of Outreach and Missions, Director of Children's Ministries, Director of Assimilation and Ministry Placement, Director of Women's Ministry, and Director of Local and Global Missions, Westlake Bible Church (Austin, TX, 1987–2005); Volunteer positions: Community Liaison/Minister for Westlake Partners in Ministry, Austin Bridge Builders Alliance, Communities Connecting for a Better Tomorrow, and Community Action Network (Austin, TX, 1979–86); Director, King David's Children's Center, Westside Baptist Church (Austin, TX, 1976–78). MA Curriculum and Instruction, University of Texas (Austin, TX).

Words for Susan: Considerate. Unassuming. Enthusiastic.

MEET KAREN MOY

Currently: Management consultant and speaker. (Seattle, WA, 1996–present). ***Formerly:*** Legislative Correspondent to U.S. Rep. Jim Talent (Washington, D.C., 1996–97); Consultant to Secretary of Health and Human Resources for the Commonwealth of Virginia (Richmond, VA, 1994); Deputy Associate Director of Presidential Personnel, Executive Office of President George W. Bush (Washington, DC, 1991–93); board member, InterVarsity Christian Fellowship/USA (1998–2005).

Words for Karen: Caring. Intense. Clear-thinking.

MEET SARAH SUMNER

Currently: Study group participant, Evangelicals and Catholics Together (2004–present). Editorial Council member and writer, *Christianity Today* (2010–present). Writer, *Relevant Magazine*. Advisory boards: *Leadership Journal* and PreachingToday.com. Consultant, Sumner Consulting (Redding, CA, 2007–present). ***Author:*** *Leadership above the Line* (Tyndale House, 2006) and *Men and Women in the Church* (InterVarsity, 2003). Co-author: *Just How Married Do You Want to Be?* (with J. Sumner, InterVarsity, 2008). Contributing author: *A Faith and Culture Devotional* (K. Kullberg, Zondervan, 2008) and *Women, Ministry, and the Gospel* (M. Husbands and T. Larsen, IVP Academic, 2007). ***Formerly:*** Dean, A. W. Tozer Theological Seminary (Redding, CA, 2010–12); Professor of Theology and Ministry, Haggard School of Theology/Azusa Pacific University (Azusa, CA, 1997–2009); Teaching Pastor, New Song Church (San Dimas, CA, 2000–2009). MA Theology, Wheaton College; MBA, Azusa Pacific University (Azusa, CA); MDiv and PhD in Systematic Theology, Trinity Evangelical Divinity School (Deerfield, IL).

Words for Sarah: Energetic. Multi-faceted. Kind-hearted.

MEET LAVERNE TOLBERT

Currently: Founder and President, Teaching Like Jesus Ministries (Pasadena, CA, 2001–present); Director, The Society for Children's Spirituality: Christian Perspectives conferences (Pasadena, CA, 2003–present); and Adjunct Professor Christian Education and Spiritual Formation, Biola University (La Mirada, CA, 2006–present). ***Author:*** *How to STUDY and Understand the Bible in 5 Simple Steps without Learning Hebrew or Greek* (Xlibris, 2012); *Keeping You and Your Kids Sexually Pure* (Xlibris, 2007); *Teaching Like Jesus* (Zondervan, 2000); and *I've Got the Power Abstinence Curriculum for Middle and High School Students* (A. C. Green Foundation, 1995). ***Formerly:*** Adjunct Professor, Haggard School of Theology/Azusa Pacific University (Azusa, CA, 2001–11); Director of Christian Education, Crenshaw Christian Center (Los Angeles, CA, 2004–8); Assistant Professor of Christian Education, Talbot School of Theology (La Mirada, CA, 1989–98); and Director of Christian Education, Faithful Central (Inglewood, CA, 1989–2000). MA in Christian Education and

PhD in Christian Education, Talbot School of Theology (La Mirada, CA). Website: www.teachinglikejesus.org.

Words for LaVerne: No-nonsense. Sweet. Impassioned.

MEET JEANETTE YEP

Currently: Pastor of Global and Regional Outreach, Grace Chapel (Lexington, MA, 2007–present). ***Editor:*** *More Than Serving Tea* (InterVarsity, 2006). ***Co-author:*** *Following Jesus without Dishonoring Your Parents* (with P. Cha, P. Tokunaga, and G. Jao, InterVarsity, 1998). ***Formerly:*** U.S. Director of Staff Training and Development, International Fellowship of Evangelical Students/InterVarsity Christian Fellowship (Madison, WI, 2005–7); Vice President and Director of Multiethnic Ministries, IVCF (Madison, WI, 2003–5); National Field Director/Special Director of Staff Training and Development, IVCF, (Madison, WI, 1999–2003); Divisional Director, IVCF (Chicago, IL, 1993–99); Area Director, IVCF (Chicago, IL, 1983–93); Coordinator, Asian American Staff Fellowship, IVCF (1982–83); Campus Staff Member, IVCF (Boston, MA, 1977–82). MS in Managerial Communication, Northwestern University (Evanston, IL, 1995).

Words for Jeanette: Warm. Humble. Servant.

AND . . . ? OR, "SO WHAT HAPPENED?"

How did these women come face to face with their questions about women's roles—what caused their awakening to the issue? What happened to them *after* they encountered those situations that brought them face to face? What did they decide and how did they decide it?

Aside from reading portions of the mentors' journeys throughout the text of this book, you can find answers to these particular questions on this book's website, www.womenleadershipbible.com,[2] in these articles:

- "The Mentors' Awakenings"

2. You may also link through via my website, www.natalieeastman.com.

- "The Mentors' Final Decisions and Implementation"

I urge you, however, to read the entire book and be well into your own study, prayer, and research before you read those articles. The more you set yourself up to approach your own research without predisposed feelings, the more objective you can be in making your own determination. That is one of the primary reasons those portions of their accounts are not included in this volume.

Appendix B

Resources, A Strategy

"WHERE DO I START, Natalie?" you might wonder. "I want to understand this issue, but don't know how to select the best books. I don't have a lot of time. And I don't understand a lot of the technical jargon theologians seem to love to use."

If you want to cover a lot of ground and become as informed as possible in the shortest possible time, start with this reading list. Building a library for researching this issue, and a theological library in general, can become pricey. You might try to borrow someone else's book or buy them used online, as on Ebay's www.half.com or alibris.com.

Your strategy, should you decide to accept it, will be to begin with resources that provide overviews of the debate and move gradually toward those that discuss specific passages and theological issues from a particular perspective.

Here is a "map" to help guide your way:

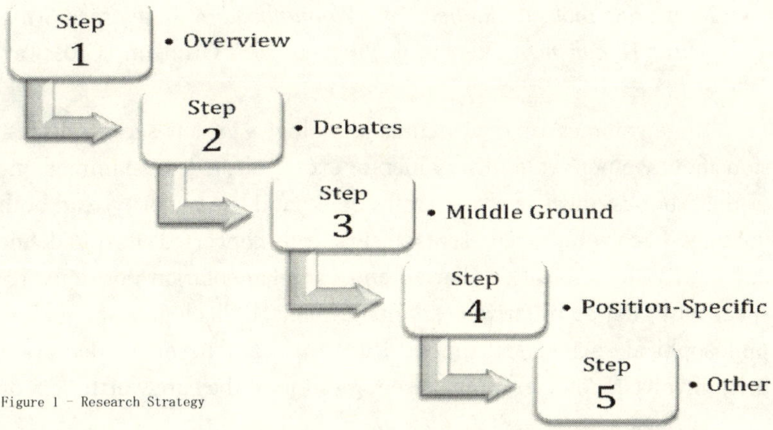

Figure 1 – Research Strategy

Unless specifically noted, all authors or editors of these resources align with evangelical principles, such as the inerrancy, accuracy, and authority of the Scriptures. Still, read every work critically. Take nothing for granted. And certainly, take nothing as "gospel truth." Remember, each contributor to the debate over this issue is a fallible human being. The whole counsel of Scripture must be your guide; then use these additional resources to shed further light on any particulars and peculiarities you identify in Scripture, as well as on historical and cultural contexts. Remember, as we discussed in step one, "Prepare" (see page 25), be sure to write down your questions as you go, along with your reactions, ideas, and other comments.

Note that resource lists are presented in alphabetical order within each list in this appendix. If a mentor mentioned a book, her comment is included after the reference. Only author(s) or editor(s), publisher, and publication year are included in these listings. For complete bibliographic information, please see the Bibliography.

STEP 1: BOOKS PROVIDING AN OVERVIEW OF THE DEBATE ON THE "WOMEN'S ISSUE"

Any woman seeking to grasp and understand these issues in the fastest possible timeframe will thank herself afterward for the time she saved by consulting these resources first:

- *Discovering Biblical Equality: Complementarity without Hierarchy.* Edited by R. Pierce, R. M. Groothuis, and G. D. Fee. (IVP Academic, 2004)
- *Recovering Biblical Manhood and Womanhood: A Response to Evangelical Feminism.* Edited by J. Piper and W. Grudem. (Crossway, 2012)

These volumes are the essential anthologies for any serious discussion about women's roles. Every mentor except one at least skimmed one of these books; most read the entire book; and the majority read both volumes. Each volume represents the first truly concerted effort to define and clarify the biblical egalitarian and complementarian positions, respectively. They summarize every major biblical, theological, exegetical, philosophical, sociological, practical, historical, and hermeneutical argument involved. You can mine these tomes for all they are worth, too, by looking further for works cited in their bibliographies and footnotes. This can save you a lot of research time.

However, those great benefits aside, certain chapters may seem technical to readers who have no background in either theological study or exegetical Bible study. Some of the chapter authors use Greek and Hebrew references, although you don't have to know the languages to benefit from and understand this book. The editors aimed for a general audience. Therefore, by and large, it is not *overly* technical, even for a lay reader with little exposure to "deep Bible study" methods.

STEP 2: THE DEBATE FORMAT

A handful of editors has helpfully endeavored to present issues important to Christians, including the issue of women's roles, in a debate format. These volumes, perhaps even more than those in Step 1, above, are aimed at a general, lay audience; therefore, no ancient language skills are required.

Chapters are written by scholars and ministry folk who hold different positions. Each summarizes his or her position's main points. Typically, the other authors, or perhaps the editors, respond to each chapter. Such titles include

- *Women in Ministry: Four Views.* Edited by B. Clouse and R. G. Clouse (InterVarsity, 2004)
- *Does Christianity Teach Male Headship? The Equal-Regard Marriage and Its Critics.* Edited by D. Blankenhorn, D. Browning, and M. S. Van Leeuwen (Eerdmans, 2004)
- *The Role of Women.* Edited by S. Lees and J. G. Baldwin (InterVarsity, 2001)
- *Two Views on Women in Ministry.* Edited by J. Beck and C. Blomberg (Zondervan, 2001)
- *Women, Authority and the Bible.* Edited by A. Mickelsen (InterVarsity, 1986)

These resources have, in my opinion, two benefits. First, they aid a reader's personal understanding of the positions and how they all relate to each other. Second, and possibly even more important, they hopefully encourage unity among Christians through understanding each other's discernment of Scripture.

Several of the mentors commented on some of these books:

> [Kay Daigle] In the book *Two Views on Women in Ministry*, one of the editors—it may have been Craig Blomberg—responded in an appendix that he called "*Neither* Hierarchicalist Nor Egalitarian." I *have* heard people say, though, that he was wrong to call it that, and that he really *was* complementarian. But, I really liked his essay. I'm not sure he *convinced* me entirely, but it was pretty much what I already thought anyway! [*Laughs!*] I liked it because it was balanced and not an extreme position.

> [Barbara Fletcher] A book that was extremely helpful to me is called *Women in Ministry: Four Views*. It has a man presenting a hierarchical view, somebody refuting it; then a partnership view and a rebuttal; egalitarian view and rebuttal, and I can't remember the fourth view but it was such a fine line or inappropriate breaking up the various views into the four views they identified.
>
> I'm much more comfortable with three views; four views complicates my life! It's all semantics at some point. I am wondering whether it's splitting hairs to come up with four views. It would be simpler to stick with three views—hierarchical, egalitarian, and partnership in the middle, which gives complete freedom to women to do anything that God calls them to do, but women are still *different* from men. We are wired differently and there are differences in what we bring to the table as leaders.

> [Karen Moy] Some of the books that I particularly liked and that were helpful would kind of take it from different angles and not present any one view. *Women, Authority and the Bible* is one of those. It has something like twenty-five different theologians, from one extreme to the other. Each writes their own piece and responds to each others' pieces. That one has post-its sticking out all over the place!
>
> InterVarsity Press did a whole series called "Four Views." One of them was *Women in Ministry: Four Views*. Same kind of thing as the other book.

Susan McCormick and LaVerne Tolbert also named these books as key resources.

STEP 3: MIDDLE GROUND RESOURCES

Once you familiarize yourself with the main arguments and positions, you would do well to read books that attempt to find middle ground—or, perhaps, that explore the question of whether there *is* any middle ground. We will look at three resources here:

- *Men and Women in the Church: Building a Consensus on Christian Leadership*. S. Sumner (InterVarsity, 2003)
- *Slaves, Women & Homosexuals: Exploring the Hermeneutics of Cultural Analysis*. W. J. Webb (InterVarsity, 2001)
- "Women and the Nature of Ministry" (article). W. Liefeld (*Journal of the Evangelical Theological Society*, 1987)

Men and Women in the Church

Mentor Sarah Sumner's book *Men and Women in the Church* has reached the hearts and minds of many women who have been frustrated with the arguments on both sides of the equation. Sandra Glahn and Karen Mains both highlighted it as one of their most helpful resources:

> [Sandra Glahn] At a point when a lot of factors were coming together for me, Sarah Sumner came out with her book, *Men and Women in the Church*. She was the first female PhD in Systematic Theology coming out of Trinity Evangelical Divinity School. Like Bill Webb said in his book, she said both sides of thought are doing some gymnastics with the truth. Traditionalists can't say they have a long-term tradition of *intimacy* being the purpose of marriage, which most of them are teaching today. They simply don't have tradition on their side, because the church throughout history has *not* taught that *intimacy* is the purpose of marriage—reproduction was.
>
> Her book was really good. In fact, I found it was the favorite of some of my students because she had *struggled*. They also identified with a theological woman's view today.

> [Karen Mains] I am always amazed and shocked when I run into these groups retrenching the same ideas. Sarah Sumner's book *Men and Women in the Church* was *excellent*. She brought out excellent points I had never thought about—there was new and fresh thinking. I was glad that IVP published it and that I was given a review copy. I probably would not have picked it up and read it otherwise. I just thought she did a great job. There was not a whole lot of angst. I could easily recommend it to everyone. The fresh thinking was good.

In my opinion, Sumner brought unrecycled, honest questions and reasoning to bear on the scriptural, theological, and cultural/mindset issues regarding women's identity and roles in the church. She challenges the "standard" questions asked by theologians of all types who approach the "restrictive passages" and proposes a new set of questions for each area of stalemate. She avoids the labels "complementarian," "egalitarian," "feminist," or even "pro-woman." She prefers instead to be considered "pro-Christ."

Nearly half of the women I interviewed for this book cited Sarah's book as pivotal in finally understanding the issues. The primary expressions I heard revolved around relief at reading someone who spoke plainly about the church's "gymnastics with the texts" (Sandra Glahn's description) and the ugly demeanor that Christians who disagree sometimes display toward one another. Sumner speaks directly, also. So, readers accustomed to the traditional, dry presentation so prevalent in academics will find this book the equivalent of wearing a cool cotton dress rather than a wool suit.

Slaves, Women, and Homosexuals

During their interviews, several of the mentors spoke at some length regarding the impact of William J. Webb's book, *Slaves, Women and Homosexuals*. Webb argues for what he calls a progressive, developmental hermeneutic, meaning that the Bible reveals God's redemptive plan throughout human history. Overall, Webb says, the biblical message communicates that God's desire is for humans to treat each other with justice, compassion, and equity, but that this is progressively revealed throughout Scripture in movement toward the "eschatological ideal"—meaning, what God's perfection might look like, as best we can understand it, through our study of the end times and the judgment of humanity as discussed in the Bible. In the case of women's roles in the church, Webb argues, this progressive movement is present.

In terms of the debate on women's roles, I call this book a "middle ground" work, because his method cannot be categorized as egalitarian or complementarian. Some will disagree with this assessment and that's okay. However, he makes the case that when his method of studying Scripture is employed, the researcher unavoidably finds herself concluding with a softer version of *either* position. His goal is to bring the evangelical community back together.

> [Sandra Glahn] At one point, two of our Dallas Seminary theology profs flip-flopped on the issue, from being complementarians to being egalitarians. In fact, one of them had *taught* me the complementarian point of view. The reason they both switched their positions was Bill Webb's book *Slaves, Women and Homosexuals*. Bill Webb is a DTS grad. He could get very much within our *paradigm* and how we process truth, and show us where our holes were.
>
> That was my first exposure to his book and it was exactly what I needed, because he didn't play gymnastics with the texts I thought were being played with by others.
>
> He said things like, "No, that's what it *said*: 'wives keep silent' *meant* 'keep silent'; *but* we see movement—*redemptive* movement—on the issue of slaves; we see redemptive movement on the issue of women," meaning that God is always trying to push the culture to a little more generosity on those issues.
>
> One of the big obstacles for me had been that the assumption that if you "move" on one cultural issue, you're gonna move on *all* of them. Webb showed us the paradigm for how to process cultural material and find the "absolute" in it—what's movable and what's not movable. It was incredibly convincing. (It is also a *very* technical, semi-boring book.) [*Laughs!*]

> [Candie Blankman] William Webb's *Slaves, Women and Homosexuals* was an excellent resource. What Webb's book does is gives you seventeen criteria to determine whether something is cultural or trans-cultural.
>
> So, what I see is that from Genesis to Revelation you have God saying over and over again, "I don't do it the way you do it."

> Human beings set up all these systems, whether it's white over black, or male over female, or rich over poor, and God says, "That's not the way *I* see it." Over and over again, he calls the youngest; he affirms the poor.

> [Kay Daigle] William Webb's book I found very intriguing and interesting. To me, he has given the best big-picture type of argument I've seen for being an egalitarian. I actually enjoyed—appreciated—it. He said if you understand his argument and agree with it at all, you can't be an extreme position-holder; you end up either an egalitarian or a "soft" complementarian. And I don't think I'm extreme. I think I'm as close to an egalitarian position as I can be without actually *being* one! [*Laughs!*]

"Women and the Nature of Ministry"

Finally, in the area of middle ground resources, one other piece that is helpful for anyone beginning to inquire about this issue is Walter Liefeld's brief article, "Women and the Nature of Ministry." In it, he proposes an approach to addressing the stalemates between Christians who believe a restricted view of Scripture and those who believe a full-inclusion view. He spends the bulk of the article discussing the nature and theology of ministry—a profitable exercise for anyone exploring this overall issue.

STEP 4: POSITION-SPECIFIC RESOURCES

At this point, it is time to focus on books arguing particular interpretations and positions. An overwhelming number of these exists. I hope to give you a place to begin by offering resources used and recommended by the mentors, along with several I found to be most helpful. Typically, these will fall into either the complementarian or egalitarian category. However, some will have shades of differences one way or another, in terms of advocating limited roles for women or no limits on roles for women. Therefore, I have generally categorized them under the descriptions "limited roles" and "no limits on roles."

Limited Roles, Equal Value

- *Different by Design: Discovering God's Will for Today's Man and Woman.* J. MacArthur, Jr. (Chariot Victor, 1994)
- *Does Christianity Squash Women? A Christian Looks at Womanhood.* R. Jones (Broadman & Holman, 2005)
- *Evangelical Feminism and Biblical Truth: An Analysis of More Than 100 Disputed Questions.* W. Grudem (Multnomah, 2004)
- *The Five Aspects of Woman: A Biblical Theology of Femininity.* B. Mouser (WinePress, 1995)

Barbara Mouser's *The Five Aspects of Woman* contributes to the discussion with a Bible study to show the basis for complementary roles for men and women from Genesis to Revelation. Mouser leads students through an examination of five passages from the Bible, which she proposes define the five subsequent "aspects" of woman.[1] Each aspect is studied from three perspectives: as it was created, as it was distorted by sin, and as it is redeemed and restored in Christ. Mouser's husband, William Mouser, developed a complementary Bible study on masculinity, *The Five Aspects of Man.*

- *Leadership for Women in the Church.* S. Hunt and P. Hutcheson. (Zondervan, 1991)
- *Male Spiritual Leadership,* Special Study Edition. F. L. Smith (21st Century Christian, 1998)
- *Man and Woman in Biblical Perspective.* J. Hurley. (Zondervan, 1991)

James Hurley's *Man and Woman in Biblical Perspective* is a complementarian work not to miss.[2] Hurley faithfully exegetes all of the controversial passages and attempts to ascertain a whole-Bible view of women's roles and worth, taking apostolic writings into account, as well. His *applications* tend to be hierarchical rather than moderate. His tone is irenic and his work extremely helpful overall.

1. Genesis 1: Mistress of the Domain; Genesis 2: Helper-Completer; Genesis 3: Life-Giver; Proverbs 1–9 and 31: Lady of Wisdom; 1 Corinthians 11 and Ephesians 5: Glory of Man.

2. It bears mentioning that Bilezikian's *Beyond Sex Roles* was written as a direct rebuttal to this book.

- *Men and Women, Equal Yet Different: A Brief Study of the Biblical Passages on Gender*. A. Strauch (Lewis & Roth, 1999)
- *Women and Men in Ministry: A Complementary Perspective*. Edited by R. L. Saucy and J. K. Tenelshof. (Moody, 2001)

Some consider this resource to be similar to *Recovering Biblical Manhood and Womanhood*, but more up-to-date.

- *Women and the Word of God: A Response to Biblical Feminism*. S. T. Foh. (Baker, 1979)

Susan Foh represents a position that attempts to mediate between what some view as too liberally or too hierarchically interpreting the "restrictive" biblical texts. Foh's interpretive decisions were made before the term "complementarian" was coined in *Recovering Biblical Manhood and Womanhood* in 1991. Her work is important, because she is one of the first women to undertake a thorough exegetical analysis, determine a theological interpretation in favor of limited roles, *and* achieve her goal responsibly in terms of its scholarly qualities. She also critiques the hermeneutical approaches of Christian feminists.

- *Women, Creation, and the Fall*. M. A. Kassian (Crossway, 1990)

In this work, Kassian offers one of her best contributions to the ongoing discussion of women's roles: modeling her critical thought process. She not only presents her conclusions, she examines different possible interpretations and explains why she finds each tenable or untenable.

No Limits on Roles

- *Beyond Sex Roles: What the Bible Says about a Woman's Place in Church and Family*. G. Bilezikian (Baker, 2006)

Prior to the advent of *Discovering Biblical Equality*, many considered Gilbert Bilezikian's *Beyond Sex Roles* (originally published in 1985) to be the definitive work for the egalitarian position. Adela Carter and Barbara Fletcher both listed this book as influential in their research.

> [Barbara Fletcher] I remember reading Bilezikian's *Beyond Sex Roles* and it was eye-opening to read and profoundly encouraging to me. It hit my heart.

- *Beyond the Curse: Women Called to Ministry*. A. B. Spencer (Thomas Nelson, 1985)

In this resource, Spencer wrote a biblical defense of evangelical feminism.

- *Finally Feminist: A Pragmatic Christian Understanding of Gender.* J. G. Stackhouse (Baker Academic, 2005)

Finally Feminist follows the same type of thinking as William Webb's book, *Slaves, Women and Homosexuals*, deducing that the biblical and theological *ideal* appears to be possibly more akin to an egalitarian image. However, Stackhouse finds the trajectory argument to be out-and-out in favor of egalitarianism. This book explores hermeneutics, but not in depth. On the other hand, this book is a *lot* shorter and much less technical than Webb's. It could be a good place to begin looking at the trajectory arguments. Both egalitarians and complementarians may feel a measure of fairness from his treatment, because he observes that the interpretive methods and conclusions of both sides have, at times, been faulty.

- *The Blue Parakeet: Rethinking How You Read the Bible.* S. McKnight. (Zondervan, 2008)

McKnight explores and explains biblical interpretation, helping readers to sharpen their skills and think of the Bible as story. He uses the issue of women's roles as the primary case study.

- *Gender or Giftedness: A Challenge to Rethink the Basis for Leadership within the Christian Community.* M. B. Smith (World Evangelical Fellowship, 2001)

Gender or Giftedness is a Bible study prepared by a committee for the World Evangelical Fellowship. This work aims to educate Christians who desire a deeper understanding of how to begin personal biblical research on this specific topic. It instructs on understanding the importance of hermeneutical framework and other interpretive considerations, such as issues that arise during Bible translation. It then attempts to assist the reader toward constructing a biblical theology regarding women's roles.

- *God's Women, Then and Now.* D. M. Gill and B. Cavaness (Grace and Truth, 2004)
- *God's Word to Women: One Hundred Bible Studies on Woman's Place in the Divine Economy.* K. Bushnell (Christians for Biblical Equality, 1923)

In considering books arguing for full equality, one might think it would be difficult to find solidly biblical resources on this topic that were published before the 1960s, or even the 1970s. However, in 1923 Katharine Bushnell published *God's Word to Women*, a series of one hundred exegetical Bible study lessons on the "woman question." She actually began her research before 1900! Bushnell was egalitarian before the term existed. Her exegesis includes some persuasive exegetical ideas that no other scholars on record had identified at that time—including some not widely known even today.[3]

- *Man and Woman, One in Christ: An Exegetical and Theological Study of Paul's Letters*. P. B. Payne (Zondervan, 2009)

Payne's work on the Pauline corpus is thorough, exacting, and scholarly. It has functioned as a game-changer for some.

- *Origins of Difference: The Gender Debate Revisited*. E. Storkey. (Baker Academic, 2001)

Storkey examines the historical, theoretical, and theological underpinnings of the gender debate.

- *Woman in the Bible: An Overview of All the Crucial Passages on Women's Roles*. M. J. Evans (InterVarsity, 1984)

Mary Evans wrote *Woman in the Bible* to treat the textual piece thoroughly, which she does well and concisely.

- *Women & Church Leadership: Contemporary Evangelical Perspectives*. E. M. Howe (Zondervan, 1982)

E. Margaret Howe exhibits methodical exegesis in *Women & Church Leadership* (1982). She also includes an inquiry into the real-time experiences of contemporary women in church leadership and in seminary. Karen Moy also recommended this resource.

- *Women in the Church: A Biblical Theology of Women in Ministry*. S. Grenz and D. M. Kjesbo (InterVarsity, 1995)

3. For example, in lessons thirteen through twenty of *God's Word to Women*, Bushnell goes "beyond reasonable doubt" to show that the sense of the obscure word *teshuqa* in Genesis 3:16 was known and accepted by the early church fathers as "turning" or some similar rendering, as in the wife turning toward her husband instead of toward God. Bushnell argues that *teshuqa* only began to be translated as "desire" during the 1400s, with Pagninus' version specifically, as a result of the influence of immoral teachings of the "Ten curses placed upon Eve" of the Babylonian Talmud and the Targum of Onkelos.

Women in the Church struck me by its irenic tone and evenhanded treatment of nearly every issue involved in the exegetical, historical, and cultural debates. Grenz and Kjesbo also engaged the practical implications of their conclusions. As they explain their biblical position, they continuously encourage an atmosphere of respect toward others' interpretations.

STEP 5:
OTHER HELPFUL RESOURCES

Interpretation

If you'd like to know more about interpreting the Bible and about learning to do more in-depth Bible study, try these resources:

- *How to Read the Bible for All Its Worth*, 3rd ed. G. D. Fee and D. K. Stuart (Zondervan, 2003).

Easy to read and chock full of useful information and teaching, this has become a "go-to" book for pastors, scholars, and lay people, alike when it comes to learning or teaching Bible interpretation to lay people.

- *Interpreting Biblical Literature: An Introduction to Biblical Studies.* M. R. Cosby (Stony Run, 2009).

Designed to be extremely engaging and user-friendly, Cosby's book succeeds at presenting an important and often heavy subject in manageable, informative segments. Chapters both inform and train. Lighthearted at points, it yet provides an excellent, thorough introduction to Bible interpretation.

Learning Exegesis

You may want to try some of these resources:

- *Biblical Exegesis: A Beginner's Handbook.* J. H. Hayes and C. R. Holladay. (Westminster John Knox, 2007).

In approachable language, this book introduces a person who has no experience with exegesis to all of the basic concepts of exegesis.

- *Interlinear for the Rest of Us: The Reverse Interlinear for New Testament Word Studies.* W. Mounce (Zondervan, 2006).

I love a good interlinear Bible! Bill Mounce, my Greek professor in seminary, produced this one, my latest favorite. Mounce, ever desiring for preachers and other shepherds to have the biblical tools necessary to shepherd and teach their flocks, even if they don't know Greek, made this as painless and complete as possible. The text is given first in English word order for an English reader's natural flow, with the Greek translation (in altered grammatical order) just below it. Then, he provides the Greek word order at the bottom of the page, because in Greek the word order is often significant for translation. You can use this tool immediately, starting the second it reaches your mailbox from Amazon.

- *The Complete Word Study Bible* and the *Key Word Study Bible* series by AMG Publishers. Includes these titles and others:
    A. *Hebrew-Greek Key Word Study Bible (NASB)* by S. Zodhiates (AMG, 2008). This is also available in NIV and KJV.
    B. *The Complete Word Study Dictionary: New Testament* by Spiros Zodhiates (AMG, 1992) or *Old Testament* by Warren Baker and Eugene Carpenter (2003).
    C. *The Complete Word Study New Testament* (1991) and *Old Testament* (1994).

These are classic resources for English readers. They were my first foray into biblical word studies. Because they are so easy to use, I'm confident that you'll be off to the races with word meanings within a half-hour of inspecting their pages.

Learning the Biblical Languages

If you want to learn the biblical languages, good for you. You will reap the reward of heaps upon heaps of delightful discoveries as you dig deeper into God's Word with your growing language skills. Remember, though, that learning any language requires commitment and time. Learning an ancient, dead language, though, adds an extra level of necessary commitment. I don't want to discourage or intimidate you any more than you may already be; but neither do I want you to believe that after a few lessons you will be accurately translating and interpreting Scripture.

Yet, if learning the languages is your desire, do it, and don't let anyone talk you out of it. Mentally "set your face like a flint" (nod to Isa 50:7) and just do it (nod to Nike). These resources will help you on your way:

- *Greek for the Rest of Us: Using Greek Tools without Mastering Biblical Greek*. William Mounce (Zondervan, 2007). Includes a CD-ROM.

Dr. Mounce's entire goal is to provide enough biblical Greek language skill that a person can do more thorough Bible study, including very basic translation and in-depth word studies. Early into the language learning, Mounce has you looking in your Bible at Greek words and phrases. By the end, you are learning to recognize and understand word tenses and other helpful and interesting aspects of Greek language, along with basic training in how to use Greek tools, technical commentaries for example. Learning the basics of biblical Greek will deepen your understanding of God's Word and enrich your ministry.

- *Hebrew for the Rest of Us: Using Hebrew Tools without Mastering Biblical Hebrew*. L. Fields (Zondervan, 2008)

Fields wrote this book as a companion to Mounce's and has similar goals. Both Mounce and Fields express one primary, valid concern: that language learners will think that, because they've gone through a book like these, they know as much as or more than Bible translators who have been studying Greek or Hebrew and their translations throughout their careers. Yet, I agree with them that the benefits of even a little knowledge and familiarity with the languages far outweigh the potential risks of that type of presumption.

In Fields' words, "the English-only Bible student can maximize the benefit gained from . . . original language tools. This basic knowledge empowers an English-only student to refine study techniques on the Bible itself and to read advanced secondary works such as dictionaries and commentaries that make direct reference to the original text. The goal is to move toward greater independence in OT studies."[4]

Both Mounce and Fields directly aim to help people "be careful and precise" when they study the Bible and have solidly-understood and "owned" beliefs, because they have studied the Bible for themselves.[5]

Be forewarned: these books, *Greek for the Rest of Us* and *Hebrew for the Rest of Us* are *courses*. Both require regular, consistent time investment and commitment to following them through. However, your rewards will be great. Bible study will never be the same again!

4. Fields, *Hebrew . . . Rest of Us*, ix.

5. Ibid., xii.

Historical References

In addition to exegetical and theological examinations of the Bible's words regarding women, you may want to learn more about women, their lives, and their words and witness throughout church history. Another good strategy is to examine what church leaders throughout history believed about women, their personhood, their capabilities, and their roles. One of the best ways to discover history's realities is by reading what are known as "primary-source" documents and other ancient historical evidence, along with secondary sources.

The term "primary source" refers to any document that is the actual, historic document or evidence. Primary sources can even include material evidence, such as a tomb inscription or an ancient legal document. Whatever it is, it is the original source. Secondary sources include anything else, whether documents or evidence, that was written or created by someone else *about* the actual historic document, but is not the source itself.

- *Women in the Early Church*. Message of the Fathers of the Church Series, vol. 13. E. Clark (M. Glazier, 1983)

Elizabeth Clark gathered primary source passages that are direct quotations from the early church fathers regarding women. Using these fascinating documents, you can read with your own eyes the interpretations and opinions of these important church figures, along with guidance through knowledgeable commentary from a professor of ancient Christianity.

Several other books contain both primary and secondary sources concerning women in Christian history and can give you a fuller picture of their lives and influence within and upon the church:

- *A Woman's Place: House Churches in Earliest Christianity*. Carolyn Osiek, Margaret Y. MacDonald, and Janet H. Tulloch (Augsburg Fortress, 2006)

- *Daughters of the Church: Women and Ministry from New Testament Times to the Present*. Ruth Tucker and Walter Liefeld (Academie, 1987)

- *Her Story: Women in Christian Tradition*. B. J. MacHaffie (Augsburg Fortress, 2006)

- *Maenads, Martyrs, Matrons, Monastics: A Sourcebook on Women's Religions in the Greco-Roman World.* R. S. Kraemer (Fortress, 1988)
- *Women in Early Christianity: Translations from Greek Texts.* Patricia Cox Miller (Catholic University of America Press, 2005)
- For an excellent source of other primary and secondary sources on women, and men who wrote about women, throughout the Middle Ages, check the tiny-print footnotes in *Luther on Women: A Sourcebook* by Susan C. Karant-Nunn and Merry E. Wiesner (Cambridge University Press, 2003).

Women and Theology

- *When Life and Beliefs Collide: How Knowing God Makes a Difference.* C. C. James (Zondervan, 2001)
- *The Gospel of Ruth: Loving God Enough to Break the Rules.* C. C. James (Zondervan, 2008)

I wasn't certain how to categorize Carolyn Custis James' books precisely, but knew I wanted to include these two in this resource strategy somewhere. James wants women everywhere to grow theologically and biblically in their relationship to God. In *Life and Beliefs*, particularly, she encourages this and teaches how to do it, directly and indirectly. At the same time, she encourages women that they're already "doing theology" the minute they ask "why?"[6]

More recently, she produced *Half the Church: Recapturing God's Global Vision for Women* (Zondervan, 2011), which doesn't address theological development directly, but does indirectly and still builds on her proposition of the *ezer*-warrier and Blessed Alliance ideas, put forth in her first books.

Psychological and Sociological Resources

- *Gender and Grace: Love, Work and Parenting in a Changing World.* M. S. Van Leeuwen (InterVarsity, 1990)

6. James, *Life and Beliefs*, 64.

In *Gender and Grace*, Van Leeuwen gives attention to similarities and differences between men and women, pointing out that Christians must not succumb to idolizing particular issues, but must work and strive to reflect their identities as the priesthood of believers in Christ. Karen Moy also recommended this as a resource.

- *My Brother's Keeper: What the Social Sciences Do (and Don't) Tell Us about Masculinity*. M. S. Van Leeuwen (InterVarsity, 2002)

Van Leeuwen reminds readers in *My Brother's Keeper* that the issue of women's roles does not exist in a vacuum. Men's roles, epistemologies, and socialization must be important considerations.

- *Women's Ways of Knowing: The Development of Self, Voice, and Mind* by M. F. Belenky *et al.* (Basic, 1997)

An absolutely fascinating work, not to be missed by any woman, is the seminal *Women's Ways of Knowing*. This composition provides a complement (and a bit of correction) to William Perry's epistemological studies that were an industry standard for nearly twenty years.[7] Perry's fifteen-year study, published in 1970, was based on male Harvard undergraduate subjects but accepted as highly accurate not only for all men but for women, as well.[8] The authors of *Women's Ways of Knowing* determined to understand how women identify, evaluate, and develop in knowledge. They concluded that there are five different perspectives from which women view reality, view themselves, and draw conclusions about truth, knowledge, and authority.

The Silent Knower is voiceless, unknowing that she can know anything for herself. She relies on others to tell her what to think. The Received Knower is a dualistic thinker, characterized by thinking in black and white categories only, with no gray scales whatsoever. She is unable to construct knowledge on her own, but depends upon "authorities" to inform her as to what is truth. Subjective Knowers reject all external knowledge and authorities, accepting only knowledge that comes from personal construction. Procedural Knowers, having realized that the inner voice is sometimes mistaken or misleading, actively engage in knowledge as a process for personal development. They believe in the

7. Perry, *Development in the College Years*. For a brief and helpful comparison of the works of Belenky, *et al.*, and Perry, see Mathews, *Prescription and Description*, 168–70.

8. See loc.gov/catdir/description/wiley035/98033543.html.

validity of their own, and others,' subjective knowledge, yet respect and systematically acquire external knowledge. Constructive Knowers view themselves as creators of knowledge, for themselves and for others. This epistemological perspective interacts critically and reflectively with both subjective and objective strategies for knowing.[9]

Even if you have never read a sociological study, you will find this easy to read—gripping, perhaps, as well as informative.

Feminism

Before reading about these final books in this literature review, please reach for a dictionary—or perhaps two or three dictionaries—and look up the word "feminism." After becoming familiar with a few definitions of the term, interested readers will benefit from reading

- *Feminist Thought: A More Comprehensive Introduction*. Rosemarie Putnam Tong, et al. (Westview, 2009)

You may wonder why I might recommend a non-Christian book on feminism in this book. I can provide three reasons for reading generally on the feminisms:

1. To gain awareness of exactly how broad the subject is.

Tong has compiled an essential resource for understanding the breadth of the range of the feminisms. In her own words: "feminism is not a monolithic ideology; . . . all feminists do not think alike, and . . . feminist thought has a past as well as a present and a future."[10]

2. So you can see with your own eyes exactly how feminists differ in their thinking.

Some feminists are merely "pro-woman"; other groups of feminists are extremely radical. Christians unaware of the range of the feminisms

9. William Perry was the originator of the standard epistemological categorizations with his work *Forms of Intellectual and Ethical Development in the College Years*. Perry's categories did not include a category analogous to Silent Knowing. The categories analogous to the others of Belenky, et al., were the following: "basic dualism" (received knowing), "multiplicity" (subjective knowing), "relativism" (procedural knowing), "full relativism" or "commitment" (constructed knowing). A side-by-side comparison of Belenky *et al.* and Perry may be viewed online at cs.buffalo.edu/~rapaport/perry.positions.html. A basic overview of Perry's "positions" may be found at perrynetwork.org/schemeoverview.html.

10. Tong, *Feminist Thought*, 1.

often believe and propagate the idea that who would place "feminist" after the word "evangelical" or "Christian" must by virtue of the label-sharing subscribe to the same ideas as the most radical feminists.

3. To dispel the pervasive fears many conservative Christians have about feminism.

I particularly hope that, equipped with factual knowledge and understanding, you will no longer have to *fear* either the word "feminist" or feminists themselves, or even question, "I wonder if I *am* a 'kind-of' feminist . . ." The more you read, the more you will know the facts. Subsequently, the more you will be able to speak out with greater confidence, either for or against—or somewhere in between.

As you learn more about the feminisms, should you choose to do so, you should know that some complementarians believe that feminism in *any* form undermines God's intentions for his people and contradicts his Word. Evangelical, conservative, moderate, radical—it doesn't matter where on the feminism spectrum it might lie; the understanding is that all feminist positions are based on presuppositions that are inherently unbiblical. Read more in these books:

- *Evangelical Feminism: A New Path to Liberalism?* W. Grudem (Crossway, 2006)

- *The Feminist Mistake: The Radical Impact of Feminism on Church and Culture*. M. Kassian (Crossway, 2005)

Ping, pong! It's always a volley in the ongoing published discussion on women's roles and the feminisms.

- *The Goddess Revival: A Biblical Response to God(dess) Spirituality*. A. B. Spencer, et al. (Wipf & Stock, 2010)

Spencer wrote *The Goddess Revival* as an evangelical, egalitarian response to neo-feminism.

- *What's Right with Feminism*. E. Storkey (SPCK, 1995)

Worldview

In "Mindkeeping 1," we explored the issue of our interpretive view, which is related to worldview. Read more on worldviews in these helpful resources. Note that these particular authors write from the Christian perspective, presenting a Christian worldview as normative. Still, they present basic and helpful introductions to and comparisons between major worldviews. Schaeffer's book explores Western thought in particular.

- *The Universe Next Door: A Basic Worldview Catalog.* J. W. Sire (InterVarsity, 2009)
- *How Now Shall We Live?* C. Colson, N. Pearcey, and H. Fickett (Tyndale House, 2004)
- *How Should We Then Live? The Rise and Decline of Western Thought and Culture.* F. A. Schaeffer (Crossway, 2005)

Miscellaneous Recommendations from Mentors

The resources in this section are listed in alphabetical order, by title.

- *Community 101: Reclaiming the Local Church as Community of Oneness.* G. Bilezikian (Zondervan, 1997). Recommended by Susan McCormick and Alice Mathews.

The first several chapters lay out not only a biblical theology for community, but for male and female personhood in God's image as foundational to the understanding of community.

- *Dream Big: The Henrietta Mears Story.* E. O. Roe (Regal, 1990). Recommended by LaVerne Tolbert.

> [LaVerne Tolbert] There were a number of other resources I consulted, outside of the Bible. I can't say that any one author shaped a philosophy of ministry for me on women in ministry. The one *person* who impacted me the most was Henrietta Mears, because of her *example*. She *did* the work of the ministry and she didn't have any title. But that woman did *more* to influence the Christian world!
>
> And *none* of my seminary professors mentioned her! I just kind of stumbled upon her at the end of my seminary training. I think she should be required reading for everyone in seminary. Her book *Dream Big* was a major, major influence in helping to confirm my stance for women in ministry. She didn't argue, but she trained men and women in the ministry. Every class I teach, I require my students to read about her.

- *Enduring Grace: Living Portraits of Seven Women Mystics.* C. L. Flinders (HarperOne, 1993)

[Karen Moy] It helps to read outside the evangelical tradition; so I picked up something at a monastery once called *Enduring Grace: Living Portraits of Seven Women Mystics.* It's intriguing.

- *Equal to the Task.* R. H. Barton. (InterVarsity, 1998)

[Karen Moy] I haven't read it all, but what I read has helped me.

- *Neither Slave Nor Free: Helping Women Answer the Call to Church Leadership.* P. Gundry (HarperCollins, 1990). Recommended by LaVerne Tolbert.

- "Second-Class Citizenship in the Kingdom of God." R. A. Schmidt. In *Our Struggle to Serve: The Stories of 15 Evangelical Women.* Edited by Virginia Hearn (Word, 1995).

[Jeanette Yep] I met for a while with Ruth Schmidt, who in '71 wrote the first *Christianity Today* article on "why the double standard in the church?" Ruth's story is in *Our Struggle to Serve.*

- *Sexual Ethics: A Biblical Perspective.* S. J. Grenz (Word, 1990).

[Candie Blankman] Theologically and biblically, Stanley Grenz's book *Sexual Ethics* was probably, for a long time, the most helpful resource for articulating what I believe. It's a must-read, because he was the first person who ever had a theology of *sexuality,* as opposed to a theology of the issue of women in ministry, or a theology of child rearing, or a theology of all the issues related to it. *He* starts out with a theology of sexuality, where he lays the biblical and theological (Old Testament as well as New) groundwork for what is *at the heart* of us being created as sexual beings. The idea is that there is a foundational *sameness*—equality—to men and women that is the overarching scriptural principle and it is affirmed in Scripture.

So, Grenz was helpful to me in putting theological teeth to something that I just knew in my gut and I *knew* that the whole of Scripture speaks to it when you look at it.

- *The Priscilla Papers* (CBE). *The Priscilla Papers* are a publication of Christians for Biblical Equality. http://www.cbeinternational.org/?q=content/priscilla-papers-journal. Recommended by Jeanette Yep. The equivalent publication produced by the Council on Biblical Manhood and Womanhood is their journal, *The Journal for Biblical Manhood and Womanhood*: https://www.cbmw.org/journal/.

- *Women at the Crossroads: A Path beyond Feminism and Traditionalism*. Kari T. Malcolm (InterVarsity, 1982). Karen Moy, LaVerne Tolbert, and Jeanette Yep all read and recommended Malcom's book.

- *Women in the Maze: Questions and Answers on Biblical Equality* by Ruth A. Tucker. (InterVarsity, 1992). Recommended by LaVerne Tolbert.

Appendix C

"Where Do I Start?" A Case Study in Interpretation

1 Timothy 2:9–15

INTRODUCTION TO OUR CASE STUDY

SOME PEOPLE MIGHT SUGGEST that only the "prohibitive" and controversial verses need to be studied and discussed in order to make a decision about women's roles. I believe, however, that all of Scripture is involved.

Christians seek the "whole counsel" of God on important issues. Important issues are typically complex in all of life; so, we should avoid thinking simplistically about the Bible. A passage that either "frees" or "prohibits" one believer may not have the same effect on another believer. We've already determined that simply finding verses that support what you already think won't cut it. It's also foolish to find two or three passages that seem similar and think we've "sought the whole counsel of God" on the matter.

Instead, we want to find answers that are not only workable, but biblically and theologically *defendable*. To do this, many questions need to be asked and answered.[1]

But you have to start somewhere. Therefore, we're going to use 1 Timothy 2:9–15 as a learning tool. Ironically, however, you should not

1. Reminder: you can find my list of questions at www.womenleadershipbible.com. You might use this list as fodder for a women's Bible study on women's identity and roles.

begin your case study on this passage by scrutinizing it under your critical-thinking microscope. Wait until after you read these next few pages and prep yourself for the text. In the section entitled "Get into the Text," you will begin your examination in earnest.

Why 1 Timothy 2:9–15?

I chose this passage for three primary reasons:

- Every mentor counted it as important, even pivotal, in her research.
- Every mentor commented on it during the interviews; some even expounded on it at length. Also, well over half of the 315-plus Christian women who responded to an in-depth, written survey I conducted for my doctoral research referred to this passage either as the key to their understanding of women's roles or as an enormous question-mark in their understanding of women's roles.
- A great many Christians understand this passage differently, or don't understand it at all.

This passage causes a lot of consternation for a lot of people. Many of those written-survey respondents who referred to this passage expressed that they did not fully understand it, but still believed women should not be in leadership roles in the church.

One could argue that it's the most controversial passage on women's roles in the church. I figured we might as well go for the jugular.

Many details make this passage difficult to understand. One detail involves the difficulty of defining and truly understanding at least one of the passage's key words (*authentein* in verse 12). This word appears only one time in the New Testament. The term for this type of singular occurrence is *hapax legomenon* (see discussion of this term on page 131). An additional *hapax* occurs in verse 15 (*teknogonias*), another verse that defies an easy read. Of course, this situation brings a challenge for every person who takes up the investigation.

Despite its difficulties, it remains a key passage that many who limit women's roles believe most unmistakably applies to this issue in this passage. And, of course, it remains one for which others continue to seek alternative readings.

Because it is difficult to fully understand, many people chose to "err on the safe side," limiting women's roles until they know more. And that's okay. That is, it's okay *until* you can get around to doing your own study of it.

I do believe every believer should get around to studying this issue in-depth, and this passage in particular. Its impact on the life of the church as a whole, not *only* the lives of women, is too far-reaching to ignore or to remain ignorant about it.

Note: What This Case Study is Not

This case study includes starting thoughts for every step from part 2, "Get into the Text!" The goal is for you to see how to begin to ask questions of the text in a critically thoughtful way, in order to become more informed. What you will *not* find here is a decision, position, or one-right-answer for what this text means.

WORKING THROUGH THE PASSAGE

Notice to the faint of heart—or to those like me who may not be faint of heart, but simply have a hard time making decisions:

- Eventually, you are going to have to make choices about all of these questions.
- Interpretations and conclusions *always* involve making choices.
- So, brace yourself.

Step 1: Check Your Objectivity

Begin your case study now by reading the passage, but don't apply any critical analysis to it just yet. Instead, accompany your initial reading by revisiting your two "best friends" who help with your objectivity (see page 95).

Search your heart and mind, asking yourself, "What do I currently understand this passage and the words contained in it to mean? Why do I have that understanding? Is it primarily because of my culture? My denomination? My pastor? My own prior study? A book I read? Dramas and plays I've seen? It just seemed normal or 'natural' to me? Something else?"

Folks on all "sides" of this issue are guilty of acting upon and believing in what their church or denomination says or does, or looking for what they want to see in the text, without having studied it for themselves beyond face-value. Ask the Holy Spirit to give you the ability to view the Word with fresh, unsullied eyes. Ask for wisdom. Ask for grace.

Step 2: Get Your "Mindkeeping" Done: Line Up Your Principles and Starting Points

Line up your principles and starting points; however, still don't start your exegetical scrutiny yet. Your first question to answer is,

- What interpretive principle(s) will I apply to Scripture—every time?

Go back to "Mindkeeping 2: Establish Your Interpretive Principles" (page 101). Read over the list of principles other people use and choose one (or more), or clearly state your own.

> **Your Turn:**
>
> What interpretive principle or principles have you decided upon? List them.

For example, consider whether you think this and all other passages should be read in a plain-text reading (see page 102) or differently. If differently, then how?

Remember, the principle(s) you apply today should be the principles with which you approach all of your Scripture study all the time—not just this particular study of this particular passage.

For example, Mary Ann Hawkins spoke about Scripture interpreting Scripture and how that may be affected by whichever controlling verse one chooses.

> The whole "authority" word—"I don't let a woman have authority over her husband" (or over "a man," depending on whose interpretation you're using) . . . Well, what is "authority"?
>
> And nobody—*nobody*—knows what that *particular* word for authority meant in that context.

> Everybody has agreed that it has one of three meanings. Which one you choose determines how you translate that. And everybody waffles on this: "Well, it could mean this or it might mean that and it might be this . . ."
>
> Nobody knows.
>
> Since it is the only time that word is used, why don't we throw it out and not make that a defining moment? I don't think you can make that verse a definitive, for all time, for all place type of thing.

Remember, that's what Mary Ann decided; but, as with any of the opinions expressed in this book, it's not the "gospel truth." You don't have to do the same thing, unless you agree with her reasoning and think, for yourself, that the whole of Scripture "walks" together best that way, to borrow Mary Ann's phrase.

Your second question to answer is:

- With what starting points of agreement can I personally agree?

Your Turn:

Review the examples of starting points on page 114.
With which starting points do you agree? List them.
These are foundational beliefs. Why do you believe them?

Get into the Text

Now, it's time to move to the text. Here, you can begin to apply your basic exegesis skills, as you learned to do in step 3, Study.

First, pray. Then, read the passage. From this point on, write down every question about the passage and related passages that comes to your mind. There is no such thing as a dumb question. Ebay says, "If you want something, someone's selling it on Ebay!" I say, "If *you* wonder about something in the Bible, someone else does, too." Ask the text—and yourself—a bunch of questions. You are hereby granted permission. Don't be afraid.

Also, keep notes. *Write everything down!* You'll be glad you kept track of your findings and all that you learned, because it will help you sort through the complexity of the issue.

Remember, though, this is not purely a cerebral, scholarly process. You'll have to do some soul-searching. These issues run deep, as we have already seen in the first steps. So, pray *all the way.*

Aside from commentaries, you may choose to use other books in your research. Here is a suggested reading list to help you get started. It includes varying perspectives and interpretations. Gather them (remember: beg, borrow, or Ebay!) and keep them together for easy reference.

You might begin with the pertinent chapters in *Recovering Biblical Manhood and Womanhood* (particularly chapter 9) and *Discovering Biblical Equality* (particularly chapter 12).

- *I Suffer Not a Woman: Rethinking 1 Timothy 2:11–15 in Light of Ancient Evidence.* R. C. Kroeger and C. C. Kroeger (Baker, 1992).
- *Man and Woman, One in Christ: An Exegetical and Theological Study of Paul's Letters.* P. B. Payne (Zondervan, 2009).
- *Women in the Church: An Analysis and Application of 1 Timothy 2:9–15*, 2nd ed. Edited by A. Kostenberger and T. Schreiner (Baker Academic, 2005).
- You may also want to review the suggestions included in Appendix B.

EXEGESIS STEP 1: EXAMINE THE ANCIENT CULTURE

Acknowledge the Culture Differences

Remember that the original writer was not writing to *us*. Thinking otherwise will lead us to a very misinformed interpretation! The author communicated to an audience in a specific time and involved in a specific culture. The truths may yet apply to us today; but we *must* consider their original context.

Do Your Ancient Culture Research

Using resources listed in chapter 11 for researching the ancient culture (page 120), find out all you can about Paul's world and the culture in Ephesus, in particular. Use the checklist below to prompt your studies. Write down your answers.

Table 1. Your Checklist for Exegesis Step 1: Examining the Ancient Culture

✓ Checklist: Examining the Ancient Culture What Does the Historical and Cultural Context Tell Us about This Passage and/or This Scene?	
☐	Consult a Bible atlas. What information can you gain regarding the location of the story? Is there any particular significance to that particular place? Its history? Its geography?
☐	What archaeological evidence sheds light on the culture contemporary to the story?
☐	What sociological studies of that time period give you insight into that culture? Paul? The Ephesians (they were the ones receiving this letter)? The people spoken about in the text?
☐	What would have been normal in Paul's culture?
☐	Do any extra-biblical texts (meaning outside the Bible) that were contemporary to the Bible impact your reading of 1 Timothy?
☐	What images from this passage have been passed down through Christian traditions?
☐	Are these different from the original scenario as we now see and understand it from the cultural and historical evidences?
☐	Compare those to what you've found in 1 Timothy and what you've learned about the ancient culture.
☐	Notice any differences you find, remembering that readers contemporary to the story would assume many of these images and priorities, while they are mostly foreign to us.

Examine Ancient Sociological Evidence

What sociological evidence sheds light on the passage? Ask the obvious questions (who, what, when, where, why, and how) and proceed to the less obvious ones. What would have been normal in Paul's culture? What concerns did Paul and his contemporaries have? What was he attempting to address in the book?

Choose two or three commentaries on 1 Timothy. A Bible background commentary may prove to be a helpful resource. Read through and take notes on the pages that introduce the historical and sociological context. Then glance through the pages that pertain to these specific verses.

LaVerne Tolbert shared how a sociological possibility she learned about influenced her interpretation of 1 Timothy 2.

As far as my particular scriptural questions about women in the church, the main one centered on 1 Timothy 2: "women should keep quiet in the church, let a woman learn in silence and all submission" and "I do not permit woman to teach or to hold authority over a man, but to be in silence."

Until I understood the *cultural setting* of that mandate, I wrestled with women's roles in the church.

But, I learned that the Jewish women were asking their husbands questions out of turn, screaming questions down to the floor, asking, "What do they mean?! I don't understand!"

Paul said, "Let the women keep quiet. Let them ask their husbands at home." That made so much sense to me. Certainly, God wasn't saying that women couldn't teach or speak at all in church.

The church, especially the black church, is 80 percent women. Women have leadership roles in every area. So, if women kept quiet in the church, we wouldn't *have* any church.

My second main question was regarding the next chapter in Timothy, about elders and deacons being men. Whenever leadership is talked about, it is never in the female sense, it's always in the male sense. In the context, it's definitely gender-specific. These were the things I wrestled with.

My conclusion is that these were *cultural.* In light of Jewish women's lack of education and lack of standing in their society, it made sense. Culturally, it cannot translate as a mandate in our culture today—in Western civilization.

We don't see it in other cultures of the world, for example in South Africa. When I have visited South Africa, I have seen that women hold prominent positions in the church and it is not questioned. Women are just serving.

Kathy Keller's conclusions were influenced by sociological research regarding ancient Jewish synagogue worship:

Wrestling with "what did it really mean for women to keep silent in 1 Corinthians 14 and for women not to teach men with authority in 1 Timothy 2, the most helpful person I ran into was James Hurley, who wrote *Men and Women in Biblical Perspective*. I've studied other people who've only confirmed what Hurley suggested, which was that the early church's worship was modeled on synagogue worship.

You did not have a professional minister in residence; you had traveling apostles, "wanna-be" apostles, and false teachers. Or, if you didn't have anybody coming through that day, you had somebody from your congregation who stood up.

In 1 Corinthians, the order of worship is that everybody contributes something: a word of instruction, a revelation, a tongue. Everyone speaks. And it says, "Two or three prophets should speak and the others should weigh carefully what is said." And *this* is where women are supposed to be silent.

More Ancient-Culture Food for Thought

Verse 15. As you read various resources, you will find that many scholars try to understand this verse by considering the influence a group called the Gnostics had in Ephesus. If you think that has any credibility, what light might it shed on the passage?

It is *possible* that the relationship of Gnosticism to the Christians in Ephesus impacted Paul's words and reasoning in verses 13–15. Reading it in this manner might possibly explain why verse 15 is there, when it otherwise seems rather tacked-on. What theories can you find? What can you make of it?

How Archaeology Impacted One Mentor's Understanding of the Passage

Timothy and the others for whom Paul intended the letter lived in the city of Ephesus, which is on the western coast of what is now Turkey. During a trip there, Mary Ann Hawkins gained some possible understandings on 1 Timothy 2:15 from archaeology.

> Twelve of my female friends and I had an opportunity in 1999 to go to Turkey for two weeks where we did a seven-churches tour. A Church of God missionary there was trying to get some tourism stuff happening for Christians. She hired a Muslim professional woman to be our tour guide. When we were in Ephesus, I gained so much understanding of things in Scripture.
>
> Timothy was in Ephesus at the time 1 Timothy was written. So understanding the city of Ephesus and the cultural context at that time brought a lot of clarity for me.

The Muslim tour guide and I were standing on the street beside the Celsus library. It's actually [near] a brothel that was built and had a common wall with the gymnasium where the baths were. They have found a tunnel that actually goes from the gymnasium into the library.

So a man could say to his family, "I'm going to the library to study," then take the tunnel into the gymnasium, which has a door into the brothel. So there is a connection in that process.

One of the greatest heresies of the era was Gnosticism, which taught the division of physical and spiritual. And this Muslim tour guide, as she is standing and explaining all of this to me, looks at me and says, "You know, your American theologians don't have a clue about that Timothy passage that talks about women will be saved through childbirth. Look at this." She took me over to walled-in area that looks like a well.

She said, "This is the well of the babies. If a woman, particularly a woman of the brothel, made it through childbirth, this is where her baby was pitched, because however spiritual her intention was being, they couldn't bring material things into this world and maintain their salvation because of the Gnostic belief. So, this is the well where the babies were thrown.

"See, Gnosticism was a prevalent part of the worship of Diana, also called Artemis, the female deity worshiped prominently in Ephesus. Involvement in sexual *activity* was permissible and was spiritual, but *conception* was not, because the physical was evil and the spiritual was good. So you should not *produce* anything that is evil. It has to be discarded.

"And there were many medical processes that killed women and their babies. All Paul is saying to the married women who were good Christian women is, 'Stay in a monogamous relationship and trust the Lord and he will bring you through the birth process and he will save your child. You are going to be safe.' Not '*saved*,' but 'safe.' I don't know where you Christians get the idea it says 'saved.'"

Now that's the way that Muslim, Turkish woman explained it. It makes sense to me, because the whole Gnosticism thing was part of what Paul was addressing in his letter to the Ephesians and in part of his first letter to Timothy. But there are also issues of Gnosticism that are addressed in Corinthians. Almost every time heresy is spoken of, it comes back to the Gnostic beliefs. It was incredibly prevalent in the first century of the church. (Actually, I think it's pretty prevalent now, too. I see it.)

So I am just listening to this Muslim woman's theology about this passage. She lives there. And I am thinking, "That's really interesting! It makes really good sense to me."

Whether her ideas are correct or not, I see her *interpretation* is every bit as valid as many of the other ones I have heard!

This brings me to the point of reiterating once again how we need to chew our own food. My husband, who is a trained archaeologist and went to Ephesus for archaeological study, differed with that tour guide on both the location of the structures and the existence of the tunnel.

After comparing his memory against his actual maps and checking out some things online, he told me, "Well, it wasn't a gymnasium, it was a bath [as in, Turkish baths] and the locations don't seem to match up exactly with what her tour guide told her. Lots of tour guides tell the story about the brothel and the tunnel. But, tour guides say a lot of things that simply are not accurate."

This, of course, sheds at least some doubt on the tour guide's interpretation, too, since it was supposedly based on archaeological findings.

So, like Mary Ann did not, *we* don't merely swallow whatever someone tells us, even if they're an "authority" we're paying to tell us interesting stuff we didn't already know! Even if they live right there in the location in question and we don't. We *consider* their ideas, but weigh them against other sources. In this case, it would mean that we compare the tour guide's claims against scholarly archaeological findings. This, my friends, defines critical thinking.

EXEGESIS STEP 2: EXAMINE THE LITERARY CONTEXT

Remember, the literary context of the actual passage includes both what the author has written in the passage and elsewhere in the same book, and what the author has written in other books. You can *absolutely* use commentaries to find these answers—in fact, you *should*, and you should use several. In a typical commentary, this kind of contextual information is usually included in the introductory paragraphs (or pages) of the section or chapter that covers the particular biblical book. If it's an entire commentary volume devoted to one book of the Bible, you may find it in several of the first chapters.

Table 2. Your Checklist for Exegesis Step 2: Examining the Literary Context

✓ Checklist: Examining the Literary Context The Central Message and the Greater Context of the Passage Questions to Ask, Research, and Answer	
☐	What book contains the passage?
☐	Who wrote it?
☐	When was it written or recorded?
☐	Where was the author when he wrote that book or recorded this event? Under what circumstances did he write it?
☐	To whom did he write it (who was the audience)?
☐	What circumstances were those recipients in and why?
☐	Why did the events occur?
☐	Why did the writer include this narrative or these statements? How does it (or how did they) fit in this theme or purpose?
☐	How did it come to the original recipients? In other words, what *type* of writing is it (genre)?
☐	Was it arriving as a . . . letter? Sermon? Book? Oral story/parable? A teaching by Jesus? Prophecy?
☐	Where did the events described in the passage (and in the book overall) take place?
☐	What comes before this particular passage of interest? What comes after it?
☐	What situation(s) are being addressed, or assertions being made, just before this passage? Just after? Overall in the section? Overall in the book?
☐	What happened just after the passage as a result of what occurred in the passage you're studying?
☐	Consider what this passage (and the book overall) teaches or contains: History? Laws/legal writings/contracts? Parables? Proverbs (wisdom literature)? Psalms? Poetry? Songs? Prophecy? A teaching of Jesus? Interpretation of OT Scripture?
☐	What is the *central message* of this paragraph? Its surrounding section? The book?
☐	Consider why the author may have situated this particular passage where it is within the book. What if it was *not* situated at that place? What if it was somewhere else? What if it wasn't there at all? What difference might that make?

Mary Ann Hawkins considered the verses preceding our specific passage:

> It says in the first part of that [2:8] that men are to lift holy hands in prayer. That means every time I see my husband pray (or any other

> man in the church), he'd better have his hands in the air? What was going on that Paul needed to say, "Lift holy hands in prayer"?
>
> Well, evidently there were other things going on with the men. There was another issue that was happening there.
>
> And then you come down to the whole thing about being saved through childbirth [2:15]. Well, my sister, who can't have children, can't be saved. Her own sin made it so that she was born without ovaries?
>
> You can't take them in a literal interpretation and make it stick. It will not walk with Scripture, with the whole body of the Word. It just won't.

Phyllis Bennett also addressed this passage's literary context in one of the personal position papers she shared with me:

> Paul in chapter 2 begins by making a positive appeal, not just to Timothy but to all in the body to offer prayers, intercessions, and thanksgivings for everyone, particularly those in governmental authority (kings) that the church may live peaceful quiet lives (verses 1 and 2) leading to the salvation of all men (verse 3). Keeping with this theme of lives free of turmoil creating an atmosphere conducive for salvation, Paul transitions into identifying some restrictions on the general conduct of both sexes that might also bring about this desired result. First, he addresses men, then women, using parallel phrases: "I want."
>
> 1. "I want . . ." Men are not to get their way by being angry, but are to lift up holy hands in prayer without anger or dispute (verse 8).
> 2. Next, he addresses women and lays out two restrictions. The first he begins by saying, "I also want women to dress modestly, with decency and propriety, not ostentatiously (with braided hair or gold or pearls or expensive clothes) but modestly (verse 9), implying they are not to get their identity from their clothes.
> 3. His second restriction for women begins with a similar, somewhat parallel verb form, but stated negatively: "I do not permit a woman to teach or have authority over a man; she must be silent." She is also to "learn in quiet and full submission."
>
> Woman's whole attitude toward learning should be that of learning in quietness (not silence) and full submission.

Phyllis concludes by saying, "Therefore, in context this full submission [by a woman] should be expressed mainly by not allowing herself to be put in the role of an elder."

That may seem like a bit of a leap to you, since "elders" are not mentioned in verses 9–15. To fill you in, Phyllis concluded from studying other passages that

(1) There is an "office" of the church called "elder," which consists of a decision-making role, and

(2) The office of elder is restricted to men.

Her conclusions, based on other passages, obviously influenced her reading of 1 Timothy 2. She was trying to consider this passage in its greater context. Notice, too, how Phyllis looks to the grammar and sentence structure (i.e., parallel phrases denoted by "I want") to understand what Paul was saying.

Ask questions of the text and make observations. Look for how this passage goes together with the passages around it. What situation was Paul addressing? Why are these statements together? What are they getting at? Overall, how do they "walk with the rest of Scripture," as Mary Ann describes?

This idea of "walking with Scripture" relates to the consistency with which we view and interpret Scripture. Hopefully, these situations encourage us to revisit our interpretive principles, to make sure we're applying the same standards to the Bible every time we study, especially within the same passage.

As Mary Ann says, it's all got to "walk" together somehow.

EXEGESIS STEP 3: EXAMINE THE LITERARY CONTENT

Words and Grammar

Look at the words and grammar in this passage and in other passages attributed to the author. Use the checklist below to prompt your study. Write down all of your findings.

Table 3. Your Checklist for Exegesis Step 3: Examining the Literary Content

✓ Checklist: Examining the Literary Content Words, Grammar and Points of Comparison
☐ Read slowly and purposefully through the passage, vv. 9–15. Write down any of your own questions that arise.
☐ Overall, what does the author say in *this* passage and how does he say it?
Literary Content Step 1: Examine the words in the original language.
☐ 1. What words are *actually* used in the original text? Assuming you've already begged for or borrowed (I'll stop short at thinking you might possibly have stolen one . . .) an interlinear Bible from someone or explored some online interlinear tools, look at the Greek words Paul actually used.
☐ 2. Now check several translations (or use an online parallel Bible feature). How have the words used been translated in several translations?
☐ 3. Definitions: Understand the possible meanings of the words in a sentence. There may be several variations of meaning for a particular word or words. (Use the dictionaries, wordbooks, and lexicons you've found.) For each key word, ask:
☐ • Is this word used several times in this passage? How is it used each time? Gather information on how Paul used that word throughout 1 Timothy. Eventually, gather information on how he used it in other books attributed to him, also.
☐ • Look at the English translations you have. Have any other (different) original-language words been translated into English the same way this one has been translated? (Remember the "love" example?) Again, you can use an interlinear for this.
☐ • If Paul didn't use the word again, did any other biblical authors use it? How?
☐ • Note any *hapax legomena*.
☐ 4. Now that you've studied it thoroughly, answer the question, "What do you think this word (or these words) mean in *this* text?"
Literary Content Step 2: Examine the grammar in the original language. Understand the relationships of words in a sentence and how they relate to each other. (Use the commentaries and any grammatical aids you've found.)
☐ 5. What does the grammar of this text show us? Diagram the passage's sentences, preferably in the original language. (Refer to page 132 for tips on diagramming resources.)
☐ 6. How does the author support, or "ground," his statements? (Remember "because" and "for"? See page 134.)

Literary Content Step 3: Look at the words and grammar the author uses in other passages attributed to him.

☐ 1. What words does he use in various other places for the same or similar concepts and how does he use them?

☐ 2. How does the author refer to or describe that same thing in other places?

☐ 3. Does the author use the same word(s) each time? Does he use those particular words or closely related words elsewhere in that book or other books attributed to him?

☐ 4. How does the author support, or "ground," his statements in other writings?

☐ 5. Does he use the same or different grammatical structures in other places?

☐ 6. What kinds of emphases does he choose to make throughout his writings?

Literary Content Step 4: Read commentaries on the passage and the book as a whole.

☐ 1. What theories do you find and what theological insights can you gain about the passage? Each verse? The book?

Literary Content Step 5: Look for points of comparison in the Bible, including the "silent" passages.

1. Find and compare similar theological issues.

☐ • Where else has this same *topic* been discussed in Scripture?

☐ • Has this *situation* arisen anywhere else?

☐ • Who raised it?

☐ • What did they say?

☐ • What was the argument? How was it grounded (what reasons were given for it)?

2. Find and compare different theological issues that are argued similarly or that simply shed more light on the passage or issue.

☐ • Are any other, *different* theological issues in Scripture argued the same way as some of the statements in 1 Timothy 2:9–15?

☐ • How is the issue or situation similar? How is it different?

☐ • How does this shed light on your passage of interest?

☐ • What is its trajectory? Is it continuing something? Ending something? Fulfilling something?

☐ • Do any other, *different* theological issues in Scripture shed more light on 1 Timothy 2:9–15? (Remember also the "silent" passages, as in passages that don't speak directly to the women's issue.)

Examples: Studying Words

Many of the mentors expressed how complicated the word *authentein* in verse 12 makes things, because it is a *hapax legomenon*. (Don't you feel brilliant and scholarly now, knowing what that fancy Latin phrase means?) Mary Ann Hawkins expressed the difficulty that arises in translation and interpretation because of it:

> That particular word for authority is used only in that place in Scripture and what it means is not explained.
>
> In Greek antiquity, it has three meanings. Which one do you want to pick? I can go that way with an explanation.

Karen Moy spoke about how an interpretation is always a choice, *especially* when a word is only used one time in the Bible.

> When I started encountering people who thought women should not speak or teach, I wondered why. So I did my own research, *because* I ask my own questions and I "chew my own food."
>
> And I now understand their conclusions, even though I think their conclusions are flawed. And I think their conclusions are a *choice*.
>
> At the time that we joined the church Ed and I are about to leave, their stated position was that women could not be elders.
>
> I engaged the senior pastor during our membership interview: "Do you at least agree that pretty much your entire position against women being elders hangs on one verse in the entire Bible [meaning 1 Timothy 2:12]? In that one verse, it hangs on one word [*authentein*]. That *one* word in Greek appears nowhere else in the Bible and in extra-biblical sources it is frequently translated as '*usurp* authority' rather than '*have* authority,' which would then change the meaning of that phrase to 'I do not allow women to *usurp* authority.' Do you agree that we cannot be certain as to the meaning of that word?"
>
> And he said, "Yes."
>
> "So therefore you must agree with me that you have chosen an interpretation of that word, as have I."
>
> He said, "Yes, more or less."
>
> "You have chosen a *restrictive* understanding of that word, and I have chosen a *larger* one of that word."

> He said, "Yes."
>
> I said, "Okay. I just wanted to hear you acknowledge your position as a choice and not because you have done a lot more research than I have or that you have reached some penultimate, obvious conclusion. My stated position is that there is sufficient ambiguity in the text to allow for women to be elders. And your stated position is that there is *in*sufficient ambiguity in the text to allow for that. But we *both* have to agree that it is all hinging on one word, and we are not sure what that word means."
>
> And he said, "Yes."
>
> I said, "Okay. I just wanted to be really clear about that."
>
> I think the jury is still out. Maybe there are extra-biblical sources that will come along to help us understand that Greek better some day. But right now, with all the reading I did, I incline toward saying, "I don't think it means what everybody thinks it obviously means."
>
> And I read all the stuff from Christians for Biblical Equality and I read the stuff in *Recovering Biblical Manhood and Womanhood*. I've read them all. They all seem very earnest. Still I incline toward saying that I think it's not entirely clear or specific here.

I mentioned earlier that Phyllis Bennett and other mentors wrote papers to help themselves learn about and work through these issues. In one of these, Phyllis thought through how grammatical construction may shed light on Paul's commands. Notice her emphasis on the conjunction *oude* and what a difference it can make in one's interpretation.

> [Some people say,] "1 Timothy 2:12 says women are not to teach or exercise authority over men; And these are two different ministries, each of which are restricted to men."
>
> Although it is true that these two can function as two separate ministries, I don't believe that Paul's intent was to speak of them as separate in this passage. Paul is saying there that he does not allow a woman to teach "or" (*oude)* have authority over a male. *Oude* can be used as a disjunctive, "this or that," as in "male or female," or it can be used as a conjunctive, implying teach *and* have authority over.
>
> In that Paul moves from this topic to his next topic with a connecting phrase, "It is a trustworthy saying," this connective expression implies linkage between the role of elder [in 1 Timothy

3] and that which comes just prior in 2:11–15. By this connection Paul is implying that an elder is commissioned to the same dual role from which a woman is restricted to participate, namely that of teaching *and* exercising authority.

Therefore, I believe Paul is saying in 2:11–12 that a woman is not to be in the role of an elder and therefore not to carry out the responsibilities of final authoritative teaching and exercising authority over a body of believers. This role distinction is limited only to the men of a local congregation. Therefore, it was not Paul's intent in 1 Timothy 2:12 to say that women were excluded from two separate ministries, but from one office, that of elder.

Tidbits to Stimulate Your Thinking about the Words

Consider these key-word questions as you study:

Verse 11. Do a word study on the Greek word *manthaneto*. What range of meanings do you find for that word in your theological wordbook or dictionary? Note that it is the only imperative (command) in the sentence, indeed in the whole passage. What purpose do you think this imperative verb serves in this context?

Verse 12. The "authority-word," *authentein*, in verse 12 appears one time in the New Testament—a *hapax legomenon*. With no other instances in the Bible to which to compare it in an apples-to-apples way, finding a range of its meanings or understanding its use in this passage is difficult. Paul here could have used the word for "to lord it over" or "to rule" or "to manage," but he did not, although he used those words elsewhere.

- How does this fact inform your interpretation of that word, *authentein*?
- Use your word resources to consider the range of possible meanings of *authentein*. Make your list.
- Consider the word in its passage and think about which definition might fit best.
- Now consider it in light of its connection to "to teach" (*didaskein*).
    - As Phyllis said, the connective word *oude* is used between "to teach" and "to have authority," which places the latter as a modifier of the first. Therefore, it was teaching *of a certain sort* that these women were prohibited from. (If right now you're

thinking, "Hey, this is grammar, not strictly words!" you're right. Sometimes these things have to be considered outside of their designated section.)

- What do you think, then? Was Paul prohibiting women from thrusting their own teaching on the men? From teaching men independent of authorization? From teaching contentiously? From teaching licentiously or murderously? In a domineering manner? Some other option?

Verse 12. Is *andros* referring to "a man," "men," or "husband"?

Verse 13. In verse 13, Paul used the word *plasso* (its form in the verse is *eplasthe*), which is translated "to mold or shape or form," instead of *ketidzo*, the word commonly used for "to create." He said the man was "molded/shaped/formed" first. Why do you think Paul would do that?

Verse 15. The word for "childbearing," *teknogonias*, is another *hapax*. How unhelpful, Paul! Although, we should grant that this was presumably a fairly common word at that time, so it may simply mean what it seems to mean. However, that still leaves us scratching our heads about the entire verse and its presence in context of this passage. Note that it has an article before it ("the"). The construction is the genitive, often translated as "through" or "by." Read the grammar tidbit I give at the end of the following section on grammar ("More Fodder . . ." on page 266) and read a handful of commentaries to find out some theories about it; then make a stab at your understanding of it all.

Examples: Studying the Grammar

Phyllis Bennett examined Paul's basis, or ground, for the commands in the passage:

> Paul grounds his argument for elder restriction of a woman in the creation account giving two reasons:
>
> 1. "Adam was formed first, then Eve" (v. 13). God has chosen man to be the head. He has placed man in that role in the home and, I believe this passage implies, in the church as well.
> 2. "Adam was not the one deceived. It was the woman who was deceived and became a sinner" (v. 14). Paul could not be saying here that Adam did not sin. They both sinned, but Eve's sin was a result of her deception. Adam also sinned, but with full

> knowledge that he was disobeying God's command. Are women in general more easily deceived than men? I'm not sure. Are men more willing to be outwardly rebellious than women? I don't know. But Paul does seem to be making these implications by his statements.

It's not 100 percent obvious from this quote, but you probably reasoned that Phyllis decided at some other point, based on other passages, that "God has chosen man to be the head," etc., because "head" is not mentioned in this passage. Many people infer from the Adam-being-formed-first situation that it indicates that the male should be the "head" role in the home, especially when combining it with other passages that *do* contain the word "head."

Before moving on, notice that Phyllis honestly acknowledged her remaining questions. In like manner, acknowledge any of your own remaining questions.

Fodder for Your Grammar Studies

Verse 15. Note that, in this (rather perplexing) verse, "*she* will be saved [third person *singular* verb, *sothesetai*] . . . if *they* continue [third person *plural* verb, *meinosin*] . . ." This is an interesting construction, because the grammatical person changes within the verse. Compare how these words have been translated in several versions. Remembering that all translation requires interpretation, which translation do you think is best?

Things to Read about in Commentaries

Think through some of the Genesis "Trump Card" questions (see 134–35) you have as they relate to this passage. List them and look for answers.

Of course, list every theological question you can think of and look for those answers, too.[2]

Also, you may want to look up what various early church fathers said and assumed about women, their personhood, and their roles. This is instructive and can be fairly shocking. Elizabeth A. Clark's book *Women and the Early Church* provides fascinating insight into how the early church fathers perceived and portrayed women.

2. Reminder: you can find my article, "Questions We Can Ask of the Text," at www.womenleadershipbible.com.

Examples: Comparing Similar Theological Issues in Different Texts

Elizabeth Inrig compared 1 Timothy 2 to the situation involving Priscilla and Aquila teaching Apollos.

> I think the best I can understand the command passage in 1 Timothy is that I do not take a lead authoritatively in the church to preach *propositional* truth, teaching the church when it comes together. But it seems there are times when a woman's teaching *is* acceptable, because Priscilla certainly modeled that and so did others who worked with Paul.
>
> So, what about teaching men? Well, I teach men in the context of a small, adult class. I am teaching how to study the Bible now and maybe fifteen people might sign up for it. I teach them how the Bible works. I always have a couple of guys in there.
>
> Is there a paradigm for this? There is a paradigm in Acts 17 or 18, when Paul meets Aquila and Priscilla. Then Paul goes on to Ephesus and Apollos shows up in Corinth. They listen to him and they find out that he hasn't understood the *whole* counsel of God.
>
> And they take him home. And in the Greek it is interesting that Priscilla's name is mentioned first. Why is that important? When you go through the history of Acts, you can see when Barnabas is trying to convince the apostles to accept Paul, we have Barnabas and Saul. Then, they go on their missionary journey and then we have Barnabas and Paul. Then they come home and report and then you have the council at Jerusalem (Acts 15) and all of a sudden, Paul is involved and it *changes* to Paul and Barnabas, and *Paul* is taking the lead. For the rest of the book, he is basically the leader. Barnabas takes John Mark off and basically sails into the sunset. There's not a lot mentioned after that. The literary emphasis there is that when there is a name used first in the list (for instance, the twelve apostles: Peter is always listed first because he was the spokesman), there's an indication of leadership.
>
> It seems like there is what I call the "Priscilla principle" where she, in the context either of her own home or a small group, is teaching with Aquila and she is helping Apollos understand the way of the Lord more clearly.

> Let me give you a definition, which I learned through personal experience, of what this is *not*. A few years ago, I went to Dallas Seminary to speak in chapel there when I accepted their offer to speak (which I did *not* solicit). In retrospect, I think I let such an opportunity override what my beliefs are.
>
> I prepared my talk as a teaching talk (meaning, teaching propositional truths concerning the Bible), rationalizing it by thinking, "Well, that's not the church and I will tell them that when I stand up to speak."
>
> I argued to myself that it was strictly a very large "Priscilla-Aquila experience," as in, "I am inviting you to into my kitchen to have a cup of coffee with me."
>
> But, teaching in a seminary chapel context is a public thing in the way the "kitchen" is private. If I ever have it to do over again, I would not teach them anything! I would talk about something like "Serving Women in the Passing Postmodern Culture," which is something I just taught at a Phoenix Seminary Women's Conference and which is a "how-to" subject, more befitting a public, mixed-gender-audience situation.
>
> It is without doubt that Paul had women on his team. Aside from Priscilla, look at the end of all his letters. He gives greetings from so and so, and so and so. Then in Philippians 4, he says, "Euodia and Syntyche, you stop arguing! You are useful in the ministry!"
>
> Still, all of that to say, I do not believe that women should be exchanged, in terms of role, for men.

When Sarah Sumner began making comparisons among Scripture passages using the same interpretive principles scholars and folks within her Christian community did, she found inconsistencies in their approaches.

> I was all ramping up for [studying Scripture in support of all-male leadership] and I started making some observations: "Wait, *this* is so inconsistent. *That* doesn't make sense. This doesn't make sense, *either*. Women aren't saved by childbirth. . . . None of these commentaries are convincing me! What about Priscilla?"
>
> You know, it says [in 1 Timothy 2:12], "I do not allow a woman to teach a man."

And these commentators all said, "No, Priscilla can't teach *men*."

And I'm like, "That's not the *text*. The text is '*a* woman,' '*a* man.'"

And a lot of people go, "Oh, don't get that picky."

And I say, "Hold it! We've been so nit-picky in these other things and all of a sudden you want us to ease up? I don't like that! Let's go nit-picky all the way down the line."

But when you do that, it's a mess.

It's quite *illogical* to have this theology that's so confusing and just *riddled* with inconsistencies. And there are inconsistencies at a rational level, not just on an experiential level.

For example, 1 Timothy 2 says "*a* woman" can't teach "*a* man." So, you can't rationalize that it means, like, "Oh, 1 Timothy 2 means he doesn't allow a woman to speak to *men*. You can't take it literally and say, *a* woman to *a* man, because Priscilla showed that's not what it *means*. So, it *can't* mean that, so it's *gotta* mean *men*."

That just doesn't work, because that's *not* what it *says*. You're not being *honest*. It doesn't mean what it sounds like it means, because of Priscilla?

Priscilla lived, of all places, *in Ephesus*, right there where Paul *wrote* that letter. Come *on*. Let's get *so* honest. We're *all* in pain; we'll all just suffer together right here in this land of honesty! You're in pain, I'm in pain; we all *hurt* with all this honesty! [*Laughs!*]

But let's spit it out and *be honest!*

Your Turn:

Examine every relevant passage you can find. When making your comparisons, try to do so fairly using the same interpretive principles throughout. Aim for consistency.

Example: Comparing Theological Issues that are Different but Argued Similarly

Laverne Tolbert looked at a whole cross-section of related issues:

> I believe in Paul's teachings he affirms women and their leadership in the church and he affirms women's roles in ministry. I also see in

> Scripture an emphasis for women on ministering to the family and to other women. I *also* see the emphasis on us being submissive one to another, to avoid foolish arguments, and to strive for peace. So, when we look at it altogether, what I see is a role that is nonconfrontational, but one that is effective.

Consider how Sandra Glahn compared the Sabbath to Paul's emphasizing the male being born first:

> Because the primogenitor argument (that is, "the man was created first") is what Paul always refers to when he pulls out the Genesis "trump card," I am not yet ready to say there is nothing about the man that is different in that sense.
>
> The "first-ness" of the male's creation happened before the Fall. In other words, I have not figured out yet if that is cultural or if that is part of design. As a point of comparison, the Sabbath also got established before the Fall, but we don't *always* follow the Sabbath commands in the Church Age.

Candie Blankman looked all through the Bible trying to discern God's heart on women's roles. She reflected long and hard on "silent" passages, as well as passages directly related to women, particularly as they related to 1 Timothy 2.

> Maybe it was Catherine Clark Kroeger who in one of her books talks about all the passages in both testaments where women are profoundly involved in ways that are shocking when you look at their culture. Obviously the most prominent one is that Mary gives witness to the resurrection. In a culture where women aren't even allowed to give testimony in a court of law, God allows a woman to give testimony to the resurrection.
>
> But you have the same thing in Exodus. Among the first people mentioned in Exodus are Puah and Shiphrah, Hebrew midwives. Their names are given, even though the Pharaoh's name is not given. In a historical context where the Pharaoh is the highest power there is, the Pharaoh's name is never given. And yet you have these two little midwives whose names are written for all eternity. Two little midwives become critical, central to the deliverance of not only Israel but of salvation of the world *for eternity*.

Other key players are Miriam and the mother of Miriam. So you have *that* kind of stuff over and over again. Scripture, even in revealing who God is, turns upside-down who does what and how it's done.

Then you have Deborah, who was a judge. Many people pass her off; but clearly, she's there. You can't dismiss her. And then you have the women at the resurrection. And you have all these incidences where Paul talks about a woman being able to sanctify a man within the Jewish culture, where normally in that culture all she could do was contaminate him.

And, certainly, it's clear that leadership is primarily servant leadership. There's no domination; there's no usurping authority. And *Jesus* is the example: as the prime leader, he served. He died for people.

It's not *my* authority by which I lead, but the authority of the Scriptures and the authority of Christ in my life that I try to encourage other people to submit to. I am not anybody's boss, not anyone's last word. I appeal to Scripture and I appeal to what God has called us to do. I am a *conduit* of God's authority. I don't have it in and of myself.

I find it interesting that the evangelical community is *so* against women in leadership, because it usurps authority or whatever. Everything Jesus said was, *That's the way the Gentiles do it. Their leaders lord it over others. With you, it ought not be so. With you, the first shall be last. If you want to be a leader, get down and wash some feet.*

That's how you lead.

Human beings set up all these systems, whether it's white over black or male over female or rich over poor, and God says, *That's not the way I see it.*

Over and over again, He calls the youngest, He affirms the poor.

It just turns everything upside down.

So you have all this biblical evidence, but it's a little more complicated. It's not like Romans 12:3 that you can just *quote*. It's more complicated and harder to discuss quickly and easily. But, rather than proof-texting, if you do a clear study of Scripture from Genesis to Revelation, I don't think there's any *doubt* that God is in the business of calling men and women to do all *sorts* of things.

CONSIDER THE CATEGORY OF MEANING

As you recall, if the original author made a statement that appears to have been meant for *all* believers in God, it may be "enduring," or applicable to all believers in all time periods. (See chapter 12 on page 144 for reminders and examples on this.) Here is your checklist to help you weigh our case study passage further.

Table 4. Your Checklist for Discerning Categories of Meaning

✓ Checklist: Categories of Meaning Some of the checklist questions overlap; many are distinct. They are loosely grouped to guide your thinking for each category. Overall, they are cumulative; meaning, use all of them, working your way down the list, to determine categories of meaning for this passage.	
	Category 1: Enduring Truths
☐	1. Has the writer identified principles that reflect highest norms and standards taught in the Bible, such that it is nearly unmistakable?
☐	2. Have any other Bible writers either interpreted Old Testament Scripture or evaluated an event in such a way as to demonstrate the timelessness of this passage?
☐	3. Has the writer summarized a truth at the end of or elsewhere within a book?
☐	4. Consider Jesus' teaching. Was Paul reinforcing, reiterating, or contradicting anything Jesus taught? Recall that if anything seems to contradict Jesus' teaching or practice, we need to consider why it seems so.
	Category 2: Restricted Commands
☐	1. Make a list of the references you find difficult to understand because so much time and culture have elapsed.
☐	2. Does anything, at least on first pass, seem obviously specific to the situation?
	Category 3: Historical Records
☐	1. Does this passage appear to be recording some historical event?
☐	2. Are its actions or tenets explicitly commended elsewhere in Scripture? Disapproved?
☐	3. Does any portion of this account go against Jesus' teachings? How?
☐	4. Did New Testament authors comment on it? If so, what did they say? How did they interpret it for the church to which they wrote or ministered?

☐	5.	Can you discern a pattern throughout the Bible that shows some kind of redemption of the original actions?
☐	6.	On the other hand, can you discern a pattern that shows that it is actually unapproved by God and eventually was or will be ended?

One distinct argument between groups who interpret the Bible differently on women's roles involves categories of meaning, the question of which verses apply for all time, and how to determine that. Kathy Keller gave her estimation of an aspect of this ongoing discussion, which is that if it made the canon, it's still relevant today:

> As far as 1 Timothy, the classic way of excluding that text is saying, "Well, that was just written for a specific time and a specific place and a specific set of women who were out of control." Well, *everything* Paul wrote was for a specific time and specific place—everything. He never said, "This is for *all* churches for *all* time and in *all* places, wherever they might be and in whatever century."
>
> That was not relevant in assembling the Canon. The fact that he was an apostle and this is God's truth was the only rule of thumb in whether it made the canon or not, assuming that God's truth is for all time. God, being immutable, is not going to change tomorrow what he thinks about a subject today. It's not going to be "new and improved" in a thousand years: "Well, now we're going to do it a different way."
>
> Actually, if you do a close study of 1 Timothy, if there's *any* book in the New Testament that *might conceivably* be called a letter for all churches in all times and all places, that would *be* 1 Timothy. Paul wrote a church-planting manual for Timothy, saying, "If I'm delayed, this is how I want you to set up the churches, which are the household of God. I want you to take these house churches—that are doing everything every which way—here is a template. I want you to supply them all. This is how I would have the women act; I want the elders chosen this way, church discipline carried out this way."
>
> So if there's any book that is proof against thinking that says, "that was for that time only and it doesn't have any universal application," that would be 1 Timothy. Therefore, that didn't fly as a "get rid of 1 Timothy 2" strategy.

Your Turn:

Based on your answers to this set of questions, what category or categories of meaning do you think apply to 1 Timothy 2:9–15? Is it restricted to that time, place, and people? Does it apply to us today? Is it a historical record that simply serves as a reminder? Do you think different categories apply to different verses? Whatever your decisions, think through your reasons and write down those reasons. Write it *all* down!

SO, WHAT DO YOU THINK? INTERPRETIVE DECISION-MAKING-TIME

Remember what Karen Moy said about getting people to see, "Okay, do you really know what you believe and why you believe it, or are you just repeating something you've heard?"

Now it's time to face the music. However, this time you're not sight-reading or merely "winging it," because you're more familiar with the score!

Your Turn:

Go back to "Check Your Objectivity" on page 248. What was your own understanding of this passage and the words contained in it before beginning to study it more closely? Why did you have that understanding?

What is your overall understanding of the passage now? The same? Different (very different or slightly different)? In what *ways* is it the same or different?

Remember, you're still simply making choices. But *now*, you're making informed, thoughtful, theologically and biblically based choices. I found something Karen Moy said during her interview very freeing:

If, in fact, you're sure that you've studied this thoroughly, then can we just agree that you're just going to have to choose a position on this issue? Because there's all this stuff the Scripture doesn't say and because there is this particular word in there that nobody's sure what it means.[3]

And if you can get that far, then I'm happy that at least we're to a point where everybody's being *honest*.

I've picked a position. I think I've done it intellectually honestly; but I *have chosen* a position.

> **✍📖Your Turn:**
>
> Write down your answers to some important questions,"(see Table 5 on page 278) along with any other notes you wish to add. Remember, give your reasons *why* you now think what you think.

Avoid making statements, such as this one, *without backing it up with a "why"*: "In Paul's next statement (saved through childbearing), I believe Paul is referring to the Genesis account (Gen 3:15) of our being saved through *the* childbirth of Christ."

If you use the words "I believe," be sure you can follow that up with "because."

Note: Plenty of questions exist for this passage's immediately-surrounding context, such as, "Why do you think these statements went along with Paul's statements about men lifting holy hands in prayer?" For the purposes of this case study, though, you will notice in Table 5 that I stuck with listing questions that are directly related to verses 9 through 15.

> **✍📖Your Turn:**
>
> Record your current, *informed* understanding of the situation, knowing full well that you've not exhausted the issue and that there's still more studying to be done.

Free yourself from pressure by resting assured that you are simply formulating a "working belief" from everything you've researched and

3. Karen is referring to *authentein*.

learned thus far. Some questions truly are unanswerable for now, no matter how tidy we'd like it all to be. That doesn't mean you'll never get your answers, although it might mean that—at least until heaven, as we've already acknowledged.

Eventually, you can revisit your questions, particularly as you study and compare other passages. Plenty of other passages and overarching biblical issues still remain to be explored. But this important exercise of declaring your choices will help you move forward as you move toward a "working conclusion" about what you think women's roles should or shouldn't be in the church.

The Benefits of Questions

I love the movie *O Brother, Where Art Thou?*[4] A favorite line is the one Holly Hunter's character would repeat when comparing her new, respectable suitor to her kind-of-ex-prison-breaker husband, which was George Clooney's character. To rub in her husband's less-than-desirable life choices and lack of prospects, she'd say of her suitor, Vernon, "[He's] got prospects! He's *bona fide*!" Of course, you have to pronounce that with as thick a southern twang as you can possibly muster for it to have the same effect.

Congratulations! Now, *you* are *bona fide*! *You* have prospects!

From now on, in any conversation with anyone on the topic of women's roles in the church, 1 Timothy 2:9–15 in particular, you have something biblically and theologically thoughtful to say. You may still choose to remain quiet, depending on the situation; but you would be *choosing* to remain quiet on it. You would not be quiet because you actually didn't know and didn't have anything to contribute to the discussion. At this point, you have done credible, extensive study—your own. At least you've started on it. You're on your way to doing more study like this, too. You've even got a list of other passages and issues you have questions about.

Let me also encourage you that *questions are okay*, even healthy.

In a court case, the prosecution must show a "burden of proof"; the defense must show "reasonable doubt." Why these ambiguous terms? Because with people and life and deciding others' fates, there can rarely be 100 percent certainty. Similarly, there will never be a biblical issue that

4. *O Brother, Where Art Thou?* Directed by J. Coen and E. Coen.

arises about which you don't have one or two, or even a handful, of questions remaining.

The big question is, "Can you live with those questions unanswered, at least for the time being, and live into what you have decided, based on what you do know?"

In terms of contributing well to a discussion, sometimes that involves raising a question, much like Mary Ann Hawkins and so many of the other mentors do. Take this assurance with you: you can raise questions, because it's *valid* to do so. As I've said, questions typically remain after studying any issue. They always will, until we "know fully, even as [we are] fully known" (1 Cor 13:8–12).

You now can identify many remaining questions that are involved with interpreting 1 Timothy 2:9–15. *Good questions are good contributions to a good discussion.*

✍📖Your Turn: More Lists

- **List 1:** List any remaining questions you have about 1 Timothy 2:9–15. Try to answer those questions as you study in the future.
- **List 2:** List any questions that remain in your mind about the issue of women's roles, in general, and do the same.

  For example, you may wonder how this passage interacts with other New Testament passages that clearly indicate female *non*-silence in the worship setting, such as 1 Corinthians 11:5. Record that as a "future to-study item."
- **List 3:** Make a list of the passages and issues you want to explore next.

You can follow this same interpretive and exegetical process to find answers and make more "working decisions" about those other questions.

One thing at a time.

Table 5. Questions to Answer (as Well as You Can Right Now)

1. What is Paul saying to Timothy and to the church at Ephesus overall in 1 Timothy? What major themes do you find? Key issues? Tone? Does the tone change?
2. What is Paul saying overall in verses 9–15? What is his central message?
3. Why was he saying it? What had occurred to cause Paul to write these statements?
4. What does he want to have happen or to see and why?
5. What is he allowing, perhaps even encouraging, in this passage?
6. How is he allowing it? Can you theorize why he wants it to be that way?
7. Is he prohibiting anything?
    - Do you think he was preventing women from teaching?
    - If you think he was, was he preventing them from teaching *entirely* or from teaching *men*?
    - If only men, was he preventing them from teaching men in every situation and occasion?
    - If there's a prohibition, are there any circumstances under which that prohibition might be removed?
    - Perhaps you've come to some other conclusion that is a variation on these. Write about that.
8. What do you think Paul meant when he chose and linked the words translated as "authority" and "teaching"?
9. What kind of "silence" is this in verse 12?
10. What reasons (ground) does he give for his statements?
11. Do you understand those reasons? How do you understand them at this point?
12. What do you currently make of verse 15? Why do you think that verse is it there?
13. Was this passage for every Christian throughout time or for the church in Ephesus?
14. Does it mean something for us today? If not, why? If so, what? Why?
15. What is God trying to teach you? If you have concluded that this is indeed meant for Christians today, how can you apply it to your life, your calling, and/or ministry?

Please Keep in Touch!

Contact info:

Natalie@womenleadershipbible.com
WomenLeadershipBible.com
NatalieEastman.com

On the websites, look for these downloadable resources, which complement *Women, Leadership, and the Bible*:

Downloadable eBooks

- *Interpreting Courageously/Facing Fears and Hesitations—And Overcoming Them*
- *Facing Interpretive Conflict—And Rising Above It/Making Sense of Conflicting Authoritative Voices in Our Lives*

Articles (added regularly)

- Going Further with History: Behind Every Great Man . . .
- Is It Too Late for Me?
- Questions We Can Ask of the Text*
- Reading Lists for Further Exploration*
- The Sacred Question (And Women's Confusion over It)
- "What is A 'Call'? Am *I* Called?" Some Thoughts
- Why Are Christian Women Confused? (Essay)

Appendices

- The Mentors–First Awakenings*
- The Mentors–Final Decisions and Implementation*
- The Mentors–Parting Words*

*For those who have purchased a copy of the book, use coupon code IBOUGHTTHEBOOK during checkout to download these selected book supplements for free. If you have any trouble with this process, please contact support@womenleadershipbible.com

As you read this book or download any of the resources from either website, know that God has prompted me to pray for you for more than twelve years. God bless you.

Bibliography

BOOKS AND ARTICLES

"Agape." *Encarta Dictionary English*. No pages. Online. Accessed September 15, 2009 at encarta.msn.com/dictionary1861668827/definition.html. No longer online.

"Agape." *Oxford Dictionaries*. No pages. Online. Accessed March 22, 2013. Available at http://oxforddictionaries.com/definition/agape—2.

Atwood, Craig D., Frank S. Mead, and Samuel S. Hill. *Handbook of Denominations in the United States*. 13th ed. Nashville: Abingdon, 2010.

Augsburger, David. *Caring Enough to Confront: How to Understand and Express Your Deepest Feelings toward Others*. Ventura, CA: Regal, 2009.

Baker, Warren, and Eugene Carpenter. *The Complete Word Study Dictionary: Old Testament*. Chattanooga, TN: AMG, 2003.

Barton, Ruth Haley. *Equal to the Task*. Downers Grove, IL: InterVarsity, 1998.

Baugh, S. M. "The Apostle among the Amazons: A Review Article." Review of *I Suffer Not A Woman*, by Richard Clark Kroeger and Catherine Clark Kroeger. *Westminster Theological Journal* 56 (1994) 153–71. Available at http://www.cbmw.org/resources/reviews/suffernot.php.

Beck, James R., Craig Blomberg, and Craig S. Keener. *Two Views on Women in Ministry*. Grand Rapids: Zondervan, 2001.

Belenky, Mary Field, Blythe McVicker Clinchy, Nancy Rule Goldberger, and Jill Mattuck Tarule. *Women's Ways of Knowing: The Development of Self, Voice, and Mind*. 10th anniversary ed. New York: Basic, 1997.

"Bias." *The American Heritage Dictionary of the English Language*. 4th ed. Houghton Mifflin, 2000, updated 2009. No pages. Online: www.Dictionary.com.

Bilezikian, Gilbert. *Beyond Sex Roles: What the Bible Says about a Woman's Place in Church and Family*. Grand Rapids: Baker Academic, 2006.

———. *Community 101: Reclaiming the Local Church as Community of Oneness*. Grand Rapids: Zondervan, 1007.

Blankenhorn, David, Don S. Browning, and Mary Stewart Van Leeuwen. *Does Christianity Teach Male Headship? The Equal-Regard Marriage and Its Critics*. Grand Rapids: Eerdmans, 2004.

Blomberg, Craig. "Response to Catherine Kroeger on 1 Timothy 2." *Journal of Biblical Equality* 1 (1989) 44–49.

Bruce, F. F. *The Epistle to the Galatians: A Commentary on the Greek Text*. Grand Rapids: Eerdmans, 1982.

Cavaness, Barbara, and Deborah M. Gill. *God's Women, Then and Now*. Springfield, MO: Grace and Truth, 2004.

Clark, Elizabeth A. *Women in the Early Church*. Message of the Fathers of the Church 13. Wilmington, DE: Glazier, 1983.

Clouse, Bonnidell, and Robert G. Clouse. *Women in Ministry: Four Views*. Downers Grove, IL: InterVarsity, 1989.

Colson, Chuck, Nancy Pearcey, and Harold Fickett. *How Now Shall We Live?* Carol Stream, IL: Tyndale, 2004.

Cosby, Michael R. *Interpreting Biblical Literature: An Introduction to Biblical Studies*. Grantham, PA: Stony Run, 2009.

Danker, Frederick, W. *A Greek-English Lexicon of the New Testament and Other Early Christian Literature*. 3rd ed. Chicago: University of Chicago, 2001.

De Bono, Edward. *Lateral Thinking: Creativity Step by Step*. New York: Harper & Row, 1970.

Easton, M. G. "Tittle" and "Jot." *Illustrated Bible Dictionary*. 3rd ed. Nashville: Thomas Nelson, 1897. No pages. Online: www.BibleStudyTools.com.

"Eisegesis." *Merriam-Webster Dictionary*. Accessed Sept. 10, 2012. http://www.merriam-webster.com/dictionary/eisegesis?show=0&t=1347417521.

Ericson, Jon. "What is the Difference between Historical-Grammatical and Historical Criticism?" No pages. Online: http://hermeneutics.stackexchange.com/questions/422/what-is-the-difference-between-historical-grammatical-and-historical-criticism/731#731?newreg=5ff7b40971cb48bb99523c604e000d04. Accessed Nov 27, 2013.

"Eros." *Dictionary.com Unabridged*. Random House. No pages. Online: http://dictionary.reference.com/browse/eros. Accessed March 22, 2013.

Evans, Mary J. *Woman in the Bible: An Overview of All the Crucial Passages on Women's Roles*. Downers Grove, IL: InterVarsity, 1984.

Fee, Gordon D. "Reflections on Church Order in the Pastoral Epistles, with Further Reflection on the Hermeneutics of *Ad Hoc* Documents." *Journal of the Evangelical Theological Society* 28 (1985) 141–51.

Fee, Gordon D., and Douglas K. Stuart. *How to Read the Bible for All Its Worth: A Guide to Understanding the Bible*. 2nd ed. Grand Rapids: Zondervan, 1993.

Fee, Gordon D., and Mark L. Strauss. *How to Choose a Translation for All Its Worth*. Grand Rapids: Zondervan, 2007.

Fields, Lee M. *Hebrew for the Rest of Us: Using Hebrew Tools without Mastering Biblical Hebrew*. Grand Rapids: Zondervan, 2008.

Flinders, Carol Lee. *Enduring Grace: Living Portraits of Seven Women Mystics*. New York: HarperOne, 1993.

Foh, Susan T. *Women and the Word of God: A Response to Biblical Feminism*. Phillipsburg, NJ: P & R, 1979.

"Genre." *The Mirriam-Webster Dictionary* online. No pages. Online: www.merriam-webster.com. Accessed November 22, 2011.

Grenz, Stanley J. *Sexual Ethics: A Biblical Perspective*. Issues of Christian Conscience Series. Dallas: Word, 1990.

———. *Sexual Ethics: An Evangelical Perspective*. Louisville: Westminster John Knox, 1997.

Grenz, Stanley, and Denise Muir Kjesbo. *Women in the Church: A Biblical Theology of Women in Ministry*. Downers Grove, IL: InterVarsity, 1995.

Grudem, Wayne A. *Evangelical Feminism and Biblical Truth: An Analysis of More Than One Hundred Disputed Questions*. Wheaton, IL: Crossway, 2004.

———. *Evangelical Feminism: A New Path to Liberalism?* Wheaton, IL: Crossway, 2006.

Gundry, Patricia. *Neither Slave Nor Free: Helping Women Answer the Call to Church Leadership*. New York: HarperCollins, 1990.

"Hapax Legomenon." Random House, 1998. No pages. Online: randomhouse.com/wotd/index.pperl?date=19980723. Accessed Mar. 17, 2005.

Hayes, John H., and Carl R. Holladay. *Biblical Exegesis: A Beginner's Handbook*. Louisville: Westminster John Knox, 2007.

Hearn, Virginia, editor. *Our Struggle to Serve: The Stories of 15 Evangelical Women*. Waco, TX: Word, 1979.

Henderson, Debbie, Gerry Breshears, W. Robert Cook, Robert A. Krupp, and Bruce A. Ware. *Ordination of Women Study Packet*. National Coordinating Council of Conservative Baptists, 1988.

Howe, E. Margaret. *Women & Church Leadership*. Grand Rapids: Zondervan, 1982.

Hunt, Susan, and Peggy Hutcheson. *Leadership for Women in the Church*. Grand Rapids: Zondervan, 1991.

Hurley, James B. *Man and Woman in Biblical Perspective*. 1st ed. Grand Rapids: Zondervan, 1981.

"Illumination." In *Collins English Dictionary, Complete and Unabridged*. New York: HarperCollins 2003. No pages. Online: http://www.thefreedictionary.com/illumination. Accessed Feb. 7, 2012.

James, Carolyn Custis. *The Gospel of Ruth: Loving God Enough to Break the Rules*. Grand Rapids: Zondervan, 2008.

———. *Half the Church: Recapturing God's Global Vision for Women*. Grand Rapids: Zondervan, 2011.

———. *When Life and Beliefs Collide: How Knowing God Makes a Difference*. Grand Rapids: Zondervan, 2001.

Jones, Rebecca. *Does Christianity Squash Women? A Christian Looks at Womanhood*. Nashville: Broadman & Holman, 2005.

Karant-Nunn, Susan C., and Merry E. Wiesner. *Luther on Women: A Sourcebook*. Cambridge: Cambridge University Press, 2003.

Kassian, Mary. *The Feminist Mistake: The Radical Impact of Feminism on Church and Culture*. Wheaton, IL: Crossway, 2005.

———. *Women, Creation, and the Fall*. Wheaton, IL: Crossway, 1990.

Keener, Craig S. *The InterVarsity Press Bible Background Commentary: New Testament*. Downers Grove, IL: InterVarsity, 1993.

Keller, Timothy. "Introduction to the Christ-Centered Model and Introduction to the Christ-Centered Exposition." Lecture. No pages. Online audio podcast: https://itunes.apple.com/us/itunes-u/preaching-christ-in-postmodern/id378879885.

Kraemer, Ross S. *Maenads, Martyrs, Matrons, Monastics: A Sourcebook on Women's Religions in the Greco-Roman World*. Philadelphia: Fortress, 1988.

Kroeger, Catherine Clark. "Women in the Church: A Classicist's View of 1 Tim 2:11–15." *Journal of Biblical Equality* 1 (1989) 3–31.

Kroeger, Richard Clark, and Catherine Clark Kroeger. *I Suffer Not a Woman: Rethinking 1 Timothy 2:11–15 in Light of Ancient Evidence*. Grand Rapids: Baker, 1992.

Kuhn, Thomas. *The Structure of Scientific Revolutions*. 3rd ed. Chicago: The University of Chicago Press, 1970.

Lees, Shirley, and Joyce G. Baldwin. *The Role of Women*. Leicester, UK: InterVarsity, 1984.

Liefeld, Walter L. "Women and the Nature of Ministry." *Journal of the Evangelical Theological Society* 30.1 (1987) 49–61.

MacArthur, Jr., John. *Different by Design: Discovering God's Will for Today's Man and Woman*. Macarthur Study Series. Colorado Springs: Chariot Victor, 1994.

MacHaffie, Barbara J. *Her Story: Women in Christian Tradition*. 2nd ed. Minneapolis: Augsburg Fortress, 2006.

Malcolm, Kari T. *Women at The Crossroads: A Path beyond Feminism and Traditionalism*. Downers Grove, IL: InterVarsity, 1982.

Mathews, Alice P. "Prescription and Description: The Gap between the Promise and the Reality in Women's Experience of Hierarchical Marriage." PhD diss., University of Denver, 1996.

McClelland, Scot E. "The New Reality in Christ: Perspectives from Biblical Studies." In *Gender Matters*, edited by June Steffensen Hagen, 51–78. Grand Rapids: Zondervan, 1990.

McKnight, Scot. *The Blue Parakeet: Rethinking How You Read the Bible*. Grand Rapids: Zondervan, 2008.

Mickelsen, Alvera, editor. *Women, Authority and the Bible*. Downers Grove, IL: InterVarsity, 1986.

Miller, Patricia Cox. *Women in Early Christianity: Translations from Greek Texts*. Washington, DC: Catholic University of America Press, 2005.

Mounce, William D. *Greek for the Rest of Us*. Grand Rapids: Zondervan, 2003.

———. *Interlinear for the Rest of Us: The Reverse Interlinear for New Testament Word Studies*. Grand Rapids: Zondervan, 2006.

Mouser, Barbara K. *Five Aspects of Woman: A Biblical Theology of Femininity*. 4th ed. Mountlake Terrace, WA: WinePress, 1995.

Mouser, William E., and International Council for Gender Studies. *Five Aspects of Man: A Biblical Theology of Masculinity*. Mountlake Terrace, WA: WinePress, 1995.

Ortlund, Raymond C. "Male-Female Equality and Male Headship." In *Recovering Biblical Manhood and Womanhood: A Response to Evangelical Feminism*, edited by John Piper and Wayne A. Grudem, 95–112. Wheaton, IL: Crossway, 1991.

Osiek, Carolyn, Margaret Y. MacDonald, and Janet H. Tulloch. *A Woman's Place: House Churches in Earliest Christianity*. Minneapolis: Fortress, 2006.

Panicola, Michael R. "Making Good Decisions." In *An Introduction to Health Care Ethics*, by Michael R. Panicola, David M. Belde, John Paul Slosar and Mark F. Repenshek, 64–83. Winona, MN: Anselm Academic, 2007.

Payne, Phillip B. *Man and Woman, One in Christ: An Exegetical and Theological Study of Paul's Letters*. Grand Rapids: Zondervan, 2009.

Perry, William G., and Harvard University Bureau of Study Counsel. *Forms of Intellectual and Ethical Development in the College Years: A Scheme*. Cambridge: Harvard University Bureau of Study Counsel, 1968.

Pierce, Ronald W., Rebecca Merrill Groothuis, and Gordon D. Fee. *Discovering Biblical Equality: Complementarity without Hierarchy*. Downers Grove, IL: InterVarsity, 2004.

Piper, John, and Wayne A. Grudem. *Recovering Biblical Manhood and Womanhood: A Response to Evangelical Feminism*. Wheaton, IL: Crossway, 2006.

Powell, C. "A Stalemate of Genders? Some Hermeneutical Reflections." *Themelios* 17.3 (1992) 15–19.

Roe, Earl O. *Dream Big: The Henrietta Mears Story*. Ventura, CA: Regal, 1990.

Saucy, Robert L., and Judith K. Tenelshof, editors. *Women and Men in Ministry: A Complementary Perspective*. Chicago: Moody, 2001.

Scanzoni, Letha, and Nancy Hardesty. *All We're Meant to Be: A Biblical Approach to Women's Liberation*. Waco, TX: Word, 1974.

Schaeffer, Francis A. *How Should We then Live? The Rise and Decline of Western Thought and Culture*. 50th L'Abri Anniversary ed. Wheaton, IL: Crossway, 2005.

Schmidt, Ruth A. "Second-Class Citizenship in the Kingdom of God." *Christianity Today* 15.7 (January 1, 1971) 13–14.

Scholer, David M. "1 Timothy 2:9–15 and the Place of Women in the Church's Ministry." In *Women, Authority and the Bible*, edited by Alvera Mickelsen, 193–219. Downers Grove, IL: InterVarsity, 1986.

———. "Feminist Hermeneutics and Evangelical Biblical Interpretation." *Journal of the Evangelical Theological Society* 30 (1987) 417–18.

Sire, James W. *The Universe Next Door: A Basic Worldview Catalog*. Downers Grove, IL: InterVarsity, 2009.

Smith, Marilyn B. *Gender or Giftedness: A Challenge to Rethink the Basis for Leadership within the Christian Community*. Shafter, CA: World Evangelical Fellowship Commission on Women's Concerns, 2001.

Smith, Mont. "The Temporary Gospel." *The Other Side* (Nov/Dec 1975) 36–37.

Spencer, Aída Besançon. *Beyond the Curse: Women Called to Ministry*. Nashville: Thomas Nelson, 1985.

Spencer, Aída Besançon, Donna F. G. Hailson, and Catherine Clark Kroeger. *The Goddess Revival: A Biblical Response to God(dess) Spirituality*. 2nd ed. Eugene, OR; Wipf & Stock, 2010.

Stackhouse, John G. *Finally Feminist: A Pragmatic Christian Understanding of Gender*. Grand Rapids: Baker Academic, 2005.

Storkey, Elaine. *Origins of Difference: The Gender Debate Revisited*. Grand Rapids: Baker Academic, 2001.

———. *What's Right with Feminism*. Grand Rapids: Eerdmans, 1986.

Strauch, Alexander. *Men and Women, Equal Yet Different: A Brief Study of the Biblical Passages on Gender*. Colorado Springs: Lewis & Roth, 1999.

Sumner, Sarah. *Men and Women in the Church: Building Consensus on Christian Leadership*. Downers Grove, IL: InterVarsity, 2003.

Surburg, Raymond F. "The Presuppositions of the Historical-Grammatical Method as Employed by Historic Lutheranism." *The Springfielder* 38.4 (October 1974) 279–88. Accessible at http://natalieeastman.com/wp-content/uploads/2013/11/Surburg-Historical-Grammatical-Method-Explained.pdf.

Thayer and Smith. "Greek Lexicon entry for Agape." *The NAS New Testament Greek Lexicon*. 1999. No pages. Online: http://www.biblestudytools.com/lexicons/greek/nas/.

———. "Greek Lexicon entry for Phileo." *The NAS New Testament Greek Lexicon*. 1999. No pages. Online: http://www.biblestudytools.com/lexicons/greek/nas/.

Tong, Rosemarie, Blythe McVicker Clinchy, Nancy Rule Goldberger, and Jill Mattuck Tarule. *Feminist Thought: A More Comprehensive Introduction*. 3rd ed. Boulder, CO: Westview, 2009.

Tucker, Ruth. *Women in the Maze: Questions and Answers on Biblical Equality*. Downers Grove, IL: InterVarsity, 1992.

Tucker, Ruth, and Walter L. Liefeld. *Daughters of the Church: Women and Ministry from New Testament Times to the Present*. Grand Rapids: Academie, 1987.

Van Leeuwen, Mary Stewart. *Gender & Grace: Love, Work & Parenting in a Changing World*. Downers Grove, IL: InterVarsity, 1990.

———. *My Brother's Keeper: What the Social Sciences Do (and Don't) Tell Us about Masculinity*. Downers Grove, IL: InterVarsity, 2002.

Webb, William J. *Slaves, Women & Homosexuals: Exploring the Hermeneutics of Cultural Analysis*. Downers Grove, IL: InterVarsity, 2001.

Zodhiates, Spiros. *The Complete Word Study Dictionary: New Testament*. Chattanooga, TN: AMG, 1992.

———. *The Complete Word Study New Testament*. Chattanooga, TN: AMG, 1991.

———. *The Complete Word Study Old Testament*. Chattanooga, TN: AMG, 1994.

———. *Hebrew-Greek Key Word Study Bible (NASB)*. Chattanooga, TN: AMG, 2008.

POSITION PAPERS AND SEMINARY CATALOGUE ARTICLES

"Aren't There Enough Pastors Already?" and "Requirements for Admission." Dallas Theological Seminary. No pages. Online: www.DTS.edu. Accessed Oct. 3, 2004.

"Inclusive Education." Fuller Theological Seminary. No pages. Online: http://fuller.edu/about-fuller/institutional-cmt-inclusive-education.aspx. Accessed Oct. 27, 2011.

"Manila Manifesto." In *International Congress for World Evangelization*. Manila: Lausanne Committee, 1989. No pages. Online: http://www.lausanne.org/en/documents/manila-manifesto.html.

Mann, Sharon Cairns. *Called and Gifted: A Reaffirmation of the Biblical Basis for the Full Participation of Women in the Ministries of the Church*. Chicago: Covenant Publications, 2004. No pages. Online: http://www.covchurch.org/resources/called-and-gifted-material/. Accessed Oct. 10, 2011.

Patterson, Dorothy. "Should Women Serve as Pastors?" White Paper. Fort Worth: Center for Theological Research, October 2006. No pages. Online: http://www.baptisttheology.org/documents/ShouldWomenServeasPastors.pdf. Accessed Feb. 14, 2012.

"Position Paper on the Ordination of Women." General Assembly of the Evangelical Presbyterian Church (June 1984). No pages. Online: http://www.epc.org/about-the-epc/position-papers/ordination-of-women/. Accessed Mar. 4, 2012.

"Position Paper: The Role of Women in Ministry," the Assemblies of God. No pages. Online: http://www.ag.org/. Accessed July 9, 2001.

"The Human Witness." In "The Twenty-one Affirmations of the Manila Manifesto" in *International Congress for World Evangelization* (Manila: Lausanne Committee, 1998). No pages. Online: http://www.lausanne.org/en/documents/manila-manifesto.html. Accessed Oct. 27, 2011.

"The Role of Women in Ministry as Described in Holy Scripture." Position paper for the Assemblies of God denomination, adopted August 9–11, 2010. No pages. Online: http://ag.org/top/beliefs/position_papers/pp_downloads/PP_The_Role_of_Women_in_Ministry.pdf.

"What Do You Have for My Wife?" The Master's Seminary. No pages. Online: http://www.tms.edu/FAQAdmissions.aspx. Accessed Oct. 27, 2011.

"Women at Gordon-Conwell Theological Seminary." In *Catalogue: 2000–2001*. South Hamilton, MA: GCTS, 2000.

OTHER

Coen, Joel, and Ethan Coen, directors. *O Brother, Where Art Thou?* Touchstone Pictures, 2000.

Gilbert, W. S. and Sir Arthur Sullivan. "I've Got A Little List." In *The Story of the Mikado.* London: Daniel O'Connor, 1921.

Goldman, William. *The Princess Bride*. Orlando: Harcourt Brace Jovanovich, 1973. Movie: *The Princess Bride*. Directed by R. Reiner. MGM Studios, 1987.

Wachowski, Andy, and Larry Wachowski, directors. *The Matrix*. Warner Brothers Pictures, 1999.

Index of Mentors

Subject Index

Scripture Index

Luke

John

Acts

Romans

1 Corinthians

2 Corinthians

Galatians

Ephesians

Philippians

Colossians

1 Thessalonians

1 Timothy

2 Timothy

Philemon

Hebrews

1 Peter

2 Peter

1 John

Revelation